Reality and Research

GEORGE GALSTER
Editor

Reality and Research

Social Science and U.S. Urban Policy since 1960

THE URBAN INSTITUTE PRESS
Washington, D.C.

THE URBAN INSTITUTE PRESS
2100 M Street, N.W.
Washington, D.C. 20037

Library of Congress Cataloging in Publication Data

Reality and Research: Social Science
and U.S. Urban Policy since 1960 / George C.
Galster, editor.

1. Urban policy—United States.   2. Cities
and towns—Research—United States.
3. Policy sciences.   I. Galster, George
C., 1948–   .

HT123.R395   1995   95-23616
307.76'0973—dc20   CIP

ISBN 0-87766-639-3 (paper, alk. paper)
ISBN 0-87766-638-5 (cloth, alk. paper)

Printed in the United States of America.

Distributed in North America by:
University Press of America
   4720 Boston Way
   Lanham, MD 20706

THE URBAN INSTITUTE is a nonprofit policy research and educational organization established in Washington, D.C., in 1968. Its staff investigates the social and economic problems confronting the nation and public and private means to alleviate them. The Institute disseminates significant findings of its research through the publications program of its Press. The goals of the Institute are to sharpen thinking about societal problems and efforts to solve them, improve government decisions and performance, and increase citizen awareness of important policy choices.

Through work that ranges from broad conceptual studies to administrative and technical assistance, Institute researchers contribute to the stock of knowledge available to guide decision making in the public interest.

Conclusions or opinions expressed in Institute publications are those of the authors and do not necessarily reflect the views of staff members, officers or trustees of the Institute, advisory groups, or any organizations that provide financial support to the Institute.

ACKNOWLEDGMENTS

This book could not have been produced without the generous financial support provided by the Tokio Marine Research Institute (TMRI), under the auspices of its director, Dr. Shimokobe. In 1993, TMRI commissioned the Urban Institute to produce "U.S. Urban Problems and Policy Responses: Lessons from the Past and Challenges for the Future," which focused on the role of policy think tanks in shaping public policy. From this work grew *Reality and Research*. To TMRI, and to Makiko Ueno, who was instrumental in securing this support, go many thanks: *arigato*.

Of course, the worth of an edited volume is measured primarily by the insights of the contributing authors. I was blessed with an unusually talented set of contributors who produced marvelously concise histories and cogent analyses under tight constraints of time, page length, and resources. They were also unusually responsive to my request that they attempt to fit their remarks within the conceptual framework I established at the outset. As a consequence, the chapters are not only of uniformly high quality but share a consistent analytical perspective that sets *Reality and Research* apart from most edited volumes. My deepest thanks to: Chris, Patrick, Pam, Jenny, Bill, Tom, Paul, Adele, and George.

The draft manuscript was carefully critiqued by two anonymous external reviewers. Their excellent suggestions contributed substantially to the book. Diane Hendricks provided her usual flawless assistance in preparing manuscripts and Tim Ware again demonstrated his expertise with graphics production. I offer my gratitude to all the named individuals and organizations above, and to others who contributed to this project whose names I do not know. Finally, I acknowledge the outstanding institutional and intellectual support provided by the Urban Institute that made this book possible.

George Galster
Washington, D.C.
Oct. 31, 1995

CONTENTS

Figures

FOREWORD

As the United States approaches the 21st century, there is a pervasive perception that the nation's capacity for making effective policy is becoming more and more limited. One of the reasons for this is a declining faith on the part of the public in the ability of government to recognize problems and carry out solutions. Implicated in this declining faith is the role of policy analysts and the apparent disconnect between analysts and the public.

This book's objective is to evaluate critically the role of policy analysis over the past three decades in a wide range of urban policy arenas, including community development, education, family support and social welfare, intergovernmental financial relations, drugs, and racial discrimination. The authors structure their discussions chronologically, tracing how key urban problems, and their policymaking and research components, have evolved since the early 1960s, when confidence in the power of government to develop wise policies based on research findings was at a high point. But their focus is not only historical. Within this historical structure each author traces the links among the analysts' conception of a problem, research related to it, and associated policy responses.

The record is mixed. In some areas research has played a constructive role in identifying the problem and in helping develop effective policies to combat it. In other areas the research was on target but was ignored in the formulation of policy. In still other areas research followed rather than led the policy debate. It is my hope that the record examined here and the lessons drawn will help analysts, practitioners, and citizens in their continuing efforts to improve the decision-making process that leads to effective policy.

William Gorham
President

Chapter One

URBAN ISSUES, POLICIES, AND RESEARCH: EXAMINING THE INTERFACE

George Galster

Those of us in the business of policy research and program evaluation often talk, write, and act as if the value of our work in guiding wise and effective policymaking were self-evident. We would all agree that politics and ideology are also important, but we rarely take a hard cold look at whether our work makes a difference and, if so, what kind of a difference. As we approach the 21st century, the public seems increasingly disenchanted with the record of government, and less and less inclined to believe in the value of empirical analysis as a guide to action. In such an environment, it behooves us to reflect on the historical role of applied social science vis-à-vis urban issues and policy responses. To what extent is the reality of policymaking influenced by research on the social issues in question? Is social research more a shaper of our programs or is it more shaped by the realities of history and ideology? *Reality and Research* explores these questions.

THE PURPOSE AND ORGANIZATION OF THIS BOOK

This book charts the evolution of American urban policy in nine issue areas during the last 35 years, but goes well beyond a mere descriptive history. It examines the complex interrelationships among our conception of an urban problem, policy initiatives for addressing it, research related to the problem, and associated policy responses. The reflections contained here demonstrate that our perceptions of the most urgent urban problems and what the federal government should and could do to respond to them have been remarkably volatile. In addition, this book demonstrates how the influence of policy research in the United States has waxed and waned considerably over the past three decades since its initial ascendancy.

The conceptual framework and historical illustrations presented here are designed to dispel several common notions about policy research. Specifically, this volume's contributing authors challenge the notions that policy research: (1) is always influential because decision makers choose a policy course after rationally weighing objective evidence; (2) is never influential because decision makers choose policy on the basis of political pressures; (3) has always clarified the issues or resulted in better public policies when used; and (4) is independent of prevailing ideologies, conceptions of the problem, or past and current policies.

This last point warrants amplification, because it is most often overlooked. This volume's authors do not see policy research as occurring in an epistemological, moral, or ideological vacuum, nor do they believe that it should. On the contrary, public policy decisions should be normative, with ethics and democratic philosophy playing important roles in policy research, because policy always affects people. For policymakers or policy researchers to pretend otherwise is dangerous. As we are reminded by Robert Formiani (1990), "Science is a tool, not a method by which we can avoid making value judgments."

Ultimately, then, this book's purpose is to help readers better understand how we as a nation have attempted during the last three and one-half decades to make our metropolitan areas more livable places, and what these attempts tell us about the policymaking process in general and the role of policy research in particular. It is hoped that this enhanced understanding aids us all, in whatever special roles we play as citizens or practitioners, to work more effectively to improve the wisdom of our social policies.

Each chapter of this volume employs a historical approach, tracing how key elements of specific American urban problems, and their policymaking and research components, have evolved since the early 1960s, when applied social science emerged as a major claimant to the role of adviser to the policymaker. Nine topics that have been consistently at the core of the urban social agenda are analyzed: economic development, poverty, family support and social welfare, housing, transportation and land use, education, drug abuse, racial discrimination and segregation, and intergovernmental financial relations. Although the focus is on federal urban policy, the nature of intergovernmental relationships in the U.S. federal system is such that reference to state and local government initiatives often cannot be avoided.

The contributing authors of this book come from many disciplines—economics, education, history, sociology, political science, and urban planning—but all share two things in common. First, they are practicing policy researchers who have firsthand experience with the interface between their research results, public opinion, and policymakers' perceptions and motives. Second, they believe that the facts, concepts, and methods flowing from policy research *have* been important in changing American urban policy, although not directly, not independently, not uniformly across time and policy issues, and not necessarily for the better. This premise is self-serving on its face, but it also is supportable, as this volume's essays demonstrate.

This book is designed to be a nontechnical introduction to the recent history of urban problems, policies, and applied social research. It is intended for undergraduate and introductory graduate courses in urban problems, applied social research, and public policy analysis, and should also be of interest to informed citizens and policy practitioners.

To keep the text accessible, coverage of each issue is necessarily selective and illustrative, not exhaustive. Each chapter organizes the discussion chronologically and attempts to demarcate eras distinguished by different views of either the nature of the problem, the appropriate programmatic response, or both. As stated earlier, the text goes beyond descriptive history by interweaving hypotheses about the influence of policy research during these eras. Given the introductory nature and relatively brief treatment of each topic, we view these hypotheses as suggestive and provocative; the lists of Suggested Reading accompanying each chapter allow readers to explore topics in more depth and to evaluate these hypotheses more rigorously.

The essays in this volume share an overarching conceptual framework and are in agreement concerning the changeable efficacy of policy research. The remainder of this chapter describes this framework, outlining the causal links among urban problems, policies, and research, and reviewing the debate over the relevance of policy research to the policymaking process.

INTERRELATIONSHIPS AMONG URBAN PROBLEMS, POLICIES, AND RESEARCH: CONCEPTUAL FRAMEWORK

The overall conceptual framework of this book is portrayed in figure 1.1. This framework embodies the authors' belief that fully assessing the role of policy research can only be accomplished by positing mutually causal relationships among three key elements: policymak-

Figure 1.1 INTERRELATIONSHIPS AMONG URBAN PROBLEMS, POLICY, AND
RESEARCH

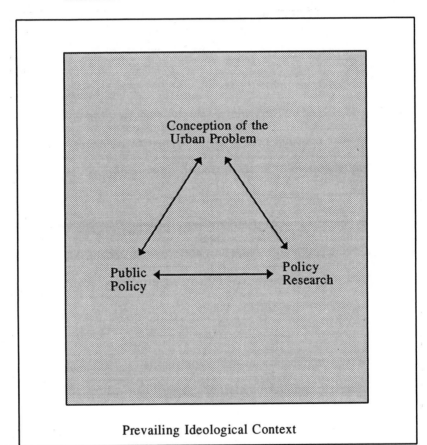

ers' conception of the problem, public policy initiatives, and policy
research results. The strength of these interrelationships is not presumed to be equal or invariant over time or issue area; indeed, the
book is replete with examples of such variability. As stated, this
framework is offered as a working hypothesis. The chapters illustrate
its applicability and analyze the nature and relative strengths of the
causal connections it embodies. The key terms in these three elements
are defined as follows.

The *conception* of the urban problem refers to policymakers' ideas
relating to the nature, impact, causes, and significance of the phenomenon in question. What are its manifestations? Who is affected directly and indirectly? What are its consequences? Why does it occur?

Can the problem possibly be eliminated or abated? The term *policymakers* refers not only to elected officials and senior civil servants but also to a broad segment of society that may reasonably be presumed to influence them. This segment includes lobbyists, intellectuals, journalists, interest groups, commentators, and citizens who actively participate in the political process.

Public policy comprises legislation, rule making, and executive orders promulgated by elected officials and senior civil servants who consciously attempt to respond programmatically to the concerns of their constituencies. (Alternative views about how the policymaking process works are described later in this section.)

Policy research refers to applied social science directed at documenting trends, conceptualizing interrelationships, diagnosing causes, and assessing alternative treatments. *Applied social science* means any of a variety of research methods aimed at systematically increasing understanding of social phenomena or public policy impacts. Some methods might be theoretical, such as developing conceptual paradigms or computer simulations. Other methods may employ qualitative empirical methods such as history or ethnography. Still other methods may be highly quantitative, such as gathering and econometrically analyzing statistical data.

As stated, explorations into the nature and variability of the causal interconnections among the conception of the problem, policy responses, and policy research form the substance of this book. Consider, first, how the conception of the problem at hand may influence policy formulation. One view is that policy is a proposed prescription rationally connected to a diagnosis. An illustration is provided in my review of civil rights policy in chapter 9: if racial inequality is caused by de jure discrimination in voting, employment, housing, and education, then the remedy implied is a panoply of new legal guarantees of equal treatment. Another view is that the form of policy is constrained by who is involved in the problem activity. Adele Harrell describes in chapter 8 how the willingness to assess severe penalties for drug use has varied greatly depending upon whether the predominant use has been marijuana by the middle class or crack cocaine by the poor. Yet another possibility is that political will for undertaking *any* public policy is shaped by the conception of who is harmed. As shown by Pamela Holcomb in chapter 4, the public reluctance to support guaranteed cash minimum allowances for families may be traced to its suspicions about the "undeserving poor."

The conception of the problem can also influence the nature of policy research. As Bulmer (1986) has noted, policy research is part of "the intellectual enterprise of society," and as such cannot be isolated from fads and conventional wisdom related to the issue or to social science methodologies. Researchers' worldviews and interests cannot be isolated from their social context. As I note in chapter 3, for example, the dominant post–World War II impression was that growth was successfully eliminating poverty; therefore, few scholarly investigations were produced on the topic. Only when poverty was "rediscovered" in the 1960s did research on the topic explode. But then the economists predominated, relegating traditional concerns of other disciplines to positions of less prominence. This theme is echoed in chapter 6 by William A. Hyman and G. Thomas Kingsley, who describe how unquestioning faith in the efficiency of technocratic solutions after World War II led to a myopic, engineer-dominated approach to urban highway construction, with unintended consequences abounding.

Because policy research is not done in a vacuum, it cannot be viewed as portraying a fully "objective" portrait of social problems. This, coupled with the fact that methodological and theoretical disagreements among applied social scientists are typically numerous, suggests that policy research does not necessarily clarify the issues it addresses, nor necessarily lead to effective public policies. Indeed, the chapters in this volume are rife with examples of policies that embodied the best research findings of the era, yet failed nevertheless. Thus, embedding in this volume's conceptual framework the conviction that the process of policy research is mutually interactive with conceptions of the problem and with policy initiatives implies that policy research is neither independent, objective, nor infallible.

Moving to the vertex of the triangle of key elements in the conceptual framework (figure 1.1), the perceived efficacy of particular public policies can affect the public's conception of the original problem. In an optimistic scenario, a policy might well "cure" a problem, leading policymakers to shift resources to more pressing concerns. Such was argued, for instance, in the late 1970s by Martin Anderson, then of the Hoover Institution, when he declared that the War on Poverty had been won and thus its policy apparatus could be dissembled (Anderson 1978). A less optimistic scenario might be that the policy not only fails to eliminate the problem but exacerbates it or creates unintended consequences. As Jennifer Daniell and I point out in chapter 5, widespread perceptions of the public housing program in the 1980s matched this scenario.

Policy form and results can also affect the conduct of subsequent social research (the third point of the conceptual triangle—figure 1.1). The connection may be direct if policymakers commission and fund evaluation research on extant programs, as was recently the case with the congressionally mandated evaluation of the Fair Housing Initiatives Program under the U.S. Department of Housing and Urban Development. Similarly, small-scale policies may be tried in a demonstration mode, accompanied by rigorous evaluations, as occurred in the 1970s with the income maintenance experiments (see chapter 4) and the Experimental Housing Allowance Program (see chapter 5). The connection may be less direct, but past policies may spawn evaluations from policy researchers whether policymakers seek such evaluations or not. A perennial illustration is the series of critiques of the effect of home mortgage interest deductibility on metropolitan spatial structure, the vertical equity of the tax code, and the federal budget deficit. George Peterson demonstrates in chapter 10 how the emphasis on federal grants for narrowly defined categories of uses during the 1960s stimulated research showing the inability of such detailed designs to be implemented in the field, thereby setting the stage for a new generation of consolidated block grants.

Finally, consider how policy research may influence both the conception of the problem and the policy response. In what Carol Weiss (1986) has called the "enlightenment model," policy research may radically redefine the entire social agenda. Research can provide a cognitive backdrop to decision making, sensitizing decision makers to new issues and to what is intolerable. Indeed, as several chapters show, research has exposed entirely new issues and helped crystalize opinion that these issues represented "social problems." Perhaps nowhere is this more clear than in the case of the Kerner Commission (see chapter 9), which reported in 1968 on the causes of urban civil disorders. Although the commission's report produced few tangible policy responses, it did change public opinion more generally and served an educational function that even today shapes our conception of urban racial issues. As noted previously, because the conception of the problem crucially shapes any policy ultimately formulated in response, the impact of research on problem conceptualization provides a potentially powerful, if indirect, means of influencing public policy.

But there may well be more direct influences as well. Weiss (1986) has suggested two other ways in which research can be utilized: for "problem solving" and for "political" purposes. The problem-solving mode arises when policymakers have reached agreement about the goals but have inadequate information about the alternative means of reaching them. Research can close this gap. Perhaps the clearest illustration of this model is the commissioning of demonstration research in such areas as housing allowances, personnel training, and welfare reforms. In the political mode, policymakers may use selectively those research findings that support their position in an attempt to neutralize opposing positions, bolster supporters, and convince those who are wavering. A clear example amplified in chapter 3 is the effective political use by conservatives in the early 1980s of certain simplistic analyses of poverty and welfare, even though these analyses subsequently were effectively debunked by more sophisticated research.

Finally, this volume's authors believe that ideology acts as a mold that profoundly shapes and constrains the three elements of our triangle: policy, conceptualization, and research. Thus, figure 1.1 portrays ideology as the box within which the others operate. Ideology is the broad and mutually consistent set of values and beliefs concerning individuals, government, and society. Ideology plays a central role in our choice of what phenomena are defined as "social problems," what their severity and consequences are, and what range of governmental responses is appropriate. More recently, radical political economists have stressed the ways in which the ideology of capitalism limits the sorts of questions that can even be considered by policymakers when diagnosing problems or devising solutions. The dimensions of this ideological box are explored in several chapters. For instance, Holcomb notes in chapter 4 how the tension between values supporting mothers' responsibilities for both nurturing their children and working in the labor force has hamstrung efforts at welfare policy reform. Daniell and I show in chapter 5 how research attacking the social disutility of continued suburban development of single-family homes can be thoroughly discounted because it flies in the face of the sacrosanct American value of individuality. Related implications of this value for automobile-dominated transportation systems are explored by Hyman and Kingsley in chapter 6. Harrell indicates in chapter 8 how public indignation over the immorality of marijuana use can dominate the policy discussion, despite credible evidence on the lack of long-term harm from smoking marijuana. And faith in the efficiency of private development decisions, argue Christopher Walker and Patrick Boxall in chapter 2, has resulted in public indifference to the metropolitan impacts of many national policies. Research on the optimal allocation of responsibilities among levels of government has had no impact within the context of a rising tide of sentiment in favor of shrinking the federal government, as shown by Peterson in chapter 10.

DOES RESEARCH MATTER?
ALTERNATIVE VIEWS OF POLICYMAKING

Given the power of the conception of the problem, existing policy initiatives, and ideology to influence policy research, one might well ask: Does policy research matter in understanding the evolution of American urban policy over the last three decades? The more appropriate question to ask is: Under what circumstances does policy research matter and how is its influence exerted? Unfortunately, the former question too often dominates discourse on the topic, perhaps because of two polar views of the decision-making process that have arisen.

One view, the "rational model," posits that policy formulation is conducted in a linear, objective, highly rational fashion. Policymakers are seen as: (1) identifying problems, (2) establishing goals, (3) laying out alternative means of achieving these goals, (4) analyzing the consequences of each strategy, (5) comparing predicted outcomes with goals, and (6) settling upon the best strategy. In this model, policy research plays an indispensable and clearly identifiable role, inasmuch as it crucially informs steps 1, 3, and 4 above.

In contrast, the second view, the "group theory" model, posits that the outcome of the policymaking process is a complex function of competing group pressures, not a logical weighing of evidence. In this process, partisans act on behalf of their constituents and interact in ways that resolve differences in the original programs advocated. Such policymaking is characterized by what Charles Lindblom (1980) has termed "disjointed incrementalism" and "partisan mutual adjustment." According to this view, only a narrow range of policy alternatives is considered. This produces only incremental, small-scale changes from the status quo and thereby minimizes the import of theory or facts enumerated by policy researchers. The "best" policy chosen is the one that achieves agreement among the competing groups after considerable interaction and negotiation, not dispassionate reflections about the "facts." Indeed, policymakers subscribing to this view may be reluctant to accept new evidence when it does not support their political interests. Thus, for many reasons the "group theory" minimizes the impact of policy research.

This volume's authors believe that the truth about the policymaking decision process lies somewhere in between these two extremes, although the precise position undoubtedly varies depending on the particular policy area and the prevailing ideology. The rational model is naive and unrealistic, and has been criticized on numerous grounds. Decision making in a pluralistic political context cannot be separated into distinct segments of a linear process. This model ignores the extent to which one group's solution may be another group's problem, and the role of power in ultimately determining the redistributive effects of policy. Policy research itself may provide conflicting answers. Yet, rejection of the rational decision-making model of the policy process need not imply the negation of all influence of policy research. At the other extreme, the group model minimizes the role of research because it is apparently not considered in a clear and rational fashion in the policymaking process. Yet, this overlooks the possibility that research can shape the underlying view of the problem that all the partisans hold implicitly. Furthermore, through their use of knowledge, negotiators can use research as a means of exerting control over the policy process.

The position of this volume's authors can be summed up by reference to a metaphor provided by Richard Nathan (1988): the "drama of social actions." The stage upon which the action occurs is circumscribed by ideology. The three players are conception of the problem, public policy, and policy research; the performance of each is influenced by the others, but not equally in all scenes. Policy research steals only those scenes in which policymakers are open to new conceptualizations or genuinely interested in answers, are uncertain about them, and, in addition, are willing to wait for them. Of course, policy research must deliver its lines clearly, simply, and in a single voice if it is to act effectively in any scene. In other scenes, policy research waits in the wings or works as a stagehand responding to cues being given on stage. The conditions under which these alternatives have been "played out" is a recurrent theme examined in this book.

SUGGESTED READING

Role of Policy Research

Aaron, Henry. 1978. *Politics and the Professors: The Great Society in Perspective*. Washington, D.C.: Brookings Institution.

Bulmer, Martin, ed. 1986. *Social Science and Social Policy*. London: Allen & Unwin.

Formiani, Robert. 1990. *The Myth of Scientific Public Policy*. New Brunswick, N.J.: Transaction Publishers.

Lindblom, Charles. 1980. *The Policy Making Process*, 2d ed. Englewood Cliffs, N.J.: Prentice Hall.
Lindblom, Charles, and D. K. Cohen. 1979. *Usable Knowledge: Social Science and Social Problem Solving*. New Haven, Conn.: Yale University Press.
Nathan, Richard. 1988. *Social Science and Government*. New York: Basic Books.
Weiss, Carol. 1986. "The Many Meanings of Research Utilization." In *Social Science and Social Policy*, edited by Martin Bulmer (31–59). London: Allen & Unwin.

Urban Problems and Policies

Ames, David, Nevin Brown, Mary Helen Callahan, Scott Cummings, Sue Smock, and Jerome Ziegler, eds. 1992. *Toward an Urban Policy Agenda for the 1990s*. Greenwich, Conn.: JAI Press. (Special issue of *Journal of Urban Affairs* 14 (3/4): 197–496.)
Gorham, William, and Nathan Glazer, eds. 1976. *The Urban Predicament*. Washington, D.C.: Urban Institute Press.
Kaplan, Marshall, and Franklin James, eds. 1990. *The Future of National Urban Policy*. Durham, N.C.: Duke University Press.
Peterson, Paul, ed. 1985. *The New Urban Reality*. Washington, D.C.: Brookings Institution.
President's Commission for a National Agenda for the Eighties. 1980. *Urban America in the Eighties*. Washington, D.C.: U.S. Government Printing Office.
Report of the Advisory Commission on Civil Disorders (Otto Kerner, Chair). 1968. New York: Bantam Books.
Solomon, Arthur, ed. 1980. *The Prospective City*. Cambridge, Mass.: MIT Press.
"The Urban Crisis: The Kerner Commission Report Revisited." 1993. *North Carolina Law Review* 71 (5, June): 1283–1786.
Urban Institute. 1992. *Confronting the Nation's Urban Crisis*. Washington, D.C.: Urban Institute Press.

Other References

Anderson, Martin. 1978. *Welfare: The Political Economy of Welfare Reform in the United States*. Stanford, Calif.: Hoover Institution, Stanford University.

Chapter Two

ECONOMIC DEVELOPMENT

Christopher Walker and Patrick Boxall

In the 1990s national attention has turned again to the problems of wealth creation in urban areas. In the wake of civil disorders in Los Angeles and continuing demands from urban constituencies for a re-articulation of federal interest in the economic fate of central cities, the Clinton administration implemented several new, if limited, initiatives to stimulate new investment and preserve these areas' dwindling economic assets. With the election of a Republican-led Congress in 1994, federal urban economic development policy is likely to undergo further scrutiny. Every reexamination of central-city economic problems studies old, dusty policy formulations and program proposals in light of new conceptual understandings of how urban places function in regional and national economies, and recasts them into a new set of programmatic and political specifications.

The subtext of continuing policy discussion of urban economic development problems is the maldistribution of wealth-creating and income-earning opportunities across urban space. However, emphasis tends to shift among the multiple dimensions of this uneven allocation of economic assets. Federal investment has variously been directed toward supporting urban commercial real estate markets, neighborhood residential property values, industrial and manufacturing employment generation, and small business creation and expansion. The scope of national policy attention has also widened and narrowed. Through the years it has included concern for central-city commercial districts, neighborhoods experiencing middle-class emigration, other neighborhoods with high concentrations of poverty households, and entire metropolitan areas and multistate regions experiencing loss of manufacturing employment.

This chapter examines the record of direct federal intervention in urban economies. How have federal policymakers conceptualized the core problems of urban economic development? What have been the concrete results of policies and programs? How have these efforts been shaped, if at all, by social science research? This chapter's discussion is primarily limited to federal efforts, although state and local initiatives are noted in passing. Furthermore, the focus is on capital assistance policies only, to the exclusion of employment and training programs. This is because by design, the former tend to be spatially targeted and place-specific.

Historically, the links between national economic policy and urban policy have been weak, at best, although the economic fate of U.S. regions and their urban centers has been influenced decisively by national economic choices. From the earliest years of the Republic, national debates over tariffs, farm subsidies, railroad rates, monetary policy, and other macroeconomic policies have sparked (occasionally furious) sectional conflict. Although economic policy over time has favored one region, then another, rarely have national policies explicitly promoted regional or urban economic development. Instead, these policies have been designed to promote increased aggregate employment and national wealth, positive balances of trade, and other macroeconomic goals. Recent decades are no exception. At times, the federal government has made weak attempts to formulate policy for urban places, but never over sustained periods or with more than piecemeal deployment of special aid programs. And although federal "nonurban" policies in housing, transportation, and taxation have encouraged overall investment in metropolitan areas, they have accelerated disinvestment in the urban core of these areas.

This indifference to the urban impacts of national policy results from two fundamental features of the American polity—confidence that economic efficiency and equity are well-served by private-sector investment decisions, and support for constitutional decentralization of political authority. The national government is loath to intervene where myriad individual investment decisions "naturally" produce local economic growth or dislocation. Insofar as these events are place-specific, subnational levels of government are the appropriate makers of policies to magnify or offset the effects of these decisions. Therefore, primary urban policy responsibility lies with states and localities, and these policies are driven fundamentally by the need to create conditions for private-sector capital formation.

Both devolution of political responsibility and dependence on private-sector decisions to encourage or sustain urban economic health introduce a striking degree of interjurisdictional competition among states, metropolitan areas, and county and municipal governments. The fiscal health of subnational governments depends on their ability to tax residential and commercial assets and income; unequal abilities to generate funds to provide urban services are offset only partially by transfers from higher levels of government. As a result, both local governments (which depend on local revenues) and local owners of residential and commercial property (who demand city services and expect competitive returns on invested capital) hold a common stake in local economic development. In almost every major urban center, the resulting "growth coalitions" of public- and private-sector leaders have devised a set of generic strategies to attract new investment, retain existing industries, and foster creation of new, indigenous lines of business. For these purposes, local governments, at times supported by states, have created a bewildering variety of development incentive programs including property and other tax relief, favorable land-use policies, targeted public works spending, and direct capital assistance programs to influence private investment decisions. Within metropolitan areas, states, and multistate regions, competitive pressures to attract private capital hold down tax rates, serve as a brake on public-sector spending, and encourage provision of investment subsidies.

Nevertheless, state and local governments face structural limits on their ability to encourage economic development. These limits are tied to national and international economic shifts, changes in manufacturing and commercial technologies, and federal policies that have promoted residential deconcentration. From the standpoint of urban areas and central cities, in particular, the net result has been increasing concentrations of low-income residents who place the most demands on urban services but are least able to pay for them. Moreover, suburban jurisdictions have reinforced this pattern, by virtue of their land-use authority and its ability to restrict affordable housing development. The fiscal and social consequences of this pattern of income segregation, rather than the economic role of central cities, have prompted episodic federal efforts to craft and implement urban policies and programs.

Throughout the decades of national policy development described in the sections following, it is difficult to find genuinely influential contributions of economic and social science research to the policy process. Perhaps more than any other policy area discussed in this volume, urban economic program development has been driven by political definitions of policy problems that have been largely uninformed by systematic and technically competent social science research. Other policy arenas have responded similarly to political rather than analytic assessments of problems and feasible solutions, but urban economic development policy has benefited neither from widely shared and relatively stable understandings of national purpose nor a body of applied policy research supported by federal agencies.

There are several reasons for this. First, most federally supported economic development efforts have been short-lived, reflecting underlying doubts about the legitimacy of federal involvement. No strong constituency of beneficiaries or bureaucrats has emerged to support consistent federal policies and programs and attendant demands for program improvement that generate evaluation research. Second, perhaps more than most other program areas, urban economic development efforts have combined multiple and often conflicting objectives. No easily characterized set of expected outcomes is available to guide design and conduct of evaluation research. Third, economic development efforts are highly contextual in terms of both implementation and expected benefits. Unlike standard program delivery technologies that typify other federal efforts, economic development programs in the hands of local administrators take on an extreme variety of implementation arrangements, subsidy mechanisms, and intended beneficiaries. Finally, economic development program benefits are highly diffuse and largely unmeasurable. Direct investments in urban real property or business assets may aim to create jobs directly, but generally create a set of general market conditions that encourage more extensive, indirect investments that are not readily observable or easily linked to initial program outlays. As a result of these factors, federal agencies tend not to sponsor large-scale, highly professional research on urban economic development. To the extent that policy analysts do inform the policy development process, they do so through popular writings that draw attention to one or another dimension of urban economic ills, or through applied analyses that examine specific tools and techniques.

EMERGING FEDERAL INTEREST

In the aftermath of World War II, the nation renewed its focus on the unattended social problems that accompanied the Great Depression, including the problems of the urban poor. The cities' slums, with their extreme population density and high rates of substandard housing, were seen as breeding grounds of tuberculosis, juvenile crime, and chronic dependency on charity and government largess. In particular, poor-quality housing—ill-ventilated, rodent-invested, and unsanitary—was viewed as an imminent threat to both the health of occupants and that of all urban dwellers. Moreover, the urban population had swelled through immigration from abroad and internal migration, signaling that the problems of the urban poor were expected to mount.

Urban Renewal Program

Cognizant of the scale of the problem and of the limited ability of municipal governments to respond, the Redevelopment Act of 1949 authorized creation of the Urban Renewal Program, destined to leave a stamp on federal involvement in central-city problems that continues through the present. The act's immediate objective was to promote physical revitalization. It authorized federal expenditures through local renewal authorities to acquire land, demolish property, and relocate residents and businesses to create areas in which new, high-quality housing and commercial areas would be constructed. The act also aimed for a "public-private" partnership by intending that the land assembled and cleared be sold to private-sector investors motivated by prospective investment returns. Finally, the act mandated, in effect, that state governments accord the appropriate authority to their constituent counties and municipalities to acquire land for private benefit—another core ingredient in subsequent development incentive programs.

Throughout the 1950s and 1960s, the Urban Renewal Program registered some spectacular successes in central-city redevelopment. Among the most dramatic of these occurred in Pittsburgh, which created a new core of urban parkland, commercial buildings, and civic facilities—all on land once occupied by old industrial buildings, railroad facilities, and dilapidated residential properties. The city's Urban Redevelopment Authority acquired hundreds of individual parcels, cleared them of existing buildings, and financed relocation of their residential and business occupants. Thus, the city took on the risk of large-scale redevelopment, and through its power of eminent domain, held down the otherwise massive costs of parcel-by-parcel acquisition. For its part, the private sector under the leadership of the Allegheny Conference—a pro-growth coalition of business, finance, and government—promoted investment in the land made available. This flagship effort in central business district revitalization was to be replicated in other cities, and set the stage for two successive waves of city renewal in the 1970s and 1980s.

However successful as a magnet for commercial investment and a generator of new property tax revenues to finance urban services, urban renewal did little to alleviate the plight of residents of substandard housing, the program's intended beneficiaries. Rather, few of the low-income residents displaced from their homes could afford the new housing built under the program, nor could business owners afford rents in newly developed commercial properties. In effect, the national Urban Renewal Program had been "captured" by local growth coalitions. Moreover, not all residents or property owners received the relocation payments to which they were entitled, and many who did resented the destruction of once-vibrant neighborhoods. Not surprisingly, most city programs encountered organized opposition to urban renewal by those who suffered its ill effects. Derided in some quarters as "Negro Removal," the program's social costs were borne disproportionately by African-American residents, who were prominent in local efforts to forestall large-scale clearance.

Research by local and national scholars supported some of the claims made by local political opponents of urban renewal efforts. Studies in Boston and elsewhere found adverse psychological effects of forced relocation on long-time residents of neighborhoods in the path of redevelopment. Neighborhoods to which residents moved tended to be no better, and sometimes worse, than the communities they had left. Studies at the national level confirmed the costs imposed on city residents, and further exposed the program's mixed record of success, nationally, in promoting increased local tax revenues. The most influential of these studies—Martin Anderson's *The Federal Bulldozer*, published in 1964—documented shortfalls in expected private-sector investment, local tax revenues, and pace of redevelopment.

Despite criticism from local opponents and national observers, the Urban Renewal Program continued until 1974. Indeed, successful programs in Pittsburgh, Baltimore, and other cities demonstrated that under the right circumstances, with the appropriate leadership, and pursuant to a coherent strategy for renewal, the program could work. Encouraged by these examples, urban renewal's national supporters responded to critics by pressing for limited program reforms, arguing that earlier expectations for widespread and swift success had been unrealistic and that the benefits of urban renewal would become manifest as local programs matured. Nevertheless, the program would eventually succumb to Richard Nixon's "New Federalism," discussed in a later section.

Suburban Flight and Its Effect on the Inner City

What the federal government gave central cities with one hand, it took away with the other. Throughout the decades of the 1950s and 1960s, the government articulated a national interest in central-city revitalization, while at the same time promoting massive redistribution of population and capital investment from central cities to suburbs through highway and housing programs. The Federal Aid Highway Act of 1956 authorized federal financing of a national system of interstate highways on a scale many times the amounts made available for urban renewal. Intended primarily to forge connections among regions and metropolitan areas, the federal highway program also funded urban expressway networks that dramatically reduced commuting times from suburban areas to central business districts. At the same time, federal mortgage insurance programs, by reducing risks to residential mortgage lenders, stimulated construction of modestly priced housing in areas newly opened by highway construction. Reflecting migration induced by direct and indirect federal support for suburban housing development, the 1970 decennial census showed that the national suburban population exceeded the central-city population for the first time.

The loss of more affluent central-city residents and large portions of the largely white middle class to the relative privacy, safety, and affordability of suburban neighborhoods accelerated an already apparent trend toward minority and low-income population concentrations in central cities. At the same time, the economic role of cities changed dramatically as a result of interregional population migration, innovation in industrial technologies, and national shifts in the sectoral composition of the economy. The net effect of these developments would be the substantial erosion of central-city employment opportunities for minority and low-skilled workers.

First, the 1960s witnessed the emergence of the services sector—finance, real estate, insurance, and information—as a primary employer in central cities. The relative efficiencies of concentrated centers of services activity gave central cities a competitive advantage in the location of new services firms. Although the emergence of the service sector was important as a spur to new investments in central-city commercial property, it began a trend that analysts later would identify as a bifurcation in labor markets: high-skill/high-salary employment in one portion of the new city economy and low-skill/low-wage jobs in another. Second, redistribution of population opened new regional markets in the South and West, redirecting national investment from traditional manufacturing centers of the Northeast and Midwest. Third, improvements in manufacturing technologies rendered central-city industrial plants functionally obsolete. Older vertical processes gave way to land-hungry horizontal processes, and decreasing transportation costs as a share of total production costs diminished the attractiveness of central-city proximity to urban markets. Suburban and nonmetropolitan areas became the location of choice for new manufacturing enterprises.

Driven first by the persistence of poverty in America, particularly within ethnic minority communities, and then by an upsurge in urban violence in the mid-1960s, the federal government responded to the problems of deteriorating central-city residential neighborhoods and diminished job opportunities. The Demonstration Cities Act of 1966 created a new program for comprehensive neighborhood renewal, with an emphasis on strategic investments in housing renovation, neighborhood facilities, urban services, and job creation activities. The Economic Development Act of 1965—primarily intended to respond to problems of rural underdevelopment—authorized limited federally subsidized investments in central-city manufacturing facilities. These programs are discussed in turn next.

Model Cities Program

Lyndon Johnson's administration created the Model Cities Program (a product of the Demonstration Cities Act of 1966) to channel federal aid to neighborhoods through specialized city agencies. In contrast to the social service and job training focus of the earlier Community Action Program, Model Cities strove for comprehensiveness, including both physical revitalization and improved social services. Demonstration agencies were to tap earmarked streams of federal assistance channeled through the departments of Housing and Urban Development (HUD), Health, Education & Welfare (HEW), Labor, and other bureaucracies.

Underfunded from the outset and hobbled by federal agencies that were unwilling and largely unable to effect genuine coordination of program delivery, Model Cities did not achieve much in the way of comprehensive neighborhood renewal. Moreover, although concentrated neighborhood planning seemed to promise genuine strategic interventions in poverty neighborhoods, the program quickly became hobbled by increasingly complex planning, procedural, and evaluation requirements. As a result, funding for Model Cities was sufficient to establish an elaborate network of governmental agencies, but failed to deliver much in the way of housing, social services, or business development.

Model Cities had been crafted and implemented based on considerable faith in the ability of social science—sociology, economics, and public administration—to devise effective solutions to complex social problems. The evident failure of Model Cities did much to shatter this belief. Partly, the failure stemmed from the sheer complexity of the policy problem: the multiple and often obscure causes of persistent poverty and unemployment defied analysts' best attempts to model real world problems. Partly, the failure stemmed from the complexities of urban governance. The problems of poor areas are multidimensional, whereas the organization of government is functional and problem-specific: housing agencies provide rental assistance, police departments fight crime, welfare departments provide income supplements, and so on. One enduring but illusory appeal of area-targeted programs is their promise to impose a coherent pattern on an otherwise fragmented public service delivery system.

Economic Development Act

Attacks on urban unemployment did not rest only on neighborhood-centered solutions. The Economic Development Act of 1965 established the nation's first area-targeted business investment program intended to create jobs for the unemployed. The act authorized a package of programs under the auspices of the federal Economic Development Administration (EDA) that offered cut-rate investment capital to business, and land and infrastructure development grants to cities and rural areas. Although this dual program focus advanced the concept of the public-private partnership, it did little to spur new business investment in central-city manufacturing.

Primarily designed as a rural development effort, the EDA's programs were ill-suited to remedy urban employment problems because of the types of investments they supported, the nature of unemployment, and the types of subsidies offered to business. First, the program's support for infrastructure investments enhanced the competitive position of rural areas that lacked basic highway, water, and sewer facilities. Urban areas that were already well-provided with basic infrastructure faced more fundamental barriers to private-sector manufacturing investment, including regional transportation bottlenecks, high labor costs, and above-average security and property insurance expenses. Second, rural areas suffered a dearth of employment opportunities, a lack remedied fairly simply by new manufacturing plant sitings. In contrast, urban unemployment stemmed primarily from the problems of a core group of unemployed among a large number of easily employed. This core group of the chronically out-of-work possessed few of the job skills needed by specialized manufacturing concerns and never developed the work habits instilled by continuing attachment to the labor force. The capital investments supported by the EDA did not attack these problems. Finally, EDA funds subsidized capital, not labor. Discounted loans encouraged business to invest in plants and equipment. Such incentives are most attractive to capital-, rather than labor-intensive, industry. Therefore, these subsidies tended to be rather inefficient as employment-generating incentives.

Ironically, among economic development efforts of the period, only Economic Development Administration programs, targeted to rural areas, were informed by the previous research of regional economists. Earlier European and American research on "growth poles"—spatial nodes in regional economies that represented high-payoff investment opportunities—followed traditional central-place concepts of regional economic geography. Because of the agglomeration effects conveyed by geographic proximity of producers, concentrated public investments in designated growth centers promised to generate high returns to public capital in the form of increased employment and private investment. New EDA programs therefore encouraged designation of growth centers in rural locations, and also supported regional economic development planning efforts intended to promote strategic rather than scattered investments. Nevertheless, despite well-intended design, the practical politics of EDA grant-making together with continued expansion of areas eligible for assistance ultimately resulted in an extremely wide distribution of federally supported projects.

URBAN POLICY AND "NEW FEDERALISM"

Neither Model Cities nor Economic Development Administration programs were funded at levels sufficient to make a serious dent in urban economic problems. Moreover, by the early 1970s, numerous government-sponsored and academic research efforts had shown the discouraging results of federal assistance efforts across a wide spectrum of programs. On the whole, Model Cities, Urban Renewal, and Economic Development Administration programs proved expensive, cumbersome to implement, sometimes inappropriate to local needs and conditions, and disappointingly short of concrete successes. Indeed, the entire intergovernmental aid system came under fire. The War on Poverty had been less a strategic and coordinated assault on urban ills than a series of piecemeal and ad hoc attacks on specific problems. As a result, by the early 1970s state and local administrators confronted a bewildering array of federal regulations attached to literally thousands of separate grant-in-aid programs. In sum, federal efforts to promote urban revitalization were perceived as both ineffective and needlessly complex.

Two related developments aimed to improve the quality of federal intervention and streamline the system. First, despite criticism of federal efforts to plan and implement economic renewal efforts, considerable optimism remained within the policy community that well-conceived federal efforts to intervene in local economies could bear fruit. In 1970, senior governmental and congressional staff urged the formulation of a national urban policy intended to guide program development in all domestic agencies. Agencies were to coordinate efforts to combat the breakdown of the inner-city social fabric, reduce economic and social disparities between central cities and suburbs, and build state and local institutional capacity to respond to urban problems. In 1972 the new Nixon administration created the Council for Urban Affairs (later renamed the Domestic Policy Council) to bring together executive branch department heads to develop strategies for urban renewal—strategies to be enshrined in a national urban policy document.

Second, the Nixon administration embarked on a policy of "New Federalism" that would consolidate multiple streams of federal assistance into three or four super-programs or block grants. This policy would retain the overall national objectives of the programs replaced, but devolve decision-making authority to localities. Henceforth, state, county, and city administrators would determine what kinds of programs to implement locally to meet the employment, social services, community development, and other objectives of federal legislation. Local administrators would replace federal bureaucrats as primary decision-makers, would craft programs to respond to unique local circumstances, and would be held accountable to both local constituencies and federal program monitors.

Both the Council for Urban Affairs and the "New Federalism" policy achieved only limited success. Federal urban policy formulation never enjoyed strong presidential support. Efforts to coordinate policy across fragmented federal agencies foundered on the reef of bureaucratic turfism and jealousy among congressional committees responsible for program authorization and agency oversight. The national urban policy document presented a patchwork of federal "urban" efforts that simply repackaged ongoing programs or documented limited and weakly funded "demonstrations" of new program approaches. A brief attempt later in the 1970s to reinvigorate urban policymaking ended with the election of Ronald Reagan on a program of federal withdrawal from issues of purely "local" responsibility. In retrospect, the failure to formulate a genuinely comprehensive urban policy marked the end of an era of widespread belief in the ability of the national government to plan and execute effective solutions to urban ills. As the decade wore on, continuing depopulation of central cities, interregional and international migration of manufacturing jobs, and new and more virulent symptoms of urban social distress eroded confidence among policymakers and the urban poor that quick solutions to urban distress could be devised. Moreover, the conviction that research could unerringly guide national policy development gave way to a more realistic perception of the complexity of regional and local economies and the limits of public-sector intervention.

Community Development Block Grant Program

Attempts to streamline the intergovernmental aid system through creation of block grants achieved somewhat better success, most notably in the area of community economic development. The U.S. Congress consolidated seven "categorical" programs administered by the Department of Housing and Urban Development into a single Community Development Block Grant (CDBG) Program, which combined Urban Renewal, Model Cities, and several other programs to fund community facilities, public works, and local planning. The CDBG program allocated funds to metropolitan areas and central cities on the basis of a national formula. Communities then selected the types of activities and the neighborhoods in which investments would be made, without federal interference so long as the programs and areas funded fell within broad federal eligibility guidelines. At the same time, Congress authorized several national subsidized housing development programs that promoted the renovation of low-income rental and homeowner housing located in declining central cities.

Both community development and housing programs were expected to contribute directly to the improved living circumstances of the urban poor and to aid in the overall economic progress of central cities. For example, renovation of multifamily housing created standard-quality units at affordable rents and restored formerly blighted properties to city tax rolls. Investments from CDBG funds in urban infrastructure and housing rehabilitation contributed to the revitalization of some neighborhood housing markets. Nevertheless, neither CDBG nor federal housing programs successfully staved off continuing decline of central-city neighborhoods. Housing programs proved expensive, and the location of assisted properties in distressed central-city areas perpetuated segregation along racial and class lines. Community development efforts fell victim to local pressures to widely distribute investments across urban neighborhoods rather than to concentrate efforts in selected areas with the highest developmental payoff. Moreover, the small amounts of funding relative to massive withdrawals of residential and industrial capital out of central cities could produce only piecemeal successes in urban revitalization. However, the program did foster state and local capacity to deliver housing and community development programs. Prior to the CDBG program, few cities could claim expertise in housing program administration or neighborhood development planning. As a result of the program, most cities and urban counties established community development offices staffed by housing rehabilitation specialists, city planners, and experts in local public works.

The Community Development Block Grant was an emphatically neighborhood-centered initiative. Although the downtown-focused Urban Renewal Program was blended into the CDBG program, the latter's authorizing legislation and implementing regulations effectively limited the program's use in urban central business districts to relatively few communities and a small share of funds. Moreover, the scale of public funding needed to attract private-sector investment to downtown commercial projects typically amounted to sums that approached or exceeded cities' annual CDBG allocation. To replace lost federal support for central-city economic development and bolster the central-city competitive position in urban commercial and retail markets, the administration of Jimmy Carter supported legislation to create a new grants program that would carry on the work of the now-defunct Urban Renewal Program.

Urban Development Action Grant Program

The Urban Development Action Grant (UDAG) Program symbolized a new spirit of cooperation between the public and private sectors—the so-called public-private partnership. Of course, nearly all previously successful public efforts to spur central-city economic development had ultimately relied on the willingness of the private sector to invest in downtown real estate. Nevertheless, the UDAG program was one of the few federal efforts to directly fund private concerns through capital subsidies, even to the point of often demanding profit shares in return for discounted loans. In a departure from Urban Renewal Program practice, private-sector investment pledges were demanded up front: no public funds could be obligated to projects until binding private commitments had been made. Federal program designers hoped that public risk-sharing in untested markets would induce private investors to seize central-city profit-making opportunities. Over an eight-year period—from 1978 to 1986—the program supported thousands of downtown commercial projects, including some with national and international visibility.

The history of the UDAG program has yet to be written, and no assertions about the program's impact and legacy can be made with confidence. Nevertheless, in some cities the program appeared to establish the preconditions for local participation in the subsequent commercial property boom of the 1980s. Leading investments supported with public funds demonstrated the market potential of downtown locations, even as suburban office center development outpaced that of the central business district. Subsequent changes in federal tax policy, continuing sectoral shifts in national employment toward services industries, and local financial inducements to spur downtown office construction accelerated a trend that was begun in the late 1970s and was abetted by UDAG support.

Community Reinvestment Act

Despite the sometimes flashy success of particular UDAG projects and the program's role in stimulating at least some private investment in central cities, the program did not attack structural barriers to more general urban revitalization. Both neighborhoods and downtowns continued to suffer from shortfalls in private- and public-sector investment relative to suburban jurisdictions. Racial prejudice and aversion to the risk of lending in inner-city neighborhoods had prompted banks to "redline" areas within which they would not place mortgages on residential or commercial property. To reverse this withdrawal of capital, in 1977 Congress passed the Community Reinvestment Act (CRA) to force financial institutions to reinvest in the neighborhoods from which they took deposits. In addition to routine monitoring of loan processing exercised by the comptroller of the currency, regional Federal Reserve Banks reviewed CRA compliance of banks proposing to acquire other financial institutions. In addition, organized citizens' groups advocated for increased investments where the pattern of bank lending had disfavored central-city neighborhoods. (Subsequent amendments to the CRA strengthened oversight of financial regulatory institutions.) No systematically gathered evidence attests to the effectiveness of the new regulations, but anecdotal and single-city studies show that the act at least partially offset the drain of capital from residential neighborhoods.

Throughout the 1970s, calls mounted to stimulate public investments in urban economies through improvements to deteriorated infrastructure and expansion of highway, sewer, and storm drainage capacity. Cities faced with increasing public services demands and eroding revenue sources had shifted spending from capital stock replacement into operating expenses. Although the federal government continued to support regional highway and public transit investments (and in the early 1970s had added support programs for water and sewer investments), cities still found that the backlog of their capital stock investment needs exceeded amounts available from intergovernmental sources. Moreover, new federal water pollution cleanup mandates increased the financial burden on localities obliged to invest in new sewerage and treatment facilities.

Contemporary research by regional economists and economic geographers on the contribution of public capital investment to local area economic growth tended to be rather theoretical. Moreover, examinations of investment returns to public capital also tended to focus on developing countries, where the absolute lack of transportation and water and sewer facilities placed fairly obvious limits on economic growth. Nevertheless, informed by these abstract modeling efforts, most economists saw deteriorated transportation and clean-water compliance mandates as brakes on private-sector investment in urban areas, barriers that particularly affected older urban centers of the Northeast and Midwest that had already suffered huge manufacturing job losses.

In 1981, Pat Choate published America in Ruins (Choate and Walter 1981), a book intended for popular audiences that dramatized the abject condition of urban infrastructure and placed a staggering price tag of $1 trillion on the accumulated public investment need. Although this investment total was quickly seen as highly exaggerated, the book stimulated national debate about the role of infrastructure in urban economic renewal. Congress refused to authorize the proposed creation of a national development bank to finance local improvements, leaving state governments to move aggressively into the infrastructure finance business. Most large states conducted infrastructure needs assessments to document deteriorated facilities and created a variety of finance programs to channel funds into public works. (The ultimate payoff of these investments is unclear, but by the early 1990s, some economic analysts had concluded that public capital spending levels had returned to their historic levels as a percentage of gross domestic product.)

By and large, central cities did not fare well throughout the 1970s. Although urban economies grew at remarkable rates in the South and West, central business districts and inner-city neighborhoods did not share in this prosperity. The federal attempt to devise a national urban policy foundered, and programmatic and regulatory efforts to support downtown and neighborhood renewal registered mixed results. Nevertheless, states and localities did improve their ability to attract private capital to the nation's urban centers. Both the CDBG and UDAG programs sustained community and economic development capacity that had been built under the Urban Renewal and Model Cities programs, and created new capacity where none existed before. Industrial decline and infrastructure deterioration in some regions prompted states to adopt a more activist posture toward economic development. Indeed, by the early 1980s states and localities had put in place a bewildering variety of industrial and commercial incentive packages: venture capital funds, tax abatements, discount financing schemes, targeted employment and training programs, loan guarantees, and other inducements to private-sector investment. Sometimes derided as "smokestack chasing," these efforts to influence business location decisions reflected a fundamental reorientation in public-sector attitudes toward urban economic development. Throughout the coming decade, nearly every state and local tax and spending program would be framed with an eye toward its potential effect on private investment.

Contribution of Research

Research support for urban economic development efforts dramatized, on the one hand, the general plight of older industrial regions of the Northeast and Midwest and, on the other hand, focused narrowly on the applied technologies of industrial development incentives. In the late 1970s and early 1980s, a spate of books appeared that described the flight of capital and employment from older urban areas. Typical of the genre is Bluestone and Harrison's *Deindustrialization of America* (1982), which pointed to the social consequences of capital mobility and the failure of industrial capitalism to accord appropriate weight to the economic value of work-force skills and stability. Despite these and other criticisms of national economic organization, national policymakers did not respond to calls for an industrial policy that would attempt to offset structural shifts in the national economy.

Applied research, however, did contribute to the dizzying rate at which states and local governments introduced incentive programs for business. A small industry of industrial targeting that promised to guide strategic public use of development incentives emerged. A portion of this research was highly technical if not widely used, relying on economic base theories to guide development of regional input-output models that would highlight regional export opportunities. Other methodologies in wide application offered more rudimentary methods to match local labor and market assets to potential targets of industrial attraction.

These methods gained wide popularity at the same time that other analyses suggested their futility. David L. Birch's influential book, *The Job Generation Process* (1979), highlighted the role of small business in new job creation and cast considerable doubt on the ultimate payoff from public attempts to forestall job loss through attraction of large-scale industrial facilities. Rather, Birch's analysis suggested a reorientation to "homegrown" economic development efforts that focused on small business access to capital and removal of regulatory barriers to small business formation and growth. Moreover, regional economists increasingly challenged prevailing assumptions that direct public-sector incentives were at all influential in business location decisions. Numerous empirical analyses of local area performance and surveys of business decision makers produced conflicting or negative evaluations of industry's receptiveness to differences in local tax rates, capital subsidies, or training programs. These assessments had relatively little influence on national policy, and most state and local governments continued to promote new industrial plant location. But this research did prompt many economic developers to add business retention and indigenous small business promotion programs to their inventory of development incentives.

THE REAGAN REVOLUTION AND FEDERAL WITHDRAWAL

Ronald Reagan's election to the presidency on a pro-business, anti-government program inaugurated a decade-long attempt to fundamentally refashion federal support for urban economic development. The Reagan philosophy of governance held that the public-sector role in urban economic development should be limited to removal of barriers to business investment. Implied in this philosophy was the belief that the structural impediments to urban investment were not overcome by subsidies extended piecemeal to urban investors. Rather, apart from continued investment in infrastructure, government's role was limited to removal of tax and regulatory obstacles that inhibited the free flow of capital among sectors and regions. Further, the administration held that direct, spatially targeted incentives (such as those offered by the UDAG program) inappropriately redistributed investment and created no new national wealth. Indeed, spatially targeted investment incentives were viewed as representing a drag on national economic performance.

Typical of this policy orientation were the 1983 recommendations of the National Research Council's Committee on Urban Policy. Charged to review current and past urban policies and devise recommendations for the future, the committee recommended five basic policies to transform the national economy and make it more competitive in international markets (Committee on National Urban Policy 1983). These included policies to encourage capital flow to competitive sectors, promote construction and conservation of the urban capital stock, encourage investment of private capital in activities that *accelerate* transitions in local economies, encourage labor mobility, and promote investment in urban education. The committee implicitly acknowledged that the likely combined effect of these policies would be to stimulate an already painful economic restructuring that had so devastated the Northeast and Midwest, and especially central cities within those regions. The committee's urban prescriptions, therefore, centered on education and training policies to equip workers with the skills needed to participate in a restructured economy, and on creation of local public and private institutions to manage the transition.

In terms of explicit policy, the Reagan administration successfully dismantled the UDAG program, enacted deep reductions in business taxation, ended federal support for nonhighway infrastructure investment, reduced funding for Economic Development Administration programs (largely rural in emphasis), and further devolved decision making to states and localities for a variety of programs, including job training. The administration's only new initiative in urban economic development—"enterprise zones"—never received congressional approval, but the widespread adoption of such zones at the state and local levels and their final adoption (in much altered form as Empowerment Zones) in 1993 demonstrate both the emergence of state governments as dominant players in urban economic development and the unwillingness or inability of national government leaders to forge a genuine urban economic policy.

Enterprise Zones

Consistent with the Reagan belief that urban economic ills could be blamed largely on federal, state, and local policies, administration designers of federal "enterprise zones" saw them as "islands of opportunity" within which entrepreneurship could flourish unrestrained by burdensome taxation and unnecessary regulation. Federal proposals called for waiver of environmental and labor laws within zones, reduced capital gains tax rates, and tax credits for investment in new plants and equipment. Despite repeated attempts to obtain congressional approval, enterprise zone legislation failed time and again to clear congressional tax committees, whose members were skeptical of the zones' potential development payoff and wary of the concept as an opening wedge to more general business tax reduction. However, state governments, initially in anticipation of federal legislation and subsequently in imitation of other state programs, enacted their own enterprise zone variants. Originally conceived by federal sponsors as a spur to indigenous entrepreneurship in urban neighborhoods, state and local government sponsors tended to regard enterprise zones as industrial attraction devices, conceptually akin to other development tools in their inventories. Extremely diverse in terms of the incentives offered and the kinds of areas designated, enterprise zones had been enacted in 37 states by the late 1980s.

The popularity of the enterprise zone concept reflected states' uncritical willingness to use any and all devices that promised to generate private investment. Most economic development analysts agreed that as deterrents to urban economic development, regulations and taxes paled in comparison to the high land, labor, security, and insurance costs of urban areas. In addition, general tax preferences available to businesses that located in designated enterprise zones almost certainly would reward investors that would have chosen to locate in these areas anyway. Moreover, similar to criticisms of earlier EDA-funded programs, reliance on capital incentives tended to inappropriately reward capital-intensive industry, even though the goals of most state programs included hiring of surplus urban labor. On balance, the little empirical research on state enterprise zones concluded that they were largely ineffective in stimulating much new development activity.

Although the record of industrial and new residential development in central cities was poor, the 1980s witnessed an upsurge in downtown commercial construction produced by continuing national shifts of private capital into services industries and by federal tax preferences for real estate investment. Even though office space construction in suburban jurisdictions outpaced that of central business districts, central cities captured a portion of overall metropolitan area growth in the sector. Increasingly, states and localities accepted that public policy could do little to reverse urban manufacturing job loss. But as demonstrated by new commercial investment, not all economic shifts damaged central-city growth prospects. The burgeoning tourist and convention business offered cities an opportunity to share in a growth industry by creating new convention facilities, supporting new hotel construction through targeted infrastructure spending and tax abatements, and investing in urban amenities. Thus, despite Reagan administration cuts in federal aid to cities, urban county and municipal finances displayed surprising resilience as a result of new local revenue inflows.

Whereas commercial property development produced positive fiscal effects, it resulted in questionable benefits to unemployed central-city residents. Central cities gained white-collar jobs that remained largely unavailable to the chronically unemployed and underemployed, and a large share of supporting blue-collar employment consisted of low-wage positions with few opportunities for advancement. New manufacturing jobs and a large percentage of services industry jobs available to low-skill workers continued to be created in suburbs, even as suburban employers found it increasingly difficult to recruit persons to fill those jobs. Throughout the 1980s, academicians and other policy researchers highlighted this "spatial mismatch" between new job generation and potential job-holders. Transportation and job referral networks appeared ill-designed to promote the attachment of central-city workers to metropolitan area labor markets. Moreover, the continuing decline of central-city public education meant that recent secondary school graduates found themselves unprepared for jobs that demanded increasingly advanced levels of literacy and mastery of information technology.

In sum, the 1980s witnessed increased activism by state and local governments in urban economic development and positive signs of health in central-city economies. At the same time, federal withdrawal from even the limited economic development efforts of the

1970s removed a potential partner in urban development promotion. Finally, the inability of low-skill central-city workers to benefit from new job growth highlighted the intractability of unemployment problems in the poorest urban neighborhoods.

CLINTON ERA REASSESSMENT OF FEDERAL ROLE

The Clinton administration has implemented several new, but limited, initiatives that reassert the federal government's role as a partner in local economic development. Early in the administration, Congress finally passed a variant of federal enterprise zones—Empowerment Zones—on the strength of bipartisan support for a demonstration of federal commitment to urban areas in the wake of civil disorders in Los Angeles in spring 1992. These zones were limited in scope—Congress initially authorized 96 in total, but only nine with a package of incentives likely to attract more than minimal amounts of new investment. However, the Empowerment Zones appear to be an improvement over earlier proposals, emphasizing wage rather than capital subsidies and requiring strong local institutions to carry out development policy in the zones.

In another initiative, the Clinton administration obtained authorization for new, federally supported financial institutions to promote investment in urban neighborhoods. These Community Development Banks are intended to mobilize private-sector capital for direct investments in neighborhood residential and commercial property. The bank program is weakly funded, however, and holds little promise for major infusions of capital into distressed urban areas. In fact, administration efforts to strengthen federal enforcement of Community Reinvestment Act requirements may prove to have more enduring value. Although the financial system underwent a period of considerable uncertainty in the late 1980s and early 1990s, producing widespread reluctance among bankers to make loans on inner-city commercial or industrial property, recent administration efforts to encourage more aggressive inner-city lending coincide with a return to health of the banking system.

Recognizing that a major new commitment of federal funds is unlikely, the Clinton administration has augmented its modest spatial development policy initiatives with a simultaneous effort to "reinvent" HUD, including the department's economic development programs. This reinvention is intended to increase the efficiency of the agency's operations and in so doing afford states and localities enhanced flexibility in carrying out urban economic development policy, as well as to expand the impact of federal funding. In one of its early initiatives, for instance, the administration condensed the planning and application requirements for 12 separate community development programs into a single Consolidated Plan. Modeled on local successes with bottom-up, community-based planning, the Consolidated Plan is intended to enhance citizen and nonprofit involvement in the programming of federal funds. Quite apart from the goal of administrative efficiency, therefore, the Consolidated Plan represents a renewed attempt by the federal government to encourage local jurisdictions to use economic development funds more strategically.

The same themes of greater efficiency, greater flexibility, and greater effectiveness are woven into the administration's latest reinvention initiatives. In terms of economic development, administration proposals call for consolidation of 11 existing HUD programs—including CDBG and the Empowerment Zones—into a single block grant, the Community Opportunity Fund. As currently envisioned, the Community Opportunity Fund would incorporate performance-based criteria into the funding process—5 percent of the fund would be set aside for distribution, on a competitive basis, to communities that meet locally defined performance criteria. Performance-based assessment is intended to increase local accountability for the use of funds and at the same time provide another mechanism for HUD to encourage the effective use of federal resources. However, it is unclear whether a system of community-defined (and HUD-approved) performance criteria will be at odds with the administration's own goal of increasing local flexibility over the use of federal funds.

LESSONS AND SPECULATIONS

With the election of a Republican majority in both houses of Congress in 1994, the Clinton administration's reassessment of the federal role in urban economic development is, at least in the short term, at risk of being overshadowed. A Republican-led Congress clearly will be more hostile to the principle of federal participation in urban economic development than were its predecessors and, with policymakers taking aim at the federal deficit, economic development expenditures likely will come under increased scrutiny. Regardless of the outcome of the current debate, several thematic chords of post–World

War II experience in urban economic development will continue to resonate throughout the remainder of the century.

First, the legacy of federal support for spatially targeted development policies is probably unsustainable. With the single exception of the CDBG program and its likely successor, the Community Opportunity Fund, continuing national government support for urban revitalization on a scale expected to produce demonstrable results is highly unlikely. Moreover, if and when the federal government decides to move toward a balanced budget, it is likely that the CDBG program, the cornerstone of federal urban economic development policy, will be a target of major cuts.

Second, most researchers and policymakers now recognize the limited ability of public-sector adjustment policies to offset the spatial effects of market forces. State and local development policies will continue to support urban area participation in metropolitan services industry growth. Recently, private-sector developers appear to have turned their attention to the market potential of inner-city areas. Some economists and private investors have concluded that residential and commercial property values may have bottomed out in central cities, and that suburban retail market saturation makes central cities more attractive as targets of opportunity. Nevertheless, few central cities can expect major new investments in industrial facilities.

Third, public policy attention increasingly has centered on labor market failures and the continuing inability of public education to prepare central-city residents adequately for employment in the new services-based economy. Few significant changes in central-city growth prospects are likely without sustained attention to labor skills development. As yet, there are few signs of federal government support for major changes in education finance and job training or for introduction of supplemental wage payments to increase the attractiveness of labor market participation, and such initiatives are unlikely in the current restrictive budgetary environment. Moreover, any federal policy shifts are likely to be national in scope and relatively inattentive to the spatial dimensions of unemployment problems.

Finally, urban economic program development has been driven by political definitions of policy problems that have been largely uninformed by systematic and technically competent social science research. There is little reason to believe this pattern will change. In fact, with the likely erosion of federal support for spatial development programs, any link between research and national policy may weaken further. A shift in policymaking authority to states and localities may provide new, decentralized research opportunities; however, such research will focus primarily on the highly contextual issue of measuring program performance, and therefore will be of little value in terms of a wider discussion about interventions in central-city economies.

Except for episodic and weakly funded efforts, it is highly improbable that the nation will witness a resurgence of federal interest in spatially targeted urban programs. It is equally improbable that research will assume a greater role in shaping the national policy agenda for urban economic development.

SUGGESTED READING

Anderson, Martin. 1964. *The Federal Bulldozer: A Critical Analysis of Urban Renewal, 1949-1962.* Cambridge, MA: The Massachusetts Institute of Technology Press.

Bartik, Timothy J. 1994. "What Should the Federal Government Be Doing about Urban Economic Development?" *Cityscape* 1: 267–91.

Birch, David L. 1979. *The Job Generation Process.* Cambridge, Mass.: MIT Press.

Bluestone, Barry, and Bennett Harrison. 1982. *The Deindustrialization of America.* New York: Basic Books.

Choate, Pat, and Susan Walter. 1981. *America in Ruins: Beyond the Public Works Pork Barrel.* Washington, D.C.: The Council of State Planning Agencies.

Committee on National Urban Policy. 1983. *Rethinking Urban Policy: Urban Development in an Advanced Economy,* ed. Royce Hanson. Washington, D.C.: National Academy of Sciences, National Academy Press.

Consad Research Corporation. 1969. *A Study of the Effects of Public Investment.* Washington, D.C.: Office of Economic Research, Economic Development Administration.

Dommel, Paul R., et al. 1978. *Decentralizing Community Development.* Washington, D.C.: U.S. Department of Housing and Urban Development.

Eisinger, Peter K. 1988. *The Rise of the Entrepreneurial State: State and Local Economic Development Policy in the United States.* Madison: University of Wisconsin Press.

Frieden, Bernard J., and Marshall Kaplan. 1975. *The Politics of Neglect: Urban Aid from Model Cities to Revenue Sharing.* Cambridge, Mass.: MIT Press.

Glickman, Norman J., ed. 1980. *The Urban Impacts of Federal Policies.* Baltimore, Md.: Johns Hopkins University Press.

Green, Roy E., ed. 1990. *Enterprise Zones: New Directions in Economic Development.* Newbury Park, Calif.: Sage Publications.

Haar, Charles M. 1975. *Between the Idea and the Reality: A Study in the Origin, Fate, and Legacy of the Model Cities Program.* Boston: Little, Brown & Co.

Hansen, Niles M. 1972. *Growth Centers in Regional Economic Development.* New York: Free Press.

Harrison, Bennett. 1974. *Economic Development in Massachusetts.* Report to the Joint Committee on Commerce and Labor, Massachusetts State Legislature, November.

Kaplan, Marshall, and Franklin James, eds. 1990. *The Future of National Urban Policy.* Durham, N.C.: Duke University Press.

Ladd, Helen F. 1994. "Spatially Targeted Economic Development Strategies: Do They Work?" *Cityscape* 1: 193–217.

Mollenkopf, John H. 1983. *The Contested City.* Princeton, N.J.: Princeton University Press.

Moynihan, Daniel P. 1969. *Maximum Feasible Misunderstanding: Community Action and the War on Poverty.* New York: Free Press.

Peirce, Neal R., and Carol F. Steinbach. 1987. *Corrective Capitalism: The Rise of America's Community Development Corporations.* New York: Ford Foundation.

Peterson, George E., and Wayne Vroman, eds. 1992. *Urban Labor Markets and Job Opportunity.* Washington, D.C.: Urban Institute Press.

President's 1978 National Urban Policy Report, The. 1978. Washington, D.C.: U.S. Department of Housing and Urban Development, August.

Rich, Michael J. 1993. *Federal Policy Making and the Poor: National Goals, Local Choices, and Distributional Outcomes.* Princeton, N.J.: Princeton University Press.

Chapter Three

POVERTY

George Galster

The nation's perception of urban poverty over the last three decades is best described by the metaphor of a pendulum. Distinct swings have occurred in the amount of priority given to the issue, in the ways in which poverty has been operationally defined, and in understanding its causes. These changing perceptions of the social importance, definition, and causes of poverty are the focus of this chapter. Not surprisingly, along with these changes have come dramatic swings in the formulation of family support and social welfare policies; these are the subject of chapter 4.

The role of policy research either in intensifying or in deflecting these perceptual swings is unclear. At times, it appears that policy research has passively followed a shift in public opinion or political discourse, whereas at other times, policy research seems to have been responsible for damping a swing or even reversing its direction, especially when the research was reinforced by a dominant White House ideology. Although an unusual consensus on the poverty issue has recently emerged, it is doubtful that even the most robust social scientific evidence will stop the pendulum from swinging, even over common empirical ground. Rather, the center of gravity on the poverty issue seems to be defined by the deeply seated American ambivalence toward the poor. Are the poor somehow fundamentally different from the mainstream and undeserving of public support, or not? Are the observed behaviors of the poor indicators of their personal shortcomings or adaptations to the structural barriers that society has erected? Thus, although demographic and economic trends and new policy research can swing the pendulum in one direction or another, such changes will be often counteracted by this underlying ambivalence toward the poor.

REDISCOVERING POVERTY IN ERA OF OPTIMISM

By the late 1950s the post–World War II prosperity in the United States had erased poverty from the political agenda. The poverty so prevalent during the Great Depression seemed a product of another era that had forever faded amid American economic dynamism. After all, the average income of families and unrelated individuals (measured in constant 1954 dollars) had risen from $3,343 in 1936 to $5,150 in 1946, and to $6,193 by 1960. The percentage of families with incomes below $3,000 (in constant 1965 dollars) had fallen from 51 percent in 1936 to 30 percent in 1950, and to 20 percent by 1960. Surely economic growth had rendered the poverty issue moot, or would soon do so, according to optimistic contemporary thinking.

Not surprisingly, poverty was also a minor topic so far as social scientific policy research was concerned. Numerous scholarly observers at the time bemoaned the paucity of empirical data and theoretical perspectives on poverty. Sociologist Daniel Bell, for example (1968), remarked that when "poverty" burst into prominence in the early 1960s, social scientists "were not prepared, had no data, and didn't know what to do."

The often-cited prod to the popular and political rediscovery of poverty as a troubling issue was Michael Harrington's book, The Other America (1962). Through a series of powerful vignettes, Harrington riveted public and federal policymakers' attention on the hardships continually faced by the millions inhabiting the "other" America: the aged, people with disabilities, small farmers, racial minorities, and Appalachian residents.[1] Because of various structural barriers in the economy, Harrington argued, these people were not capable of being pulled out of poverty by general economic growth. As important as this book was, several other forces in the early 1960s were coalescing to raise the visibility of the poverty issue.

Demographic shifts spawned by technological changes were fundamental in this regard. The widespread introduction of the mechanical cotton picker in the South beginning in 1943 caused widespread economic dislocations that—coupled with booming industrial labor markets in northern cities—stimulated a mass migration. As a result, by 1960 over half the poor resided in cities and only 15 percent lived on farms; by contrast, in the mid-1930s half the poor had been engaged in farming. This growing concentration of the poor in inner-city areas encouraged their political organization and agitation which, in turn, enhanced their visibility in the media.

The public was also becoming concerned with several social problems related to urban poverty. Juvenile delinquency and family dissolution were widely considered "national plagues" spawned by poverty, thanks to the influential writings of researchers E. Franklin Frazier, Richard Cloward, Lloyd Ohlin, Kenneth Clark, and Daniel

Patrick Moynihan. Congress, too, was becoming impatient with the stubborn increase in the cost of the Aid to Families with Dependent Children (AFDC) program, amid rising concerns that poverty and welfare dependency were becoming "a way of life." These concerns were to resonate repeatedly throughout the next 30 years.

Arguably the most important factor in the renewed interest in the poverty issue, however, was national optimism. There was a public and professional consensus that we could devise government policies capable of eradicating poverty, and that the nation was wealthy enough to fund such eradication. As a 1962 report by the prestigious Survey Research Center at the University of Michigan asserted, "The elimination of poverty is well within the means of the federal, state, and local governments." The poverty gap could be eliminated "by the stroke of a pen," the report argued, costing only $10 billion, less than 2 percent of the gross national product (GNP). This hubris of the feasible conjoined with the morality of the desirable: if we were capable of eliminating poverty, it was unconscionable not to do so. Indeed, as Harrington (1962) had argued, poverty amid affluence was immoral.

One key indication of poverty's renewed visibility in the early 1960s was the creation of "official" measures of poverty. President John F. Kennedy's Council of Economic Advisors (CEA) sanctioned a poverty line of $3,000 for the "typical American family" of four in 1963. This figure was based on the notion that adequate nutrition was the fundamental minimum requirement in a family budget. Surveys at the time revealed that three minimally adequate meals a day would cost a family of two adults and two children $2.74 daily. Inasmuch as other surveys showed that lower-income households spent roughly one-third of their budget on food, the CEA simply multiplied their estimated food budget by three to obtain the requisite minimum complete budget. Using this procedure, the CEA estimated that there were over 34 million "officially poor" Americans in 1963.

Almost immediately there arose challenges to the appropriateness of the operational definition of poverty, a debate that lasts to this day. The CEA's definition clearly failed to adjust the presumed requisite budget for variations in family size and circumstances, and thus inadequately reflected the needs of "atypical" households. Mollie Orshansky (1968) of the Social Security Administration (SSA) undertook a painstaking revision by first adjusting for family size, then for different needs based on rural or urban residence and gender of household head. She identified 124 distinct household types and calculated a poverty line for each, based on similar assumptions as the CEA.

These SSA poverty lines continue in official use today, updated annually only to account for inflation.

The SSA definition of poverty was not without its detractors, however. Some argued that the basic food budget underpinning the poverty line estimate consisted of only the least appetizing foodstuffs and permitted little variety; "necessities" were defined in an exceedingly spartan manner. More fundamental was the criticism that the SSA poverty definition failed to account for the *relative* well-being of the poor compared to the rest of the population, because it was based on a concept of absolute biological nutritional needs. Critics argued that the sense of "relative deprivation" profoundly affected one's psychological well-being, and that the poverty line should thus be adjusted upward as the standard of living of nonpoor members of society rose.

The poverty standard one adopts has clear implications for public policy, so the debate is not purely academic. First and most obviously, by estimating the number of "poor," the poverty line chosen will crucially affect the perceived magnitude of the phenomenon. Second and more subtly, the line will also influence *who* is identified as poor, because the distribution of people by income is not constant according to age, race, family composition, or labor force participation. The choice of a more lenient standard might, therefore, include many more whites, married couples with children, and full-time workers among the poor—hardly groups one would wish to assail as "undeserving" or "culturally deviant" if trying to mobilize political support to reduce social welfare expenditures.

Policy researchers of the period also evinced little consensus on theories of the origins of poverty. Two schools of thought can be readily identified: the culturalists and the structuralists. The culturalists fundamentally saw impoverishment as a result of indelible individual shortcomings in aptitude or attitude. Those individuals performing poorly in school were presumed to be less able and motivated; those unable to secure good jobs were presumed to have previously performed poorly in school and/or to lack sufficient diligence or initiative. The origin of these shortcomings was termed the "culture of poverty"—a reinforcing set of norms, values, and aspirations that stressed fatalism, self-indulgence, and passivity. This culture was reputedly transmitted down as parents socialized their children, resulting in permanent psychological impairments such as an orientation toward immediate gratification, an inability to plan or sacrifice for the future, and various sorts of mental illness.

The structuralists, on the other hand, saw the behaviors and attitudes of the poor in a different light: as *resulting* from limited economic and social opportunities, not *causing* them. In this view, the poor's lack of achievement in school could be attributed to inferior educational institutions serving lower-income neighborhoods; discrimination on the basis of gender, race, or ethnicity; and class-based differences in social intercourse that further constrained the opportunities of the poor in the labor market. Modifications in values, aspirations, and behaviors were understandable adaptations to long-term confrontations with circumscribed opportunities, said the structuralists, but these adaptations would change if the structure of opportunities available to the poor could be altered.

This culturalist/structuralist debate on the origins of poverty holds profound implications for the formulation of antipoverty strategy. If, on the one hand, one were to see poverty as the result of immutable individual shortcomings transmitted intergenerationally, the justification for public policy intervention would be blunted. The poor would be seen as deserving their fate because they would have the opportunity to escape their plight if only they would change their values, aspirations, and behaviors. It is questionable that the government should or could intervene legally and effectively were it to try, because this would necessitate the state meddling in complex family dynamics and child-rearing practices.

On the other hand, if one were to see poverty as the result of shortcomings in social institutions, there would follow ample justification for massive programmatic interventions. The poor would be seen as undeserving of their fate because they would have been victimized by inferior education systems, depressed local economics, or discrimination. Furthermore, the government is capable in principle of altering such aspects of the social structure of opportunity. As this chapter describes, despite mounting social scientific evidence to the contrary, a sizable share of the American public has clung tenaciously to the culturalist view. This has severely constrained the type and scale of programmatic responses aimed at attacking poverty and thus, implicitly, has limited the impact of policy research.

Insecurity about whether we understood the origins of poverty or were measuring it in the most meaningful fashion proved insufficient in the early 1960s to dampen the swelling political consensus that poverty—however defined—was an intolerable problem. Similarly unimportant was the virtual absence of theoretical or empirical work from policy researchers that could inform the creation of guidelines for specific programmatic initiatives. The amalgam of optimism, indignity, affluence, and governmental hubris proved irresistible.

THREE WARS ON POVERTY

The 1960s witnessed three clear sets of public policy and intellectual responses to the powerful sentiment to eradicate poverty. The highly visible War on Poverty was a collection of new programs designed to increase opportunities for the poor. What could be called the "invisible war on poverty" was a revolution in the scale of benefits provided recipients under the Public Assistance, Social Security, and Medicare programs, coupled with unprecedented economic growth. Finally, what could be termed the "intellectual war on poverty" represented a fierce debate between the culturalists and the structuralists to settle the issue of the origins of poverty once and for all.

Visible War on Poverty

Although the highly publicized War on Poverty officially began in 1964 under Johnson's administration, several of the initiatives were based on programs originally developed during the Kennedy administration. Kennedy's 1961 President's Commission on Juvenile Delinquency and Youth Crime financed innovative demonstrations in several major cities for employment, remedial education, and neighborhood service centers. The Area Redevelopment Act was passed in 1961 to provide aid to geographic pockets of poverty through loans to businesses and capital for public works. The Manpower Training and Development Act was passed in 1962, and one year later had enrolled 2.2 million trainees in efforts to improve their productivity.

These programmatic principles, based on a doctrine of "expanding opportunity," were amplified during President Johnson's legislative initiatives of 1964. These initiatives were motivated not merely by ethical concerns, but also by pragmatic economics. As Johnson remarked:

> Our fight against poverty will be an investment in the most valuable of our resources—the skills and strengths of our people. And in the future, as in the past, this investment will return its cost manyfold to the entire economy. . . . We are not content to accept the endless growth of

relief rolls or welfare rolls. We want to offer the forgotten fifth of our people opportunity, not doles. (Johnson 1964, p. 56)

The Office of Economic Opportunity (OEO) was created in 1964 and was assigned the task of developing and overseeing the new panoply of opportunity-expanding initiatives.

The enemy that the visible War on Poverty was intended to conquer was the low labor productivity of the poor: their inability to earn enough to raise their incomes above the poverty line. This condition, in turn, was attributed to three factors: inadequate macroeconomic growth, inadequate personal skills, and unfair or unresponsive social institutions.

The growth factor was addressed by expansionary fiscal policies. The "full employment gap" became part of Johnson's macroeconomic lexicon as he justified the massive 1964 tax cut on grounds that it would stimulate employment and pull people out of poverty, just as "a rising tide lifted all boats." The appeal to "trickle down economics" was explicit: the poor would indirectly benefit even though they would receive no direct benefit from the tax cuts. Ironically, this view, originally promulgated by a liberal Democratic administration, would underpin a conservative Republican administration's antipoverty efforts 15 years later.

But the Johnson administration admitted that expansionary macroeconomic policies would not be sufficient to generate demand for the least productive laborers. Government-sponsored training, education, and health programs were devised to deal with the inadequate skills factor. Enhanced personnel training was provided by the Job Corps, Neighborhood Youth Corps, and the Work Incentive Program. Assistance for the school systems attended by the children of the poor was expanded through Head Start, Upward Bound, Follow Through, the Teacher Corps, and Title I of the Elementary and Secondary Education Act of 1965. Nutritional supports were provided through Emergency Food Aid and the school lunch program, and served as supplements to the Food Stamp Program that had been initiated a few years earlier. Neighborhood health centers and Medicaid were established (the latter in 1965) to subsidize the medical expenses of the poor.

To address the institutional causes of poverty, the visible War on Poverty tried to reform various social institutions through which the poor gained access to employment, products, and services. The Community Action program both attempted to coordinate various local public services and politically organize the poor to lobby on their own behalf. Legal Services was established to improve access to legal advice. And the Civil Rights Acts of 1965 and 1968 prohibited discrimination on the basis of race, color, gender, or religion in employment and housing, respectively.

Invisible War on Poverty

Unlike the visible War on Poverty, the invisible war on poverty was not hyped by politicians, its effects were not anticipated, and it operated not by improving opportunity but by directly transferring resources among segments of society. This second "war" consisted of an unprecedented expansion in the coverage and outlays of a variety of cash and in-kind transfer programs, many of which were not means tested—that is, did not require one to fall below an income threshold before becoming eligible. Between 1965 and 1974, expenditures on these transfer programs grew at an astounding annual rate of 7.2 percent in constant dollars, compared to 4.6 percent annually between 1950 and 1965. Transfer program expenditures represented 16 percent of GNP by 1974, up from 10.5 percent in 1965.

As a prime illustration, benefits for all elderly people were greatly expanded through Social Security and Medicare programs and, because one-third of the poor in 1965 were elderly, this had a salutary antipoverty effect. Although such non-means-tested programs consumed the bulk of the increases in federal income maintenance expenditures, means-tested outlays also rose, accounting for 2.8 percent of GNP in 1974 compared to only 1.9 percent in 1968 and 1.3 percent in 1950. Although Aid to Families with Dependent Children (AFDC) expenditures escalated as the proportion of poor households headed by females increased, considerable expansion occurred in the noncash programs that transferred goods and services in kind or were earmarked in other ways. After its introduction in 1965, Medicaid grew to a $9 billion budget by 1974. The value of public housing grew fivefold to $1.2 billion, and the value of Food Stamp outlays grew twelvefold to $4.3 billion during the same 10-year span.

The invisible war on poverty played a decisive role in reducing measured poverty during this period. Cash transfers pulled 5.1 million households (33 percent of the pretransfer poor) above the poverty line in 1965; by 1972 this number had grown to 7.7 million (44 percent). When the value of in-kind transfers was added, over 60 percent of the pretransfer poor had risen out of poverty. Put differently, without any of these government transfer programs, over 25 percent of all families would have been counted as poor in 1974; with these programs only 7 percent remained poor. It is noteworthy, however, that it was primarily the elderly who experienced the largest reductions in poverty relative to other groups. It was also the elderly toward whom the major spending efforts, especially Social Security and Medicare, were directed.

Intellectual War on Poverty

The third war on poverty during the period was waged among policy researchers who focused on better understanding the causes of poverty through new research initiatives supported by federal evaluation and demonstration grants. The establishment of the Institute for Research on Poverty at the University of Wisconsin in 1966, the initiation of the University of Michigan Institute for Survey Research's pathbreaking tracking of the well-being and behaviors of 5,000 families in 1967, and the founding of The Urban Institute in 1968 are all emblematic of this upsurge in rigorous policy research directed at the issue.

By the middle of the 1970s, it appeared that the structuralists had won the day. The empirical foundations of the "culture of poverty" view were debunked on numerous fronts. It was inappropriate, it was argued, to infer different attitudes and aspirations from observing different behaviors of the poor, because behaviors are also influenced by opportunities. Furthermore, surveys of the poor and those on welfare continued to indicate that they shared mainstream values and could clearly perceive the gap between their own aspirations (and hopes for their children) and the opportunities afforded them. Anthropologists like Elliot Liebow in *Tally's Corner* (1967) powerfully demonstrated the relationship between culture and the socioeconomic context. The intergenerational transmission of poverty appeared weak, as only about one-fifth of sons of fathers in low-status occupations ended up in such occupations. Finally, four-fifths of those who were ever poor during a decade did not remain constantly poor during the entire decade, clearly implying that indelible personal shortcomings were not the primary cause of their situation.

Despite mounting empirical evidence, new versions of the culturalist thesis emerged and continued to be influential in some policy-making circles. Most notable in this regard were Edward Banfield's *The Unheavenly City* (1970) and *The Unheavenly City Revisited* (1974). Banfield encapsulated the reputed psychological defect of those in "the lower class" as "present orientation"—an inability to imagine, plan for, or sacrifice for the future. According to Banfield, this defect, supposedly indelibly instilled by parents during a child's impressionable age, was responsible for a variety of social ills ranging from crime, violence, and school dropouts to the urban riots of the 1960s. The inescapable policy implication was that unless we could remove young children from the home, thereby isolating them from the corrupting influence of their parents, no antipoverty policy could succeed. Because such a strategy clearly was immoral, illegal, and impractical, we might as well save our money and pursue a "policy" of benign neglect instead, argued Banfield.

The popularity and widespread application of Banfield's treatise, despite much structuralist evidence to the contrary, belied a deeply ambivalent public opinion about the "undeserving poor." A 1964 national poll asked, "Which is more often to blame if a person is poor— lack of effort on his own part, or circumstances beyond his control?" One-third of the respondents said "lack of effort," 29 percent said "circumstances," and 32 percent thought both equally important. A 1967 poll revealed that 42 percent thought that poverty was caused by lack of effort, and only 19 percent attributed it to circumstances. And a 1969 poll showed that 55 percent of those interviewed thought poverty was due to "lack of thrift and proper money management by poor people" (see Feagin [1972] and Goodwin [1972]).

How could the United States commit to fighting both visible and invisible public policy wars on poverty given these ambivalent public opinions? The answers depend on which war is considered. In the case of the visible War on Poverty, the constraining influence of these ambivalent opinions was clear in two ways. First, the program constantly stressed opportunities, not handouts. By stimulating the economy, enhancing training options, and reducing institutional barriers, the War on Poverty was designed to lend a hand only to those demonstrating initiative and work effort. There was no attempt to provide broad-based income supports to the poor through Office of Economic Opportunity (OEO) programs; resources transferred were typically indirect and in-kind and only served the "deserving poor." Second, the scale of funding for the OEO was remarkably modest—a mere $1.7 billion annually, one-third of 1 percent of GNP—in stark contrast to the attendant hoopla and public prognostications about ending poverty in a decade.

In the case of the invisible war on poverty, other answers apply. First, most of the transfers were accomplished through programs that were not means tested and therefore did not permit recipients to be stigmatized. As noted previously, the disproportionate beneficiaries of the invisible war on poverty were the elderly who, because they were not expected to work, were considered "deserving." Second, most of the means-tested programs that aided the nonelderly were packaged as measures that would prevent poverty in the long run: education, housing, nutrition, and medical care. Third, and perhaps most important, the scale of the transfer was unintended. Indeed, it is arguable that these policies never would have been enacted had anyone realized how much they would end up costing. Skyrocketing expenditures were driven by demographics such as the explosions in the number of elderly eligible for Social Security and Medicare and in the number of female-headed households with children. Rapidly rising costs were also driven by categorical eligibility rules that automatically entitled recipients to benefits from several programs once they qualified for one. When these trends became more visible, there would be an attempt to roll back these unintended efforts directed at fighting poverty.

SECOND THOUGHTS

By the mid-1970s, four factors had coalesced to produce second thoughts on the poverty issue. These were by no means mutually consistent nor did they imply similar policy responses.

The first factor was a ratcheting down of the earlier general sentiment that the federal government, guided by social science, could effectively design and deliver an effective solution to a massive social problem. Policy researchers may have reached a consensus that poverty was not due primarily to cultural factors, but they came to realize that they knew little about which structural barriers should be attacked and with which policy tools. As (now Democratic senator) Daniel Patrick Moynihan remarked (1970), "Social scientists have no business prescribing. They don't know enough to even seriously consider attempting that." The minimalist scale of funding afforded the visible War on Poverty was also discouraging to many.

The second factor was a growing belief that general economic growth combined with expanding opportunity were insufficient to eliminate poverty. For those capable of working, the education and training programs sponsored by the OEO appeared to have only modest payoffs, even in a period of robust macroeconomic activity. This suggested shortcomings in the quantity and location of jobs providing decent wages, not simply in the attributes of workers. For those not expected to work (mothers of young children, the elderly, and disabled persons), job opportunities were irrelevant; targeted income support was of more concern.

The third factor was dramatic declines in poverty overall, coupled with increases in poverty for selected groups. Overall, the official poverty rate declined from 17 percent of the population (33 million people) in 1965 to 13 percent (27 million people) in 1979. After receipt of in-kind transfers, these figures dropped even further, to 13 percent and 6 percent, respectively. But poverty among unwed mothers of dependent children and among racial minorities living in central-city ghettos proved more stubborn. Increasingly these neighborhoods were seen as being inhabited by a distinct subcategory of the poor reputedly characterized by a confluence of especially distasteful problems: substance abuse, violence, criminal activity, lack of attachment to the labor force, multigenerational welfare dependency, illegitimacy, and low educational achievement.

The fourth factor was a recognition of the huge and unanticipated outlays for social welfare programs, especially those comprising the invisible war on poverty: non-means-tested programs like Social Security and means-tested programs like Dependent Children, Food Stamps, and Medicaid. From 1965 to 1975 federal outlays for non-means-tested programs rose from $59 billion to $171 billion, and means-tested programs rose from $21 billion to $72 billion (in constant 1984 dollars).

These four factors produced two widely divergent responses. Some concluded that, even if we did not know how to fight the root structural causes of poverty, we did know how to eliminate its prime manifestation—lack of purchasing power. Thus, according to this view, the focus should be on a more efficiently designed and adequately funded income transfer system. Others concluded that the War on Poverty had been won, and therefore that we should switch our resources to more deserving concerns.

The former group dominated in most policy research and policy-making circles. The favorite policy prescription of the era was the "negative income tax." This plan was touted both by liberals such as James Tobin and conservatives such as Milton Friedman, and was the subject of a large-scale demonstration proposed as part of President Carter's comprehensive welfare reform package. It was also featured as the cornerstone of urban policy in *Urban America in the Eighties*, the 1980 report by the Carter-appointed Commission for a National Agenda for the Eighties. As envisioned by its many supporters, the negative income tax would be administered by the Internal Revenue

Service and would be designed to replace the patchwork social welfare system involving various levels of government dispensing both cash and in-kind types of assistance. A floor cash income would be guaranteed irrespective of work effort. Every dollar of labor earnings would reduce the guaranteed amount by some fraction (the "negative tax rate") until, at some "break-even" level of earnings, the worker would receive no subsidy and pay no taxes. Earnings above this point would be taxed according to the regular (positive) income tax schedule. The scheme was praised for its potential efficiency of administration, work incentives, breadth and adequacy of coverage, fairness, and simplicity.

Despite its promise and widespread support in the policy community, a universal system of guaranteed cash incomes through a negative income tax was never instituted. The public never swallowed the idea of universal minimum income supports, primarily because of the public's longstanding suspicion that large segments of the poor were undeserving of governmental largess. Such suspicions were reinforced during the late 1970s by the mix of factors previously cited: growing belief that the "deserving poor" had already been helped out of their poverty, and that those who remained were too incorrigible to be effectively helped or to warrant help.

Such sentiments played into the hands of those who declared the War on Poverty "won." Perhaps most influential in this group was Martin Anderson, who wrote *Welfare* (1978). Hadn't total federal public assistance expenditures risen from $3 billion in 1965 to $63 billion by 1980? Although the pretransfer poverty rate was about 21 percent in both years, hadn't the effect of cash and in-kind transfers been to reduce the posttransfer figure to 6 percent in 1980, compared to the more modest reduction to 13 percent achieved in 1965? Buttressed by such facts, Anderson could assert, "The 'war on poverty' that began in 1964 has been won. . . . Any Americans who truly cannot care for themselves are now eligible for generous government aid in the form of cash, medical benefits, food stamps, housing and other services." Anderson's policy conclusion was that we should enact modest welfare reforms that would tighten eligibility requirements, reduce caseloads and trim costs, and expand work incentives, but not guarantee a minimum income floor. Although liberals such as Sheldon Danziger and Robert Plotnick were to rail against such complacent conclusions in their book *Has the War on Poverty Been Won?* (1980), even more draconian lessons concerning the relationship between welfare policy and poverty were about to be drawn.

BIG BROTHER, URBAN DEINDUSTRIALIZATION, AND DÉJÀ VU

By the late 1970s there was irony to claims about "solving the poverty problem," because by many indicators the overall economic status of the population had been in decline since roughly mid-decade. The poverty rate, which had fallen steadily from 22 percent in 1960 to 11 percent in 1978, had begun to climb, reaching 13 percent by 1980. The total population below the official poverty line, which had fallen steadily from 40 million in 1960 to 23 million in 1973, had risen to 28 million by 1980. From World War II through 1973, the average weekly earnings of 40-year-old men climbed 2.5–3 percent annually, after accounting for inflation; from 1974 onward, real wages stagnated and declined. Between 1973 and 1980, for example, average family income declined 7 percent, in constant dollars. This fundamental economic deterioration provided a context and a stimulant for a panoply of responses. Some sought understanding of the causes in government programs or in macroeconomic forces; others sought scapegoats or ways of perceptually minimizing the trends.

These responses were represented in the four crucial intellectual currents in poverty policy research circles that characterized the 1980s. The first was a reassessment of the negative effects of means-tested welfare programs, as part of a broader effort to reexamine the "big brother" role of the federal government. The second was a neo-structuralist analysis of poverty in urban areas as it related to changing industrial composition. The third was a preoccupation with quantifying the extent and understanding the origins of a hypothesized multiple-disadvantaged urban poverty group—the "underclass." The fourth was a heated debate over the "true" extent of poverty in the nation, a debate ultimately over the proper definition of poverty. The last two currents represent reprises of themes dominating the field in the early 1960s, hence the déjà vu description. The first current clearly resulted in the most tangible policy impacts, inasmuch as it stemmed from and ultimately fueled a rising political conservatism. The racial overtones of the first and third currents also powerfully shaped civil rights policies during the 1980s, a point amplified in chapter 9. These currents are described further in the paragraphs following.

Welfare Programs as Cause of Poverty

Although expansion in non-means-tested programs such as Social Security was by far the largest component of the growth in federal public assistance spending in the 1970s, it was the set of means-tested programs, generically called "welfare," and the AFDC program in particular, that spawned the greatest backlash in public and policy research circles. The backlash drew sustenance from the observation that cash transfers for welfare grew seven-fold between 1965 and 1980, yet rates of childbearing out-of-wedlock and of nonparticipation in the labor force also escalated dramatically, especially among urban African-Americans.

The key intellectual revolution was the hypothesized causal linking of these facts in a way that stood the War on Poverty's reputed "victory" on its head. Instead of solving the poverty problem, "big brother's" ill-conceived welfare policies were now *causing* poverty by fostering dependency and other socially counterproductive behaviors. The leading fomenters of this revolution were George Gilder in his book *Wealth and Poverty* (1981), Charles Murray in *Losing Ground* (1984), and Lawrence Mead in *Beyond Entitlement* (1986).

Gilder (1981), Murray (1984), and Mead (1986) did not, however, focus their attacks on the visible War on Poverty directed by the OEO, but instead on the less visible war that led to an expansion of means-tested welfare payments, especially AFDC. They argued first that these programs created strong work disincentives for women because they reduced welfare benefits too rapidly as earned income rose, thereby producing little (if any) net increase in total purchasing power associated with working. Second, they claimed that because AFDC only supported single mothers, there were incentives for parents to not marry and for married parents to separate. Third, they claimed that males in disadvantaged communities also were corrupted by welfare in a variety of ways, making them more prone to crime, to labor force nonparticipation, and to other irresponsible behaviors. Thus, these authors argued that welfare sucked both men and women into a cycle of self-destructive behavior and deepening dependency that rendered their poverty indelible.

These were not fundamentally new arguments, but each author added unique and rhetorically powerful twists. Gilder (1981) claimed that "the only dependable route from poverty is always work, family, and faith." Welfare destroys all three, said Gilder. The dissolution of families was especially detrimental to the fathers, because it removed from them the stabilizing impetus of being a responsible provider; instead, their "disruptive male aggressions" ran amok, with awful consequences for themselves and the neighborhoods in which they lived: indolence, violence, impulsiveness, and flamboyance. Mead (1986) argued that the fundamental problem was that welfare shielded recipients from the threats and rewards of the market economy, and thus reduced their ability to "function" effectively in modern society. Welfare fostered a lack of personal accountability and social responsibility. Work, in contrast, engendered the opposite traits and thus was to be valued for its therapeutic effects. It was both ethical and efficient, Mead argued, to enforce a new social contract whereby the poor would be obligated to perform menial tasks in society in return for welfare support. Murray's (1984) contribution was an attempt to quantitatively support the preceding claims, typically with simple correlations among annual trend data for the nation as a whole.

These charges generated a storm of controversy in policy research circles and spawned much new empirical research. Murray's work, in particular, was effectively discredited by a veritable hailstorm of critiques. The general conclusion reached by analysts by the end of the 1980s was that the empirically testable claims of Gilder, Murray, and Mead were vastly overblown. The weight of evidence suggested that the amount of AFDC payments has a negligible effect on the rate of unwed childbearing, although it apparently does increase mothers' likelihood of being heads of household by either encouraging divorce, delaying remarriage after divorce, or encouraging unwed mothers to form separate households.

Regardless of the logical and empirical rebuttals, the arguments of Gilder, Murray, and Mead held sway in federal policymaking circles, and provided the intellectual foundation for the ideologically motivated policy initiatives that emerged from President Ronald Reagan's White House beginning in 1981. The radical cutback of the scope and level of means-tested social welfare programs and an installation of "workfare" requirements for welfare recipients represented the clearest manifestations. These developments illustrate the potential force of speculations and hypotheses that, although supported only by casual empiricism, can hold sway when they are ideologically resonant with those in power and legitimated by widespread marketing and repetition.

Deindustrialization as Cause of Poverty

During this same period there arose a competing theory of the cause of poverty that had nothing to do with the role of government. Rather, it represented a new variant of the structural theory of poverty that had dominated discourse since the 1960s. This theory focused on the changing industrial landscape created by technological innovations and intensified international competition. This "deindustrialization" theory was based on the fundamental changes that had occurred in the nation's economy since World War II, especially during the last two decades. These changes were most dramatically represented by the decline in high-wage manufacturing jobs and the growth in both low- and high-wage service sector employment. From 1947 to 1969, full-time employment in manufacturing declined from 27 percent of all employment to 26 percent; by 1984, however, this figure had tumbled to 19 percent. During the same period, jobs in finance, insurance, and real estate grew from a 13 percent share of all jobs to a 28 percent share, and government jobs grew from a 12 percent share to a 16 percent share. Absolute declines in manufacturing jobs hit central cities of the North in particular. From 1967 to 1987, for example, Chicago lost 60 percent of its manufacturing jobs, Detroit lost 51 percent, New York City lost 58 percent, and Philadelphia lost 64 percent.

A concomitant rise in the educational requirements of many jobs reduced the demand for low-skilled labor. The number of jobs in which the mean educational level of employees was less than high school dropped during the 1970s by more than half in Boston, Houston, Philadelphia, and St. Louis. At the same time, over 40 percent of (especially minority) students dropped out of high school in these same cities, putting them increasingly at risk of unemployment.

Another central feature of the deindustrialization process has been decentralization: the location of remaining manufacturing jobs, as well as most new jobs of any type, has shifted out of central cities and into suburbs and small towns. These shifts, coupled with the continuing concentration of minorities and the unskilled near urban cores, have created a spatial mismatch. Potential inner-city workers' opportunities to both learn about and commute to jobs decline as their proximity to them declines. Although the empirical significance of the "mismatch" hypothesis has been much debated, there seems little doubt that labor market opportunities became more strongly differentiated over space in ways that placed central-city residents in ever more disadvantageous positions.

The two main individuals who documented these trends as an explanation for rising urban poverty since the mid-1970s were William Julius Wilson and John Kasarda. Wilson focused on the problem of inner-city poverty, especially among African-Americans, in his influential book, *The Truly Disadvantaged* (1987). To deindustrialization, Wilson added the dimension of social isolation: a reputed outmigration of middle-class African-Americans from neighborhoods suffering economic dislocations that created concentrations of unemployed poor who were bereft of middle-class role models and viable institutional and informal social support systems. To Wilson, the disturbing behaviors of those living in such concentrated poverty areas were not the results of a welfare system gone awry or a culture of poverty, but of a set of structural barriers associated with deindustrialization that foreclosed opportunities.

Many of the specific empirical hypotheses forwarded by Wilson, Kasarda, and other deindustrialization theorists have been supported subsequently, whereas others have been rejected; still others continue to be explored and tested. Regardless, the theory slowly gained widespread support in policy research, public opinion, and policymaking circles. By the start of the 1990s, this theory had become part of the conventional wisdom.

Déjà Vu: The "Underclass" and Defining Poverty

Although two new theories on the origins of poverty emerged during the 1980s, two older debates were reinvigorated at the same time: the nature of the "underclass" and the "correct" definition of poverty. Concerns about criminality, juvenile delinquency, welfare dependency, and out-of-wedlock childbearing, originally voiced in the late 1950s, resurfaced and became reified under the "underclass" rubric. The issue of how the poor should be defined grew in salience as the possible programmatic implications of conservative poverty statistics were codified during the Reagan administration.

THE "UNDERCLASS"

Although the term "*underclass*" had been used in popular and policy arenas for years, the seminal formulations of this term for the 1980s were advanced primarily by Douglas Glasgow in *The Black Underclass* (1980) and Ken Auletta in *The Underclass* (1982). These formulations differed in several key respects; ultimately, Auletta's view came to dominate the public perception. The ramification of Auletta's formulation was to divert attention away from origins to behaviors (especially to welfare dependency and birth of illegitimate children among young African-American women and to crime and nonparticipation in the labor force among young African-American males), and to attribute these failures to a neoculture of poverty.

Glasgow (1980), on the other hand, clearly saw the focus as elsewhere. He described the "underclass" as "a permanently entrapped population of poor persons, unused and unwanted, accumulated in various parts of the country." They were there because "structural factors found in market dynamics and institutional practices, as well as the legacy of racism, produce and then reinforce the cycle of poverty and, in turn, work as a pressure exerting a downward pull toward underclass status." Thus, claimed Glasgow, it was lack of opportunity that produced, among other effects, lack of labor force participation among young African-Americans. It was the virtual inescapability of their plight, not moral or ethical unworthiness, that primarily distinguished them from the rest of the poor.

Auletta's downplaying of structural causes and his focus on behaviors of the "underclass" embodied a number of categories that defined the group: passive, long-term welfare recipients; hostile street criminals and hustlers operating in the underground economy; and traumatized drunks, drifters, and mentally ill people roaming the streets. When origins were mentioned, Auletta claimed that family structure was paramount. With his emphasis on deviant behaviors and weak family structures, Auletta attracted significant attention from the popular press. "Underclass" became the new euphemism for the "undeserving poor."

Consider the following treatments of the "underclass" concept in the popular media. A 1986 cover story in *U.S. News and World Report* featured a debate between Charles Murray and William Julius Wilson on whether "a second nation" had arisen in our cities, "a nation outside the economic mainstream—a separate culture of have-nots drifting further from the basic values of the haves." Soon thereafter, an article in *Fortune* magazine by Nassar defined "underclass communities" as "urban knots that threaten to become enclaves of permanent poverty and vice." People in the "underclass" were characterized by their "behaviors—lawlessness, drug use, out-of-wedlock births, non-work, welfare dependency, and school failure." The author concluded, "Underclass describes a state of mind and a way of life. It is at least as much a cultural as it is an economic condition" (pp. 74–8). Perhaps the most influential journalist in this vein was Nicholas Lemann, who wrote on the "underclass" from a revamped "culture of poverty" perspective in the *Atlantic Monthly* in 1986. Lemann's analysis was distinctly anthropological, citing the roots of northern ghetto "underclass" behaviors in the rural southern culture of the generation before.

Whatever the nuances of the argument, the "underclass" concept served during the 1980s (and still serves at this writing) to rejuvenate the "culture of poverty" as a popular explanation of the origins of urban poverty. It also reinforced the longstanding American ambivalence about whether the poor were "different" from mainstream society. Even without its attendant associations with "criminal," "welfare bum," or "unwed mother," the very term *"underclass"* conveys an otherness and promotes what Michael Katz (1993) has called "invidious distinctions."

DEFINING POVERTY

Although scholarly work on defining poverty had continuously accumulated since the mid-1960s, the debate surrounding this issue that reemerged during the 1980s was unusually rancorous and politically charged. Conservatives, anxious to prove the efficacy of the "social safety net" of welfare reforms instituted by the Reagan administration, argued for a definition that imputed values to all in-kind transfers and medical assistance received before one could be counted as officially poor. If the remaining poor were few, it could then be argued that they must be the undeserving underclass. In 1986 the U.S. Bureau of the Census conducted such a modification and showed that this new measurement did, indeed, make a large difference in the apparent scale of the problem: the official poverty estimate of 33 million people (14 percent of the population) was thus reduced to 21 million (9 percent).

The liberal response was multifaceted. First, the official poverty line was seen as too niggardly to begin with; it had only been adjusted upward since 1963 for inflation, not in accordance with general increases in living standards. The original logic of the poverty line was now violated because the poor spent only one-fifth of their income on food (not one-third as in 1963); thus, the food budget should be multiplied by five (not three) to obtain the poverty line. Second, liberals argued that in-kind assistance should not be valued at market prices, but at the (much lower) value perceived by the recipients themselves. In addition, it was contended that medical assistance should not be added as income because an individual is compensated more highly the sicker he or she is; more medical aid does not signify an increase in standard of living or an escape from poverty. Finally, it was pointed out that official statistics do not count the homeless, migrants, and undocumented aliens (most of whom presumably are poor), because only legal households with addresses are surveyed.

The technical and philosophical debates that raged over the measurement of poverty beginning in the late 1970s persist to this day, with the respective conservative and liberal standards supported by Robert Rector of the Heritage Foundation and Patricia Ruggles of The Urban Institute. These debates should not obscure two unassailable facts, however. First, by any accounting, only a tiny fraction of all poor can reasonably be labeled "underclass." Second, by any consistent measure of definition, poverty has risen dramatically since the mid-1970s. By official estimates, poverty rose from 20.2 million people (11.4 percent) in 1978 to 35.7 million people (14.2 percent) in 1992. In addition, the poor themselves have been getting poorer absolutely. The real income of the poorest one-fifth of all families, after all cash and in-kind transfers have been included, fell 4 percent between 1979 and 1990.

AN EMERGING SYNTHESIS?

At this writing, the structuralist view appears to dominate in informing the urban antipoverty strategies of the Clinton administration, but substantial elements of "culture of poverty" and "big brother" theories are represented as well. In fact, a potentially unprecedented bipartisan consensus seems to be emerging that poverty is, indeed, a serious social problem of complex origins, although the weight placed on alternative origins varies depending on political affiliation.

For example, a structuralist view generally in line with the deindustrialization theory is implicit in widespread support for proposals for long-term human capital and public infrastructure development. Similarly, the effects of restructuring are widely seen as creating a need to help the ever-increasing number of workers who work full-time, yet cannot earn enough to raise themselves and their families out of poverty. The current bipartisan vehicle for doing so is the expanded Earned Income Tax Credit, wherein employees would receive subsidies from the Internal Revenue Service based on their hours worked and the degree to which their income falls below the poverty line. The geographic mismatch dimension of the deindustrialization theory motivates U.S. Department of Housing and Urban Development Secretary Henry Cisneros' proposals to deconcentrate central-city neighborhoods housing large proportions of poor residents.

Nevertheless, variants of the "culture of poverty" theory also appear in the contemporary policy debate. Secretary Cisneros, for example, has emphasized the need to "build community" and "fight self-destructive behaviors." His rhetoric has alluded to "culture of poverty"-like "contagion effects," wherein poverty reputedly spreads throughout a neighborhood. Other policymakers have proposed "boot camps" for troubled youngsters that would be designed to instill values of hard work and discipline. The administration's anticrime proposals involving increased police patrolling of violent neighborhoods arguably can be interpreted as responding to an underclass image of the poor.

There seems to be bipartisan consensus that welfare must be reformed to remove its pernicious work disincentives, by requiring work or training as a precondition for eligibility (à la Lawrence Mead) and by installing a time limit on eligibility. Although this aspect of the administration's antipoverty plank has been careful to eschew "undeserving poor" polemics, it certainly draws support from those who have been inculcated with that view through years of "underclass" rhetoric.

Richard Herrnstein and Charles Murray recently have added more spice to the stew of thinking about the multiple origins of poverty. Their 1994 book, *The Bell Curve*, argues that intelligence (typically as measured by IQ) is the strongest single predictor of poverty as well as a variety of behaviors classified as social problems, such as high school noncompletion, out-of-wedlock childbearing, divorce, and crime. Furthermore, they claim that intelligence is primarily a matter of heredity and that there are distinct differences in intelligence distributions among racial-ethnic groups. To the extent that a "culture of poverty" exists, it holds sway only for women of low intelligence. Claims for the genetic basis of poverty are, of course, not new. Such claims have always generated intense debate, and this case is no exception. Regardless of whether any final scholarly resolution or grand synthesis is forthcoming, however, the Herrnstein-Murray position likely will add another powerful validation to the public's perception of the poor as undeserving.

Any nascent synthesis based on a multifaceted view of the origins of poverty is tenuous, at best, and may easily dissolve when the policy debate comes firmly to grips with the emergent demography of poverty in contemporary America. This demography of poverty is characterized primarily by women and children who are increasingly concentrated in central-city neighborhoods surrounded by other poor people. In 1963 only 23 percent of all poor individuals resided in households headed by females; today this figure is close to 40 percent. Throughout the 1970s the number of children in poverty was stable, at roughly 3.5 million; between 1979 and 1983 this number jumped to 5.5 million and has changed little since. In 1990 fully 23 percent of *all* children under age six were poor; 32 percent of such youngsters were poor in central cities. Additional 1990 facts about these children confound stereotypes: 58 percent lived in single-mother families; 26 percent lived with one or more parent who worked the equivalent of one full-time job or more; 31 percent lived in a household receiving only public assistance as income; and 48 percent lived in a household receiving no public assistance. Finally, nearly half of all poor people live in central cities of metropolitan areas; the proportion of these urban poor living in neighborhoods occupied predominantly by other poor people has risen dramatically since 1970.

These demographic facts raise profoundly troubling questions. To what extent does growing up in an impoverished household affect one's likelihood of being a productive citizen as an adult? What do we expect of mothers with young children in terms of their participation in the labor force? What obligations for child care, training, or employment should the state assume? What can we do to help children without creating perverse disincentives for parents? How can moral indignation directed at "undeserving poor" parents be used to justify a niggardly social policy penalizing innocent children? Is there a point at which concentration of poor households in a neighborhood creates a critical mass, producing a culture of poverty that can become "contagious" to nonpoor in the area? If so, how can this threshold be avoided? These are the questions that policy researchers and policymakers in the field of urban poverty will be forced to grapple with as we enter the next policy era. The degree to which the answers will more reflect the findings of policy research or the American ambivalence toward the poor remains to be seen.

Note

1. "Appalachian residents" refers to poor residents in the Appalachian Mountain areas of the central eastern United States.

SUGGESTED READING

Anglin, Roland, and Briavel Holcomb. 1992. "Poverty in Urban America: Policy Options." *Journal of Urban Affairs* 14(3,4):447–68.

Ashworth, Karl, Martha Hill, and Robert Walker. 1944. "Patterns of Childhood Poverty: New Challenges for Policy." *Journal of Policy Analysis and Management* 13(4):658–80.

Danziger, Sheldon, and Daniel Weinberg, eds. 1986. *Fighting Poverty: What Works and What Doesn't.* Cambridge, Mass.: Harvard University Press.

Danziger, Sheldon, Gary Sandefur, and Daniel Weinberg, eds. 1994. *Confronting Poverty: Prescriptions for Change*. Cambridge, Mass.: Harvard University Press.

Haveman, Robert. 1987. *Poverty Policy and Poverty Research*. Madison: University of Wisconsin Press.

Haveman, Robert, and Barbara Wolfe. 1994. *Succeeding Generations: On the Effects of Investments in Children*. New York: Russell Sage Foundation.

Herrnstein, Richard, and Charles Murray. 1994. *The Bell Curve: Intelligence and Class Structure in American Life*. New York: Free Press.

Kasarda, John. 1993. "Inner-City Concentrated Poverty and Neighborhood Distress: 1970 to 1990." *Housing Policy Debate* 4(3):253–302.

Katz, Michael. 1989. *The Undeserving Poor*. New York: Pantheon.

————, ed. 1993. *The "Underclass" Debate*. Princeton, N.J.: Princeton University Press.

Mincy, Ronald, ed. 1994. *Nurturing Young Black Males*. Washington, D.C.: Urban Institute Press.

Patterson, James. 1986. *America's Struggle against Poverty, 1900–1985*. Cambridge, Mass.: Harvard University Press.

Ricketts, Erol. 1992. "The Nature and Dimensions of the Underclass," and "The Underclass: Causes and Responses." In *The Metropolis in Black and White*, edited by George Galster and Edward Hill. New Brunswick, N.J.: Center for Urban Policy Research.

Schiller, Bradley. 1989. *The Economics of Poverty and Discrimination*, 5th ed. Englewood Cliffs, N.J.: Prentice Hall.

Other References

Anderson, Martin. 1978. *Welfare: The Political Economy of Welfare Reform in the United States*. Stanford, Calif.: Hoover Institution, Stanford University.

Auletta, Ken. 1982. *The Underclass*. New York: Random House.

Banfield, Edward C. 1970. *The Unheavenly City: The Nature and Future of Our Urban Crisis*. Boston: Little, Brown.

————. 1974. *The Unheavenly City Revisited*. Boston: Little, Brown.

Bell, Daniel. 1968. "Relevant Aspects of the Social Scene and Social Policy," in *Children's Allowances and the Economic Welfare of Children*, edited by Eveline Burns. New York: Ayers.

Danziger, Sheldon, and Robert D. Plotnik. 1981. *The War on Income Poverty: Achievements and Failures*. Madison: Institute for Research on Poverty, University of Wisconsin.

Feagin, Joe R. 1972. "America's Welfare Stereotypes." *Social Science Quarterly* 52:921–33.

Gilder, George F. 1981. *Wealth and Poverty*. New York: Basic Books.

Glasgow, Douglas G. 1980. *The Black Underclass: Poverty, Unemployment and Entrapment of Ghetto Youth.* San Francisco: Jossey-Bass Publishing.

Goodwin, Leonard. 1972. *Do the Poor Want to Work? A Social Psychological Study of Work Orientations.* Washington, D.C.: Brookings Institution, 124–5.

Harrington, Michael. 1962. *The Other America: Poverty in the United States.* New York: McMillan.

Johnson, Lyndon B. 1968. "The Problem of Poverty in America." *Economic Report of the President.* Washington, D.C.: U.S. Government Printing Office.

Lemann, Nicholas. 1986. "The Origins of the Underclass (I)." *Atlantic Monthly* June, 31–43.

————. 1986. "The Origins of the Underclass (II)." *Atlantic Monthly.* July, 54–68.

Liebow, Elliot. 1967. *Tally's Corner: A Study of Negro Streetcorner Men.* Boston: Little, Brown.

Mead, Lawrence. 1986. *Beyond Entitlement: The Social Obligations of Citizenship.* New York: Free Press.

Morgan, James N. 1962. *Income and Welfare in the United States.* A Study by the Survey Research Center, Institute for Social Research. University of Michigan. New York: McGraw-Hill.

Moynihan. Daniel. 1970. *Maximum Feasible Misunderstanding: Community Action and the War on Poverty.* New York: Free Press.

Murray, Charles. 1984. *Losing Ground: American Social Policy 1950–1980.* New York: Basic Books.

Murray, Charles, and William Julius Wilson. 1986. "A Permanent Black Underclass? Debating Plight of the Urban Poor." *U.S. News and World Report* 100:20–2.

Nassar, S. 1986. "America's Poor: How Big the Problem?" *Fortune* 113:74–8.

Orshansky, Mollie. 1968. "Counting the Poor," and "Who Was Poor in 1966?" in *Children's Allowances and the Economic Welfare of Children,* edited by Eveline Burns. New York: Ayers.

U.S. President's Commission for a National Agenda for the Eighties. 1980. *Urban America in the Eighties: Perspectives and Prospects—A Report of the Panel on Policies and Prospects for the Metropolitan and Nonmetropolitan America.* Washington, D.C.: U.S. Government Printing Office.

Wilson, William Julius. 1987. *The Truly Disadvantaged: The Inner City, the Underclass, and Public Policy.* Chicago: University of Chicago Press.

Chapter Four

FAMILY SUPPORT AND SOCIAL WELFARE

Pamela A. Holcomb

The nation's welfare system is composed of a plethora of in-kind and cash assistance programs designed to provide various forms of support to economically disadvantaged individuals and families. These programs include but are not limited to nutritional assistance in the form of food stamps, medical assistance through the Medicaid program, housing assistance through subsidized public housing, and direct cash assistance to eligible poor families with dependent children through the Aid to Families with Dependent Children (AFDC) program. Policy issues pertaining to family support in general are inextricably intertwined with policy issues surrounding the existing system of welfare, but the AFDC program in particular has received the greatest amount of interest and attention.

Both as a program in its own right and as a catchall for welfare programs in general, AFDC has been a source of conflict, controversy, and concern to policymakers and the public since the 1960s. It has been a dominant and more often *the* predominant focus of all major welfare reform initiatives. Thus, a discussion of the past three decades of family support policy in the United States is best framed within the context of the history of welfare reform; examining how we have chosen to address the AFDC program and population is key to understanding the unfolding of welfare reform.

Several welfare reform policy initiatives have been introduced and debated since the 1960s, but forging a political consensus sufficient to enact policy reform has been extremely difficult and often unsuccessful. A complicated and convoluted interplay among several factors accounts for this history of controversy, gridlock, and incremental reform: disagreement over how best to respond to changing social, economic, and demographic trends; partisan politics; conflicting ideologically based beliefs about the poor, work, family, and the role of government; differing perceptions of the relationship between welfare and poverty; and differences in opinion over the appropriate goals, focus, and scope of welfare reform.

Amidst these larger forces, policy research has played a small but nevertheless increasingly important role in the formation and fate of welfare reform policy initiatives. It has served to broaden and deepen understanding about the nature of poverty and characteristics of the welfare population, influenced the development of policy through evaluations of social experiments and demonstrations, and provided political ammunition for the rejection or adoption of different policy approaches.

Although the AFDC program was intended to benefit poor children, primarily those living in single-parent households, the focus of reform has been typically less concerned with children's economic well-being than with the program's potential negative impact on the behavior of adults in matters of work, family structure, and dependency on welfare. Fashioning an appropriate policy response that addresses criticisms about the program but at the same time does not abandon the idea that federal and state government has an obligation to promote the economic well-being of poor children has proved to be an enduring challenge.

In general, more narrowly focused welfare reform efforts aimed at reducing dependency on AFDC have been successful in garnering sufficient support to be adopted as official policy, whereas more comprehensive strategies attempting to improve the economic well-being of poor and near-poor families by overhauling the entire welfare system have failed. The remainder of this chapter provides an overview of both types of policy approaches from a historical perspective, with special emphasis on the role of research in the policy process.

1962 TO 1967: EARLY EFFORTS TO REFORM WELFARE

Between the enactment of the landmark Social Security Act in 1935 and the early 1960s, "welfare," as it has come to be thought of, remained a relatively obscure and neglected policy issue. The AFDC program was one of three public assistance programs created by the Social Security legislation. The program's primary objective was to benefit children in need of economic support due to the death, continued absence, or incapacity of the family wage earner (i.e., usually the child's father). Even though AFDC eligibility was not limited to families composed only of widows and orphans, it was this type of single-parent family that formed the basis of support for such a program.

Public assistance, or welfare, represented a counterpart to the social insurance component of the Social Security Act. Its inclusion reflected the belief that our nation's social welfare system needed to incorporate the principles of adequacy as well as equity in its basic framework. For example, social insurance in the form of Social Security benefits provided a universal support system for the elderly that tied benefits to earmarked contributions made by wage earners. In contrast, public assistance programs, administered by the states with federal and state funding (i.e., taxes from general revenues), were categorical and means tested; benefits were tied to income and to categorically based eligibility criteria. States were allowed to determine the level of benefits, which led to inequities in benefits across states. For example, eligible families in Mississippi have historically received lower amounts of cash assistance than eligible families in New York. In general, benefits have been kept low so as not to make welfare receipt more economically attractive than work and to keep program costs down.

Public assistance programs were targeted to meet the immediate economic needs of certain categories of poor individuals and families—single-parent families, the aged, the blind—who were not expected to work and were therefore "deserving" of assistance. Providing benefits to single female-headed families to allow mothers to stay home and raise their children reinforced the traditional "family wage"—an informal system which divides responsibilities for family and wage work by gender, a division of labor that was also considered to be in the best interest of the child. AFDC, a program designed to help children, thus reflected the prevailing ideology regarding the appropriate roles and responsibilities of adult men and women in relation to child care and wage work.

It was also presumed that as the social insurance component matured (i.e., Social Security and survivor benefits became available to a greater share of the population), the need for public assistance would decrease and eventually "wither away" of its own accord. However, by the beginning of the 1960s it had become increasingly clear that the need for an AFDC program would not die a natural death. The AFDC caseload and expenditures steadily grew substantially after its inception in 1935, both absolutely and relative to other public assistance programs.

The changing composition of the AFDC caseload, which accounted for much of the program's growth, evoked even greater concern. By 1962, less than a tenth of AFDC children received benefits due to the death of the father. Widowed families had come by that time to be covered under Social Security survivor benefits, leaving the bulk of the AFDC caseload composed of divorced, separated, and never-married women and their children. These types of single-parent families, whose numbers were increasing, were perceived as a threat to the ideal of the nuclear family, and raised doubts about whether using public funds to support a family structure antithetical to prevailing norms was good public policy.

The racial dimension of welfare receipt complicated the picture even further. Originally primarily composed of white female-headed families, the racial composition of the caseload shifted to being disproportionately composed of single African-American female-headed families (although in absolute numbers there were until very recently more white than African-American AFDC recipients). The disproportionate numbers of African-Americans receiving welfare reinforced negative racial stereotypes and undermined public support for the program. At the same time, the controversial and sensitive nature of race made policymakers, who were not immune to such stereotypes themselves, leery of explicitly confronting the issue of race in policy discourse about welfare reform.

Beginning in the 1960s, the AFDC program became the preeminent symbol of what was increasingly perceived as a crisis in the nation's welfare system. Since the upward trend of divorce and nonmarital childbearing showed no indication of abating, and female-headed families experienced such high rates of poverty, it was reasonable to assume that more and more female-headed families would turn to AFDC for economic assistance. This proved to be correct. Moreover, concern over the socioeconomic and demographic trends that led to welfare dependency became increasingly intertwined with the perception that welfare was, in fact, not a solution to dealing with poverty but, rather, part of the problem. Welfare was thought not only to create harmful disincentives to work but to encourage the breakdown of the nuclear family and to perpetuate dependence. Thus, the "problem" to be reckoned with had two major related but still distinct dimensions—poverty and welfare dependency.

Social Services Welfare Reform Strategy

The first major effort to reform AFDC occurred in 1962 within the broader context of reforming the entire system of public assistance. The social work profession dominated the debate and influenced the direction of reform. President Kennedy's administration based its welfare reform proposal, the 1962 Public Welfare Amendments, on the recommendations of the 1961 Ad Hoc Committee on Public Assistance, which was staffed primarily by social workers. Strong and vocal support for the bill by the social work profession was also influential in bringing about its passage.

Social workers stressed that welfare dependency and the rise of single-parent families could be reduced through a services approach that stressed the need for "prevention" and "rehabilitation." Instead of simply responding to the economic needs of families on assistance by providing them with a monthly check, they argued that welfare recipients needed individualized counseling to help them become self-reliant and, in the case of AFDC families, to prevent additional nonmarital births. Such an approach required trained social workers, smaller caseloads, and increased casework. Although it was never clearly articulated how counseling alone could stem the rise of nonmarital births or reduce dependency, the social services approach was approved by Congress and financed through increased federal matching funds to the states.

In keeping with the desire to avoid further family breakdown, the 1962 legislation also authorized the permanent extension of AFDC-Unemployed Parent (UP), a program that had been approved on a temporary basis by Congress the previous year. AFDC-UP was an optional program available to states that provided benefits to unemployed two-parent families who met certain income and work history eligibility criteria. The rationale for expanding AFDC benefits to two-parent families was that it removed the existing incentive for unemployed husbands to leave their families so that their children could receive AFDC benefits. This departure from the original AFDC program eligibility structure blurred the categorical nature of the program by no longer limiting assistance to the "unemployable" (i.e., single female-headed families). However, its significance and impact was muted because the AFDC-UP caseload constituted only a small fraction of the total AFDC caseload. Only about half of the states opted to enact the program. In addition, fearing that AFDC-UP would encourage welfare dependency among an entirely new population, Congress intentionally imposed strict eligibility requirements to restrict the number of two-parent families that could take advantage of this option.

The 1962 amendments reflected both a strong sense of optimism and a consensus regarding how welfare dependency could be combatted through casework intervention to "rehabilitate" welfare recipients. Support for the potential effectiveness of the social services approach was not based on systematic research but, rather, on anecdotal evidence and the social work profession's confidence in this reform strategy.

Optimism in the power of social services alone to reduce the welfare rolls was quickly replaced, however, by ever-increasing disenchantment with this policy strategy. Instead of reducing welfare dependency, AFDC costs and caseload numbers exploded over the next several years. The failure of the 1962 welfare reform amendments to reduce welfare dependency paved the way for what was to become a long and contentious policy debate that continues to this day.

Employment and Training Welfare Reform Strategy

In 1962, 3.8 million recipients received AFDC; by 1967 this figure had increased to 5.3 million (U.S. Department of Health and Human Services, unpublished administrative data). This alarming state of affairs occurred despite the promises of the 1962 Public Welfare Amendments and the initiation of the War on Poverty (see chapter 3). Several factors contributed to the caseload increase. These factors included expanded eligibility rules; African-American migration to urban areas, resulting in economic dislocation and an increase in urban poverty; community action and advocacy efforts by and on behalf of the poor to apply for and receive benefits; continued increases in the divorce and nonmarital birthrates; and the slow and only partially realized implementation of the 1962 Public Welfare Amendments at state and local levels.

By 1967, a frustrated Congress was ready to move ahead with another welfare reform strategy. The immediate problems at hand were that too many people were on welfare, too much money was spent supporting them, and such a high rate of welfare dependency was considered unacceptable for a nation that placed an ideological premium on the work ethic and the nuclear family. A more effective solution to ending welfare dependency was still clearly needed.

Providing employment and training services to adult AFDC recipients to enable them to obtain jobs promised to be that solution. This approach was reflected in the passage of the Work Incentive Program (WIN) in 1967, which required states to administer employment and training programs for AFDC mothers in addition to their existing income maintenance responsibilities. All AFDC mothers were to be evaluated for potential participation in the WIN program, but welfare agency social workers were given discretion in deciding when a work or training referral was appropriate. An income disregard was also approved, which removed some of the work disincentives in the program by allowing AFDC recipients to earn income without experiencing a dollar-for-dollar reduction in their AFDC grant.

Until WIN's passage, it was still generally accepted that, at least for policy purposes, single mothers should be considered unemployable and should be allowed to stay home full-time to raise their children. (In reality, poor women already had a long history of labor force participation; low wages often motivated them to turn to AFDC for assistance.) As labor force participation among women with school-age children increased in the 1960s, however, the original rationale for AFDC was further eroded. Conversely, support for some form of work and/or training opportunities for AFDC mothers increased.

Although the implementation of WIN did not result in large reductions in welfare dependency any more than did the earlier social services approach, the idea that AFDC mothers should participate in employment-oriented activities was not rejected, but, rather, continued to gain support and acceptance. Very little research on the efficacy of employment and training programs, particularly for women, was available when Congress passed WIN, and no systematic research had examined the impact of this policy approach on reducing welfare dependency. The adoption of an employment-based strategy was justified because it was more consistent with current labor force participation trends and changing norms regarding the role of women. Promoting the participation of women on welfare in employment programs had started to become an acceptable means to achieve the overriding goal of reducing welfare dependency.

1968 TO 1979: INCOME-BASED STRATEGY FOR WELFARE REFORM

Whereas WIN was targeted specifically for AFDC (and AFDC-UP) recipients, substantial intellectual and political energies were directed in the years following toward designing a comprehensive welfare reform policy that would positively affect all low-income families, not just those receiving AFDC. Whereas the 1962 social services approach and the employment and training approach adopted under WIN both focused first and foremost on reducing welfare dependency, the comprehensive welfare reform proposals of the 1960s and 1970s were more equally concerned with reducing poverty and reducing dependency on welfare.

Economists replaced social workers in providing the intellectual foundation for major welfare reform proposals introduced by the Nixon and later the Carter administrations. These proposals advocated an income-based strategy to welfare reform and incorporated a negative income tax model in their design. Espoused by both leading conservative and liberal economists, a negative income tax plan would (at least theoretically) dramatically simplify the welfare system, increase economic security for the working poor and for poor single-headed families (without the stigma associated with welfare), and encourage the formation and stability of two-parent families, because there would no longer be any incentive to avoid or disrupt marriages to receive AFDC benefits. Although the concept of a negative income tax was elegant in its simplicity, its application to real-life policy proposals was extremely complicated. The welfare reform proposals supported by Presidents Nixon and Carter ultimately failed to be enacted.

Nixon Welfare Reform Proposal

President Nixon introduced his version of welfare reform in 1969. Based on the concept of a negative income tax, the Family Assistance Plan (FAP) proposed to replace the existing array of public assistance and in-kind benefit programs with a single cash-transfer program that included a guaranteed annual income for all families, adjusted for family size. In essence, the FAP aimed to eliminate the disincentive to form nuclear families that the AFDC program was faulted for creating. It would also eliminate the inequities in AFDC benefit levels across states as well as the stigma associated with receiving welfare. The level of the FAP payment would decrease as earnings increased, so as not to create new disincentives to work, and all families would be ensured a minimum level of economic security.

Despite the seemingly positive features of the plan, the FAP came under increasing attack as politicians, administrators, and advocacy groups struggled to understand how it would be implemented and administered, and the implications of such a radically different system. It was criticized by both liberals and conservatives. Some argued that the overall cost of the plan was unacceptably high; others contended that the proposed FAP payment to individual families was unacceptably low. Some criticized the plan because it represented an expansion of welfare (which would presumably create more dependency), while others objected to removing the focus from the needs of single female-headed households. An inordinate amount of attention and controversy concentrated on the potential work disincentives that the FAP created for families who had not previously been eligible to receive welfare but would be eligible for some or all of the FAP payment.

While the FAP was being debated, AFDC caseloads and program costs continued to soar. Frustrated that the WIN program was neither serving as many clients as had been anticipated nor moving substantial numbers off welfare and into employment, Congress enacted important modifications to the program in 1971 that, at least in theory, obligated recipients to engage in some form of work or work preparation activity in return for receiving benefits. Workfare, as it was called, was hotly debated but eventually passed. After 1971, AFDC mothers with children over six years of age were mandated to register and participate in the WIN program, provided that child care was available. Failure to register could result in a reduction of AFDC benefits. Programmatic emphasis was placed on job search and job placement.

A year after the WIN amendments were passed, the FAP was defeated. Although it had managed to secure sufficient political support for passage in the House of Representatives in 1970, it eventually died in the Senate in 1972. Although never enacted, aspects of the FAP were subsequently modified and approved in 1974. The public assistance programs for the aged, the blind, and those with permanent and total disabilities were combined into the Supplemental Security Income (SSI) program, a federally administered program that guaranteed a minimum level of economic assistance to those populations.

Restructuring the welfare system in ways that would have affected the incomes of able-bodied families that could participate in the labor force, however, had proved too controversial. Daniel Patrick Moynihan, then adviser to President Nixon and the chief architect of the FAP, later ruefully commented that the "FAP was devised above all to provide a guaranteed income for children and for families with children. In the end, children and families were the only groups excluded" (Moynihan 1981: 1). Thus, the basic system of support for poor families was left intact, but with new expectations regarding families' obligations to participate in work activities or activities designed to lead to employment.

In the late 1970s, another attempt was made to enact comprehensive welfare reform. The formulation of the plan's contents depended heavily on the use of a multivariate microsimulation developed by the U.S.

Department of Health, Education & Welfare to estimate the costs of various alternatives under consideration, as well as the impact of alternatives on marginal tax rates.

Carter Welfare Reform Proposal

The Program for Better Jobs and Income (PBJI), introduced under the Carter administration, attempted to combine a negative income tax plan with a jobs component. The PBJI called for (1) the replacement of the AFDC, Food Stamp, and SSI programs with a universal cash assistance program for all families whose incomes fell below specified levels, adjusted for family size; (2) a guaranteed jobs program that authorized the use of public service jobs provided through the government as employer-of-last-resort if a private-sector job could not be obtained; and (3) an expanded earned income tax credit. In an effort to resolve the dilemma of ensuring a minimum level of support to all families while not creating disincentives to work, the PBJI also included a complex system for calculating benefits that hinged on an assessment of who was expected to work.

Like the FAP, the cash-transfer component of President Carter's welfare reform proposal came under attack for expanding rather than reducing welfare dependency. The jobs portion of the proposal was criticized for underestimating the challenge of creating a potentially enormous number of public service jobs. The prospects of displacing existing workers in productive public jobs or, conversely, of consigning substantial numbers of individuals to make-work jobs were both highly contentious issues. The PBJI was also assailed for being far too expensive and too complicated to understand, let alone administer. The PBJI died in the 96th Congress before ever reaching the floor for consideration. A scaled-down version—the Social Welfare Reform Amendments of 1977—and a companion measure—the Work and Training Opportunities Act of 1979—met similar fates. In assessing the various factors that led to the failure of Carter's welfare reform effort, the role of research was not without its critics. Senator Moynihan remarked:

> What happened during the development of PBJI is that the economists took over. The entire process got caught up with economic models of how people behave and an absolute absorption in the equations and marginal tax rates of how one fools around with earnings. All of this avoided, to use D. H. Lawrence's phrase, the "dirty little secret," that the problem of welfare involves dependent women and children, not able-bodied males. (quoted in Lynn and Whitman 1981)

Negative Income Tax Experiments and Welfare Reform Efforts

By the end of 1979, hope had faded for comprehensive welfare reform that included some form of a negative income tax. Research findings from the income maintenance experiments conducted during this period undercut advocates' support for this reform strategy, and were used by detractors to further support its outright rejection.

Initiated by the Johnson administration and later supported by the Nixon administration, four large-scale, federally funded income maintenance experiments were launched that involved thousands of families. Using a random assignment methodology, the first experiment began in 1968 and the fourth one ended in 1982. This methodology allowed researchers to test the impact of implementing a negative income tax policy on one randomly selected eligible group of families compared to another group of families for whom the negative income tax was not made available. The experiments represented the most ambitious effort to date to test the potential impact of an as-yet-unimplemented policy.

According to these negative income tax studies, work effort diminished slightly among adults in families eligible to receive the guaranteed income. However, in the last of the four experiments (i.e., the Seattle/Denver Income Maintenance Experiment), researchers also found evidence that family breakup increased among those eligible for the guaranteed income. This was an unanticipated and extremely disturbing finding, given the expectation that extending income support to two-parent families would reinforce, not weaken, marital stability. The research findings provided evidence for politicians that a negative income tax strategy was not a viable policy approach.

The income maintenance experiments represent an important chapter in social policy research and its relation to public policy. Consistent with ideology that assumed that the traditional two-parent family structure with a male breadwinner was the optimal arrangement, the primary objective of the experiments was to test the impact of a negative income tax on work effort. After finding evidence that the policy might well lead to family breakdown, the question of its impact on family stability also became important. Qualitative research on the effect of the income tax on the lives of the people involved in the experiment was missing.

Despite the magnitude of the research effort, the findings tended to confuse rather than enlighten the policy debate. Preliminary findings from the New Jersey Income Maintenance Experiment seemed to indicate that a guaranteed income did not reduce work effort. But, as indicated previously, subsequent findings appeared to be much more negative. The average politician was at a disadvantage in trying to understand the results when even social scientists disagreed among themselves over the correct interpretation. The utility of this research was further limited because policymakers needed results before researchers could provide them. Results from the final income maintenance experiment were not available until after President Carter's second welfare reform proposal had already died without so much as a whimper. To this day, social scientists are debating the validity of the findings and their implications.

The failed welfare reform efforts of the 1960s and 1970s were comprehensive measures that tried to increase support to all needy families by replacing the existing categorical and means-tested welfare system with a universal system that provided a minimum floor of economic security to all families, combined with some form of work-related activities. More politicians were persuaded that antipoverty and antidependency policy objectives were inherently at cross-purposes and could not go hand-in-hand. The only enduring consensus reached in the 1960s and 1970s pertaining to welfare reform was that the federal government needed to take a proactive stance to reduce the numbers of women dependent on AFDC. This was to be accomplished by obligating AFDC mothers with school-age children to engage in work and training activities so that they could become self-sufficient. This principle continued to guide welfare reform in the 1980s.

1980 TO 1988: ENHANCED EMPLOYMENT AND TRAINING STRATEGY FOR REFORMING WELFARE

The presidential election of Ronald Reagan in 1980 heralded a dramatic shift in social policy. In terms of welfare reform, political capital and support for cash-transfer strategies were exhausted. The income maintenance research findings were used as further proof against the wisdom or efficacy of pursuing this approach. However, the Reagan administration's rejection of any form of a guaranteed income was grounded much more firmly in an ideology based on "traditional values" than on a negative interpretation of research results.

Values, Social Contracts, and Welfare Cutbacks

By 1981, almost 11 million children and adults received AFDC benefits. Charging that federal social welfare and antipoverty programs in
the 1960s and 1970s had not only failed to alleviate poverty but were
in fact a fundamental part of the problem, the new administration
reduced federal social welfare spending across the board. Insofar as
government intervention was necessary, the administration main-
tained it should take place on the state and local levels.

Given the administration's ideological commitment to reducing the
role of the federal government as well as preserving the work ethic
and the nuclear family, it is not surprising that AFDC served as the
prime rhetorical example of how government intervention reputedly
perpetuated a culture of dependency by rewarding single mothers for
avoiding work, remaining unmarried, and relying on welfare as their
sole means of economic support. These assertions were certainly not
new, but the critique did assume greater influence in an ideological
and political climate that was hostile to existing social welfare policy.
Beyond dismantling the welfare system altogether as some, such as
Charles Murray in *Losing Ground* (1984), suggested, the prospect of
constructive welfare reform appeared particularly bleak in the 1980s.

And yet, welfare reform was very much on the political agenda in
the years that followed, culminating in the Family Support Act of
1988. In the name of reducing welfare dependency, the legislation that
President Reagan signed shortly before leaving office represented an
increase, as opposed to a decrease, in federal spending and involvement in the AFDC program.

The changes initially made to the AFDC program in the early 1980s
through the Omnibus Reconciliation Act of 1981 (OBRA) did not fore-
shadow this paradoxical policy development. Yet, developments at the
state level made in response to OBRA and, to a lesser extent, under
subsequent budget reconciliation bills, played an enormously influential role in shaping the outcome of the 1988 welfare reform legislation. The immediate result of OBRA, however, was the imposition
of stricter eligibility requirements and a much weakened earned income disregard, resulting in a loss or reduction of AFDC benefits for
over 700,000 families.

The Reagan administration also pressed (with only partial success)
for attaching mandatory workfare to the receipt of welfare. Workfare
was the heart and soul of the administration's welfare reform goals.
As the administration envisioned it, mandatory workfare would require that welfare recipients work for a specified number of hours in

exchange for benefits, thereby instilling a work ethic in those receiving welfare and making it less attractive to those who might use welfare as a "free ride." Congress balked at mandatory workfare but did allow states to experiment with a variety of work-welfare demonstrations that could include but were not limited to workfare.

Spurred by the new flexibility in designing and operating work-welfare programs as well as consistent reductions in federal funding for the WIN program, states took advantage of the new option to implement demonstration programs. These state work-welfare efforts captured the interest of both federal policymakers and the media. By 1986, over half of all states operated some variation of a work-welfare program.

Between 1986 and 1988, welfare reform was again on the national political agenda, and competing versions were vigorously debated. The primary consensus reached was that federal welfare reform legislation needed to establish a social contract between the government and the welfare recipient. The intellectual justification for this position had been forwarded most persuasively by Lawrence Mead in *Beyond Entitlement* (1986). This contract was composed of reciprocal obligations in which AFDC recipients were responsible for working toward self-sufficiency and the government was responsible for providing services and activities needed for recipients to achieve that goal.

Yet, major issues of contention remained on how the social contract could best be accomplished. Should participation in activities be mandatory or voluntary? How prominent a role should workfare play? To what extent should education and training be emphasized, as opposed to short-term job search and job placement? Ultimately, a strict interpretation of workfare was rejected in favor of "new-style workfare," which included an expanded array of education, training, and employment activities as well as support services.

Family Support Act

In essence, the objective of the Family Support Act of 1988 was to do a better job than WIN and to build on the Child Support Enforcement Amendments of 1984. To achieve these goals, the FSA made changes on several fronts: it strengthened child support enforcement and paternity establishment provisions; replaced WIN with JOBS, an expanded education, training, and employment program; gave states financial incentives to target services to teenage parents and long-term welfare dependents; increased federal resources for child care while parents were participating in education, training, and employment activities; placed new emphasis on and resources for basic education, particularly for teenage parents; expanded AFDC-UP coverage in the balance of states that had previously opted out of the program; provided up to one year of postwelfare transitional Medicaid and subsidized child care; and required states for the first time to meet participation standards (i.e., a predetermined percentage of welfare recipients had to be involved in some education, training, or employment activity) that were to steadily increase over time.

Workfare, ardently supported by the Reagan administration, was limited to 16 hours a week for one parent in AFDC-UP families. Efforts to increase AFDC benefits, which had decreased in constant dollars since the 1970s, received only minimal attention and were dropped early in the legislative process.

Research and the Family Support Act

State-initiated work-welfare programs served as models for replication at the national level, but evaluations of some of these demonstrations were equally instrumental in convincing Congress that some mixture of employment, education and training, and support services should be the centerpiece of federal welfare reform. Between 1982 and 1988, the Manpower Demonstration Research Corporation (MDRC), an independent research organization, conducted several evaluations of state-initiated demonstrations.

The MDRC's research indicated that these work-welfare programs resulted in modest increases in earnings and welfare savings, and that the programs had a greater positive impact on long-term than short-term recipients. The research was based on random assignment experiments, a methodology that lent credibility to the MDRC's findings. This methodology allowed researchers to compare the impact of participating in the work-welfare demonstration on a random group of participants against another randomly selected group of nonparticipants. Separate reports on the impact of each demonstration and a summary of findings released in early 1987 provided a particularly timely body of research that policymakers utilized to fine-tune welfare reform legislation, justify the need for this type of welfare reform legislation, and help garner support for its passage under the aegis of the FSA in 1988.

Other research proved to be extremely influential as well. Research on the emergence of the "underclass" stimulated interest in long-term welfare dependency, a major characteristic of the "underclass" population. The use of longitudinal survey data to investigate welfare dynamics by poverty and welfare researchers Mary Jo Bane and David Ellwood (1983), among others, indicated that the welfare population was not a homogeneous group. Typical AFDC recipients were short-term users (who may go on and off welfare at different points in time), but a disproportionate share of program costs went to support long-term recipients. Young, never-married mothers were found to be the most likely to experience long-term welfare dependency. These findings, coupled with the MDRC's finding that long-term welfare recipients' participation in work-welfare program activities resulted in greater welfare savings than short-term recipients' participation, focused the debate on reducing long-term welfare dependency and provided the rationale for targeting additional resources to serve this population.

Policy research had an unprecedented influence on the 1988 welfare reform legislation embodied in the FSA. Although the MDRC demonstration evaluations commenced before it became clear that welfare reform legislation of this kind would be considered, the data were presented in a timely and nontechnical fashion that rendered them an integral part of the welfare reform policy process in the 1980s. Lest the importance of this research be overstated, however, it should be noted that the MDRC's findings supported a policy direction that already enjoyed strong ideological and political support.

RECENT COURSE OF WELFARE REFORM AND FAMILY SUPPORT POLICY

Continued frustration with the current welfare system has led to yet another round of welfare reform that has already taken several twists and turns and whose end result has yet to be determined. First, the Clinton administration introduced the Work and Responsibility Act in June 1993, a plan touted as fulfilling Clinton's campaign promise to "end welfare as we know it." In their capacity as officials in the Clinton administration, David Ellwood and Mary Jo Bane were given the lead responsibility for developing a welfare reform proposal for the president. Fashioning a plan consistent with mainstream values concerning the importance of work and parental responsibility formed the framework for the plan's development, but at the same time a conscious effort was made to ground the plan's particulars in empirical research on welfare caseload dynamics (including Bane and

Ellwood's own work in this area), employment and training programs, child support enforcement, and teenage pregnancy and parenting.

The main elements of the Clinton administration's welfare reform proposal were to expand the JOBS program; impose a two-year cumulative time limit on receipt of welfare, after which recipients would be required to work in publicly subsidized jobs if private-sector employment could not be obtained; expand federal resources for low-income, "working poor" families; and strengthen child support enforcement. The administration also sought and gained approval for a significant expansion in the Earned Income Tax Credit (EITC), which provides additional income to working families through the tax system, as part of its overall strategy to "make work pay" for those who "play by the rules." Health care reform, also considered a critical component of welfare reform and family support, was developed on a separate track that derailed just a few months after the administration's welfare reform plan was unveiled.

Although the administration took over a year to develop its welfare plan, congressional consideration of the plan never progressed further than a few hearings on the subject. Instead, the political and ideological landscape changed dramatically in the wake of the November 1994 congressional elections, which produced a Republican majority in both the House and Senate. Since then a wholly different version of welfare reform has taken shape.

The Republican-proposed reforms in both houses of Congress are far more dramatic and sweeping than those proposed by the Clinton administration. The most important change is to strip various family support programs, including the AFDC program, of their open-ended funding entitlement status and turn over responsibility for the social safety net to the states. States will receive funding in the form of block grants to operate programs and provide assistance to families in need as they see fit. Federal funding for these programs would be reduced between $65 billion and $100 billion over five years. In addition, both the House and Senate measures include a cumulative five-year time limit on AFDC receipt, after which time families would neither be eligible for any further cash assistance nor provided a subsidized job if they could not find employment on their own.

At present, both the House and the Senate have passed welfare reform legislation and a House-Senate conference committee must reconcile differences in the two bills. The welfare reform legislation passed by the House in March 1995 contains more restrictions on welfare benefits and block grants more programs than its Senate counterpart that was passed the following September. Once the legislation is reported out of conference and passed by Congress, it appears likely, although not a given at this juncture, that the president will not veto the welfare reform legislation and it will be enacted into law. The magnitude of the changes included in this latest version of welfare reform cannot be overstated. If enacted into law, literally millions of families will no longer be eligible to receive assistance. The federal-state partnership that was created by the original Social Security Act of 1935 would be dismantled, and the current "safety net" eliminated. Despite the magnitude of the changes proposed, Congress has spent very little time debating the proposals' merits and problems, and the role of research in informing the process has been almost totally eclipsed by ideology and partisan politics.

CONCLUSION AND PROSPECTS

Family support and welfare reform has presented an enduring policy conundrum. If success were to be measured simply in terms of whether or not a legislative initiative was enacted, incremental policy reforms that limited their focus to reducing welfare dependency among AFDC recipients would be judged more successful than anti-poverty policy reforms seeking comprehensive change in the welfare system as a whole. However, this measure of success seems almost irrelevant, given unrelenting criticism about the current system of family support and the increasing rates of poverty experienced by children.

The fact is that political rhetoric and criticisms about the welfare system have remained remarkably unchanged over the past three decades, despite long debate over the proper direction and scope of reform and the types of changes needed. Meanwhile, the factors contributing to the need for welfare reform have only become more entrenched over time. The sobering reality is that increasingly large numbers of children spend some portion of their lives in single-parent households, and that the overall economic well-being of these children has continued to decline. In 1991 nearly one out of every four children lived in poverty. The poverty rate for children has increased about one-third over the past 15 years, while the poverty rate among the elderly has decreased. As it now stands, children are twice as likely to be poor as adults aged 18 to 64, and are almost twice as likely to be poor when they are adults.

With the exception of this most recent round of welfare reform, policy research has played an increasingly important role in welfare policy debates over the past 20 years. Policy research is routinely relied upon to broaden understanding of the problems associated with welfare dependency, to form strategies to resolve these problems, to support or reject proposed strategies, and to test their effectiveness. Demonstration research and program evaluation have become more sophisticated over time and offer much promise in providing valuable information about "what works" to help inform policymakers. Survey research, particularly longitudinal analyses, have yielded much-needed information about the dynamics of welfare use and character-istics of the population.

Although policy research to date has enabled better-informed policy choices that are not based solely on ideological or political consider-ations, it is also true that these forces have influenced the type of research questions asked. As a result, we know much more about the potential effect on the work effort of welfare recipients of raising or lowering benefits, and about the impact of AFDC receipt on fertility and family structure, than we do about what types of policies and program interventions might improve outcomes in the lives of poor children and their families. The research knowledge base is often screened and interpreted through an ideological lens and distorted through the political process. At still other times, policy research analysis is simply ignored when larger political considerations and/ or ideological fervor command a course of action counter to what the research might suggest.

Given that research on family support and social welfare has so often been overshadowed by ideology and politics in the policy pro-cess, it would behoove those interested in advancing the role of re-search to consider more carefully how research might better serve the policy process. For example, researchers interested in policy need to make a more concerted effort, both when defining the research ques-tion and when disseminating the results, to clarify how their research bears upon the policy issues of the day. Since the typical policy au-dience lacks the training necessary to interpret research findings when presented in a very academic or technical fashion, a more de-liberate effort to make research results more comprehensible and ac-cessible is also needed. Finally, the sheer complexity of the problems being studied and addressed calls for greater integration of quanti-tative and qualitative research from a wide range of social science disciplines.

SUGGESTED READING

Bane, Mary Jo, and David T. Ellwood. 1983. *The Dynamics of Dependence: The Routes to Self-Sufficiency.* Cambridge, Mass.: Urban Systems Research and Engineering.

Berkowitz, Edward D. 1991. *America's Welfare State: From Roosevelt to Reagan.* Baltimore, Md.: Johns Hopkins University Press.

Ellwood, David. 1988. *Poor Support: Poverty in the American Family.* New York: Basic Books.

Katz, Michael. 1989. *The Undeserving Poor: From the War on Poverty to the War on Welfare.* New York: Pantheon Books.

Lynn, Lawrence Jr., and David deF. Whitman. 1981. *The President as Policymaker: Jimmy Carter and Welfare Reform.* Philadelphia: Temple University Press.

Mead, Lawrence. 1986. *Beyond Entitlement: The Social Obligations of Citizenship.* New York: The Free Press.

Moynihan, Daniel Patrick. 1981. "Children and Welfare." *Journal of the Institute for Socioeconomic Studies* 6 (Spring):1.

————. 1973. *The Politics of a Guaranteed Income: The Nixon Administration and the Family Assistance Plan.* New York: Random House.

Murray, Charles. 1984. *Losing Ground: American Social Policy, 1950–1980.* New York: Basic Books.

Nathan, Richard P. 1988. *Social Science in Government: Uses and Misuses.* New York: Basic Books.

U.S. Department of Health and Human Services. Various years. Unpublished administrative data. Author.

Wiseman, Michael, ed. 1991. "Research and Policy: A Symposium on the Family Support of 1988." *Journal of Policy Analysis and Management* 10(4):588–733.

Chapter Five

HOUSING

George Galster and Jennifer Daniell

Public perceptions of the problems of housing quality, quantity, and affordability have shifted during the last half-century. After World War II, the prevalence of substandard housing sparked an increased concern for the housing conditions of low-income households. By the 1960s, despite a general improvement in housing conditions, there remained a residual concentration of substandard units in specific urban neighborhoods, especially minority-occupied ghettos. Public housing in inner cities was increasingly viewed as more a problem than a solution, due to the social consequences associated with the concentration of poverty. By the mid-1970s, housing affordability concerns were in the forefront of national debate on the housing sector as prices and interest rates continued to rise. During the 1980s, housing problems evolved into a concern about the increasing incidence of homelessness and the needs of special groups, such as the frail elderly and mentally ill.

Housing policy has evolved as well, initially with a focus on increasing the supply of housing through both private development and construction of public housing. Half of this dual construction emphasis has since been abandoned: the building of public housing for lower-income renters has been slowed to a trickle. More emphasis has been placed at the federal level on demand-side policies, such as vouchers, targeted at augmenting the purchasing power of low-income households. In contrast, the promotion of private housing development and homeownership has been a constant theme throughout federal housing policy history, with continued reliance on new construction in the suburbs so that older housing can reputedly "filter down" to lower-income households and thereby help them.

These historical developments are more easily grasped with the aid of a time line, as portrayed in figure 5.1. We have demarcated periods based on salient events signaling new directions in federal housing policy; prevailing views on the nature of the housing problem have shifted more gradually than implied by the figure. As suggested in

Figure 5.1 EVOLUTION OF U.S. HOUSING POLICY

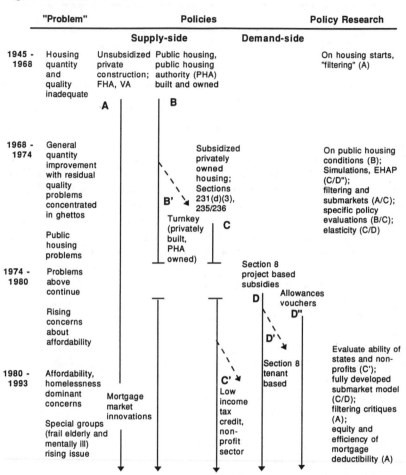

"Problem"	Policies		Policy Research
	Supply-side	**Demand-side**	

1945 - **1968**	Housing quantity and quality inadequate	Unsubsidized private construction; FHA, VA	Public housing, public housing authority (PHA) built and owned	On housing starts, "filtering" (A)

Note: Letters represent alternative housing policy strategies; policy research is
cross-referenced to these strategies by the same letters.

the figure, at least since the late 1960s considerable high-quality theoretical and empirical research has been conducted on the operation
of metropolitan housing markets, various problems that arise from
them, and current and proposed strategies for dealing with these problems. Did this research merely occur parallel with these other developments, or did it significantly shape our perception of the problems
and viable solutions? We argue that policy research did influence
policy indirectly by defining the problem to be addressed. However,

its influence was significant only insofar as its implications were congruent with central ideological tenets.

Policy research has been crucial in raising public awareness about the nature and scope of housing problems. Access to reliable and periodically updated databases funded at federal expense—specifically, the decennial Census of Population and Housing and, subsequently, the Annual (later called the American) Housing Surveys—provided unique resources for this field of research. Given that public awareness and, perhaps, discontent with particular housing issues provide a spur to political action, this indirect impact of research on housing policy seems clear in many cases.

The direct influence of policy research during this period seems, on the contrary, more circumscribed. Policy researchers provided convincing evidence that encouraged the switch from public housing and other supply-side strategies to demand-side strategies that occurred during the 1970s and 1980s. Yet, sometimes even the most persuasive research has had no impact. It is clear that, at least for those who can afford ownership, there is no longer a shortage of decent housing similar to that which confronted the nation after World War II. At the same time, the proposition that increased construction of high-priced suburban homes ultimately aids lower-income households has been assaulted by policy researchers. The social costs of this suburban development policy—sprawl, traffic congestion, inner-city decay—have long been well known to researchers and large segments of the public. Yet, the high level of subsidies for such high-priced suburban homes persists because these subsidies support central components of commonly shared values: individualism and the "American Dream" of homeownership.

1945 TO 1968: BUILDING AT BOTH ENDS OF HOUSING QUALITY SPECTRUM

More recent evolution in housing policy cannot be understood without reviewing the context of housing conditions facing the United States in the aftermath of the Depression and World War II.

Inadequate Quantity and Quality of Housing

Overcrowding and physical inadequacies were prevalent after World War II, especially in the housing occupied by low-income families in metropolitan areas. Data from the 1950 *Census of Population and Housing* report that one poor renter household in five did not have complete plumbing, that is, the family lacked hot running water or exclusive use of a toilet or shower. Twenty percent of low-income renter households and 17 percent of middle-income owners/occupants were living in crowded conditions—that is, more than one person per room.

Affordability of housing ownership also was a major issue at the time. Less than half of all households owned their own home after World War II. The common view was that this figure could be dramatically increased if a less volatile supply of credit for home purchases were made available in mortgage instruments that were more attractive to consumers. There was concern that credit supply varied with the business cycle in ways that discouraged home purchases. That is, when consumers had greater incomes during periods of economic booms, mortgage interest rates were prohibitively high; at the same time, during recessions interest rates were low, but few consumers had adequate purchasing power to buy. The mortgage instruments themselves discouraged many prospective borrowers because they required high downpayments and, instead of being repaid gradually over an extended period, required the entire principal to be repaid in a lump sum at maturity.

The "housing problem" seemed clear: the nation did not have enough decent-quality housing, and not enough of it could be owner-occupied. Given this assessment, the policy solutions also seemed clear: (1) reform the mortgage market and provide other subsidies to encourage the construction of new, single-family, suburban units for homeownership; and (2) build public housing on slum-cleared tracts in the inner city for poor renters. Thus, the "dual track" response of private and public construction was formulated.

The prevailing theoretical conception of the housing market in metropolitan areas suggested that this response would provide indirect benefits to all households of modest means, even if they were not to live in the new public housing. These benefits would arise through a mechanism known as "filtering." Filtering is, in theory, the process by which housing is passed down from upper-income households to those at the lower end of the income distribution. Affluent urban households live in newly constructed neighborhoods. As these units age, the most affluent move to the even more recently built suburbs, and the middle-income households move into the neighborhoods vacated by the more affluent, since housing prices have now declined there. As the cycle continues, the higher-income households move farther out of the city and the older housing is "filtered" down through the income distribution until it becomes affordable to the poorest households.

Boom in Private and Public Housing Production

The federal policy response to the perceived problem of housing shortage was epitomized by the Housing Act of 1949, which championed a commitment to "a decent home and a suitable living environment for every American family." The Housing Act authorized loans and grants for the redevelopment of neighborhoods and the production of quality low-cost housing through local slum clearance programs and expanded public housing authorization. But the provisions of the act also focused on providing government assistance to enable private enterprise to serve more of the total need for housing. Thus, the dual tracks of private and public production were codified (portrayed as lines *A* and *B* in figure 5.1).

Housing market responses to the 1949 Housing Act were overwhelming. There was a dramatic upsurge of new single-family home construction, spurred by several private and public forces that increased the accessibility of land and the affordability of housing. New plots of land for building became increasingly available in both cities and the suburbs, owing to federally financed highway construction and urban renewal programs. These programs, designed in part to bolster central-city economies, mainly stimulated rapid population growth and job expansion in the suburbs.

Affordability of housing increased with the introduction of low-interest, long-term mortgage loan guarantees from the Federal Housing Administration (FHA) and the Veterans Administration (VA), federal income tax incentives, and rising household incomes. The VA and FHA encouraged the use of a new, self-amortizing mortgage instrument with monthly repayment of both principal and interest at fixed amounts over the life of the loan. The FHA guaranteed the loan in the event of default, thereby reducing the risks of long-term lending. This resulted in lower interest rates and more credit available for private housing construction. Mortgage borrowing was further stimulated by provisions in the federal income tax code permitting the deductibility of interest paid on mortgages.

Rising incomes provided yet another boost to housing affordability; incomes rose faster than the cost of new housing from 1950 to 1965. Whereas in 1947, 42.3 percent of all families earned less than $5,000 (in constant 1972 dollars), by 1960 only 27 percent had an income less than $5,000. The percentage of families earning over $10,000 (in constant 1972 dollars) increased from 16.5 percent to 33.7 percent. Thus, the share of household income required to meet the monthly mortgage payments for a standard house fell considerably. By 1965 monthly housing costs were 20 percent of the median family income, down from 30 percent in 1950.

All this new construction for middle- and upper-income households was, of course, presumed to aid lower-income households through the filtering process. This presumption was so sacrosanct that a new federal program was designed to enhance filtering even further: the Federal National Mortgage Association's (Fannie Mae) Section 221(d)(3) program of expanding private construction of apartments for moderate-income households. The theory was that by removing moderate-income families from competition for low-cost housing, the supply of existing housing available to the poor through filtering would be increased. Section 221(d)(3) consisted of direct government loans for new rental housing construction both at below-market interest rates and at market interest rates with other incentives to private builders. Because these loans were issued by the government, the full value of the loan appeared on the federal budget in the first year and was offset by payments only in subsequent years. Such a large initial outlay, however—the full construction cost of the project—made the program politically vulnerable.

During the post–World War II era of extensive urban renewal programs, Section 221(d)(3) was originally designed to provide replacement housing for those who were displaced. Later, Section 231(d)(3) evolved into a more general rental housing program for moderate-income families. The below-market interest rate program provided developers with 3 percent FHA-guaranteed loans for up to 100 percent of the value of the property. The market rate program also provided high loan-to-value ratios, a long-term mortgage, and special tax advantages to induce developers to build. Income limits for tenants were set above those for public housing, thus targeting moderate-income households, and rents were regulated by the FHA. Under the below-market interest rate programs, 165,000 units were produced, mostly under 221(d)(3).

At the same time, a substantial increase in public housing construction was underway. According to the U.S. Department of Housing and Urban Development (HUD), the number of public housing units increased from 146,549 in 1951 to 643,245 in 1967. Although some critics argued that such increases in public housing were limited in terms of meeting overall housing needs, the fact that housing conditions in most urban areas did improve overall due to increases in both private and public housing construction was undisputed.

Despite the fact that newly formed households occupied many of these new units, newly built private and public dwellings outnumbered the new households. This increase in the housing supply in excess of household formation allowed for removal of many substandard units from the stock. This resulted in improved housing quality indicators and alleviated overcrowding, as multigenerational households were able to split into separate living accommodations. According to the 1960 *Census of Population and Housing*, in 1960 38 percent fewer units were in dilapidated condition than in 1950; 25 percent fewer households had more than 1 person per room; and 10 percent fewer were lacking some plumbing. By 1970, only 1 poor renter in 12 did not have complete plumbing, and only 9 percent of poor renters and 11 percent of middle-income renters were living in overcrowded conditions. This evidence confirmed the conventional wisdom about the positive effects of the filtering process combined with new public housing construction, which together increased the supply of housing available to low-income households. By most indicators, the housing "problem" seemingly was being solved rapidly, and housing policy, consequently, slipped in importance on the national political agenda.

Policy Research: Conventional Wisdom and Emerging Critiques

Policy research was mainly reactive and conventional between the end of World War II and the late 1960s. Given the unquestioned emphasis on new construction, studies were done on trends in housing conditions, the demand for housing, the determinants of housing starts, and how starts were affected by interest rates. These studies undoubtedly were influential in quantifying general impressions of housing shortages, but generally did not challenge the underlying assumptions behind the new construction fetish. The main exception was the theoretical model of filtering developed by Ira Lowry (1960). Taking the example of the rental market, Lowry criticized the assumption in previous models of filtering that depreciation and deterioration of housing are uninfluenced by the price a household is willing to pay for housing. Instead, Lowry's model claimed a direct relationship between depreciation and deterioration of a unit and rents, through the connection of maintenance inputs. Maintenance inputs are a function of revenues to the landlord; revenues are a function of the rent tenants are willing to pay. In the filtering process, when middle-income households move out, the landlord lowers rents to attract lower-income households. As rents fall, maintenance expenditures must, according to the model, fall faster to preserve the landlord's revenue from the unit. Over time, therefore, at this lower level of maintenance, low-income housing will deteriorate faster than that occupied by middle- or upper-income households. Slums, therefore, are the likely outcome of filtering older units to lower-income households. But this research was insufficient to shake conventional wisdom that more new, single-family construction should be *the* goal.

Research had more of an impact on public housing. By the 1960s, public housing had developed an image crisis due to both negative attention by the media and emerging critiques by policy researchers. Public housing was designed originally in the 1930s as transitional housing for the working class. Yet, as the rules for eligibility became more stringent in the 1960s, public housing was targeted more at the poorest of the poor, thus serving to concentrate poverty and attendant social problems. Urban renewal typically tore down more units than public housing subsequently replaced, as shown by Martin Anderson in *The Federal Bulldozer* (1964), exacerbating low-cost housing shortages, disrupting social networks, and reducing the choices available to low-income households. There were also charges that public housing projects were used to further concentrate low-income households in certain neighborhoods and, through site selection and tenant allocation policies, to perpetuate racial segregation. Suburban jurisdictions or even middle-class areas of central cities were loath, for political reasons, to accept public housing. Exclusionary zoning in the suburbs, such as minimum lot size and building requirements, created additional affordability barriers to low-income households who tried to find private apartments in the suburbs.

Revolt and Reconsideration

The urban revolts of the mid-1960s—beginning with Watts (Los Angeles) in 1965, continuing through Cleveland and Chicago in 1966, and culminating in Detroit and Newark in 1967—shook policymakers and many housing policy researchers out of their complacency. The efficacy of high-density public housing and of the filtering process for solving inner-city housing problems was dramatically challenged. The nexus of perceived housing problems began to shift to include not only physical conditions but affordability, control over living conditions and neighborhood conditions, social life, and accessibility of services and employment. The geographic scope shifted from national to urban.

A direct upshot of the revolts was the appointment of several commissions to assess urban housing problems. Policy researchers played a prominent role on these commissions. The National Commission on Urban Problems and the National Committee on Urban Housing both recommended production-oriented solutions to make additional housing available to households at low cost. The 1968 *Report of the National Advisory Commission on Civil Disorders* (better known as the Kerner Commission report), also included inadequate housing in its list of specific grievances of "first level intensity." This report advocated interest rate subsidies for construction of new, moderate-rent housing, expansion of public housing with emphasis on scattered sites, and improved targeting of programs to better assist low-income households. Although new construction programs still predominated, noteworthy among the recommendations was the "expansion and modification of the rent supplement program to permit use of supplements for existing housing." Thus, the concept of housing allowances was added to the repertoire of potential housing policies, thanks to the efforts of policy researchers. This seed of a new policy idea was to sprout in the 1970s and bloom during the 1980s.

Out of the urban crisis of the 1960s came a major reconsideration of housing needs. Policy researchers had begun to exercise some influence with their criticisms of public housing. The Department of Housing and Urban Development had been created in 1965. And housing policy jumped to a higher priority on the political agenda, as manifested in the Housing Act of 1968.

1968 TO 1973: EXPERIMENTS IN SUPPLY-SIDE INNOVATIONS

Inadequate units were still perceived as *the* housing problem in the late 1960s, but the perception had been modified to focus on a few low-income and/or minority-occupied neighborhoods in inner cities. Concentrated high-rise public housing, often prevalent in these areas, increasingly appeared to be more a problem than a solution. Thus, many policymakers and researchers were seeking to experiment with alternative approaches, and the Kerner Commission's suggestions for housing policy offered some tangible new directions. Despite this impetus toward revised strategies, old ideas were still firmly entrenched in the policy community, as evidenced by the 1968 legislative initiatives.

Modest Shifts in Policy

The continued emphasis of the 1968 Housing Act was on subsidized housing production, with the added stipulation of ambitious production goals and annual assessments of progress toward meeting these goals. What was modestly different was an emphasis on private construction and ownership of the subsidized stock, as had been begun earlier under Section 221(d)(3) (a strategy portrayed by line C in figure 5.1). Sections 235 and 236 provided direct subsidies for units targeted at moderate-income families, with the income limits for eligibility for the programs set 35 percent higher than the local public housing income limit. Low-income households were still to be served indirectly through filtering; only much later were rent supplements added to increase accessibility of the new units to the poor.

Section 235 provided direct homeownership assistance through interest rate subsidies on mortgage loans originated by banks and savings and loans that financed newly constructed (or substantially rehabilitated) private units. Eligible households were required to pay at least 20 percent of income for housing costs, including mortgage payments, property taxes, and insurance; the government subsidies made up the difference. However, the maximum subsidy payment was the difference between the actual mortgage payments and the borrowers' obligation if the mortgage interest rate were 1 percent. During fiscal year 1971, 138,000 units of the 408,000 units produced under all federal subsidy programs—34 percent—were produced under Section 235.

Section 236 consisted of interest rate subsidies on privately originated loans for rental housing construction. The shift from direct government loans to subsidies on privately originated loans was motivated more by a shortsighted political move than long-term policy logic. Direct government loans, such as those for Section 231(d)(3), would appear in full on the budget in the first year they were appropriated, whereas interest rate subsidies would appear over time only in the year incurred. Thus, the apparent budgetary outlay under the interest rate subsidy was much lower, but the long-term commitment was greater. Whatever the motive, 51,000 low-cost rental units were produced under Section 236 in fiscal year 1970 and 107,000 in fiscal year 1971. Over 90 percent of assistance under Section 236 was for new construction; the remainder was for rehabilitation of existing units.

The success of the 235 and 236 programs was limited, however. Extensive abuses of the programs were exposed along with high rates of foreclosure and default. By 1972, 1 in 15 projects was in default. Under the terms of the default insurance, HUD paid the face value of the loan and acquired the title. The number of HUD-owned homes rose from 27,000 in 1960 to 149,000 in 1972; the inventory of apartments went from 4,000 in 1960 to 54,000 in 1972. The rash of defaults was due to two factors. First, speculators were buying low-quality housing at low prices, doing cosmetic repairs with Section 235 money, then selling them for considerable profit; poor inspections failed to catch these bogus rehabilitations. It was said that real estate brokers were selling "slum housing for suburban prices." Second, the program had a design flaw: the tenant's payment of 20 percent of income did not include maintenance costs and utilities. As a result, lower-income households already receiving the maximum subsidy were paying much more of their income for total housing costs than originally anticipated. When major repairs needed to be made to cosmetically rehabilitated units, such households had no reserves upon which to draw; default was a typical consequence.

Despite the shortcomings of the programs, there was a substantial increase in subsidized housing production of various kinds during this time. More than 500,000 units were produced under Sections 235 and 236 alone.

Policy Research and Continuing Trials of Public Housing

Despite nascent concerns over the efficacy of public housing that began to be voiced in the early 1960s, public housing continued to expand through this period. Over half a million more units were added from 1967 through 1973. The proportion of public housing construction developed and built by local public housing authorities fell, however, from 62 percent in 1968 to 31 percent in 1970, as other approaches to developing public housing were initiated. For example, the "turnkey" program contracted construction of public housing to private developers; the local authorities purchased the completed projects (portrayed as line B' in figure 5.1). By 1972 there were 200,000 turnkey units out of a total of 1.3 million public housing units. Other housing authorities leased existing private housing projects for public housing. This program was not large—only 65,000 units were leased by 1972—but the program was touted as a major conceptual change. Despite the attempts to reform the construction of public housing, its problems were becoming manifest.

Public housing authorities began to face deteriorating financial circumstances, caught as they were by the federal government's failure to allocate adequate funds for maintenance and by simultaneous imposition of regulations to serve evermore impoverished households. As originally envisioned, federal public housing subsidies were to cover only the capital costs of construction. All operating costs were to be covered by rents, which were roughly based on ability to pay. Public housing authorities initially set rents at a level that would be attractive to the working poor and yet would provide adequate operating revenues, although often the lowest-income households were excluded. But new HUD regulations were instituted that required that the first eligible applicant on the public housing waiting list be granted an apartment and that the rent be set at no more than 25 percent of that applicant's income. These regulations, combined with the fact that by the mid-1970s two-thirds of public housing households contained no workers, led to a squeeze on rental revenues. Frank de Leeuw's 1970 analysis of growing financial pressures on public housing authorities in large cities epitomized the significant amount of policy research devoted to the topic that was influential in generating programmatic responses. As operating costs rose faster than rental revenues, local housing authorities found themselves in a financial crisis. Some responded by deferring necessary maintenance. Others responded with rent increases so that tenants began paying more than the officially mandated threshold of burden. A 1968 HUD survey showed that 15 percent of all nonelderly and 46 percent of all elderly households were paying 26 percent or more of their income for rent in public housing.

The Brooke Amendments of 1969, 1970, and 1971 attempted to alleviate the public housing crisis by providing: (1) rent supplements for the portion of rent exceeding 25 percent of a household's income; (2) operating and maintenance subsidies on a permanent basis; and (3) additional reserve funding. Local housing authorities, however, saw little relief inasmuch as these funds did not begin to flow until 1975.

Popular support for public housing eroded not only because of its financial troubles but for several other reasons that were identified by policy researchers. For one thing, there was growing evidence of mismanagement in some local authorities. HUD's shift in occupancy focus from working poor families to the indigent and unmarried made public housing a target for those venting resentment at the "undeserving poor." High-rise buildings, typical of many public housing projects, proved terrible places to house low-income families, with the attendant increase in social problems (such as those documented by Lee Rainwater in Behind Ghetto Walls [1970]). Many projects had been designed so that space could not be informally monitored by residents attempting to reduce potential criminal activity, as explained by Oscar Newman in *Defensible Space* (1972). The political demise of public housing is best symbolized by the demolition in 1975 of the massive Pruitt-Igoe project, built in 1954 in St. Louis.

Mounting popular and scholarly opposition to Sections 235 and 236 and to public housing led to President Nixon's moratorium on all subsidized production in January 1973. We portray this hiatus in subsidized supply programs by the breaks in lines *B* and *C* in figure 5.1. The emphasis of federal subsidized housing policy began perceptibly to shift from supply-side to demand-side policies, that is, from policies oriented toward new construction aimed at increasing subsidized housing supply to policies directed toward low-income households aimed at increasing their demand for decent housing.

1974 TO 1980: POLICY SCHIZOPHRENIA AND RESEARCH FERMENT

Despite the apparent shift in the orientation of low-income housing policy during the early 1970s, the supply-side versus demand-side debate continued unresolved, perhaps reflecting a national schizophrenia in public, political, and policy research circles. The National Housing Review Board (1974) and the Community Development Act (1974) embraced the policy shift to demand-side subsidies and enshrined the Section 8 policy for new and existing housing. Yet in 1976, President Gerald R. Ford reinstated funding for public housing and increased funding for subsidized housing construction by private builders. The program suspensions of 1973 were challenged in Congress, and in 1976 both Section 235 and conventional public housing funding were reactivated, shifting funds previously requested for Section 8. The revived Section 235 was a modified version limited to newly constructed homes and had a maximum subsidy set at the difference between the mortgage payment at the market rate and payments at a 5 percent rate (rather than the previous 1 percent subsidized rate). Later, the revised Section 235 was expanded to include existing housing and, in early 1978, the General Accounting Office recommended that Section 236 be revived as well.

But it was the Section 8 program that represented the new policy innovation of the period (portrayed as line *D* in figure 5.1). Under the Section 8 program for existing units, households located their own housing on the open market, and the local housing authorities paid the subsidy directly to the landlord whose unit was chosen. The amount of the subsidy was the difference between the rent for a standard unit, the fair market rent (FMR), and 25 percent of the household's income. Participants had some latitude as to the housing they chose. For example, they could elect to occupy housing that rented for less than the FMR and receive part of the difference; however, they could not pay more than 25 percent of their income, nor rent housing for more than the FMR. In some ways Section 8 for new construction resembled earlier supply-side programs. Private developers and state housing agencies submitted proposed housing projects to HUD. Once approved, the landlords were guaranteed the FMR for all units occupied by eligible tenants; tenants again contributed 25 percent of their income, with HUD providing the remainder. Households began receiving subsidies under Section 8 for existing housing in 1975. By the end of 1976, over 140,000 households were being assisted. Section 8 for new housing proceeded more slowly, but by 1977 about 135,000 units had been started.

Research Innovations

During the 1970s, urban economists and other housing researchers produced a surge of theoretical and empirical work on housing markets and housing policy. An important new, publicly funded database was initiated in 1973: the Annual (later, the American) Housing Survey of 60 metropolitan areas, with one-fourth of the areas sampled every fourth year. Key policy research developments during this period included extensive economic evaluations of specific housing policies, the quantification of housing supply and demand elasticities with respect to price and incomes, modeling of submarkets within metropolitan housing markets, and the use of computer models to simulate various housing policies. These works generally concluded that we should switch focus from supply-side to demand-side subsidies. However, as discussed in the paragraphs following, this occurred with insufficient decisiveness to cure the schizophrenia characterizing housing policy.

HOUSING DEMAND AND SUPPLY ELASTICITIES

The key empirical issue for housing policy research in the 1970s revolved around housing demand and supply "elasticities" (i.e., the relative sensitivity of housing consumption and production to a change in housing prices or the incomes of households). If the demand for housing were to prove price sensitive (elastic), for example, then supply-side programs would be relatively more effective than demand-side programs, for the following reason. Production programs lower housing prices for eligible households because the supply is increased. The greater the demand elasticity, the more housing will be consumed by households in response to the price decline and the greater the improvement in housing quality. In contrast, if demand were to prove insensitive to price, production programs would have little effect on consumption.

If the supply of housing were to prove sensitive to price, demand-oriented programs would be comparatively effective. Suppliers of housing would respond aggressively to the increased demand for housing, resulting in more of an increase in quantity of housing than in its price. If supply were insensitive to price, demand-oriented subsidies would primarily serve to inflate prices, since the modest increase in quantity supplied would not offset the increase in demand. If demand were to prove sensitive to income, demand-oriented policies that increased a household's effective income available for housing would markedly increase consumption of housing. Studies of the submarket for rental housing, most notably those by Eric Hanushek (1982), John Quigley (1979), Frank de Leeuw (1971, 1976), and Nkanta Ekanem (1971), concluded that supply was elastic and demand was inelastic with respect to price, implying that income transfers, or demand-side subsidies, were more likely to improve housing quality than new construction.

GOVERNMENT SUBSIDIES SUBSTITUTING FOR PRIVATE CONSTRUCTION

Much of the work done to evaluate the effects of particular housing policies questioned conventional theories. Of special note was the work claiming that, in the long run, subsidized construction programs substituted almost completely for private-sector construction that would have occurred in the absence of the policy. According to these studies' view of the market, excess demand for housing, evidenced by low vacancies and rising prices, would naturally trigger a supply response in the private sector to produce more housing. Government-subsidized construction merely provided a substitute to this response by alleviating the demand. Craig Swan (1973), for example, estimated that 85 percent of the starts produced under Sections 235 and 236 between 1969 and 1972 would have occurred without the programs.

The efficiency and equity of housing programs were also investigated. Research by Frank de Leeuw and Sam Leaman (1972), Eugene Smolensky (1968), David Barton and Edgar Olsen (1976) suggested that housing production by the public sector was anywhere from 10 percent to 42 percent more expensive than equivalent units produced by the private sector. Only a fraction of eligible households were served by housing programs, resulting in horizontal inequity, that is, households in the same income group were not made equally well off. Many of those receiving assistance were made better off than those just above the income eligibility limits for the programs, creating vertical inequity. Another target of persistent criticism for equity reasons was mortgage deductibility. Homeowners can deduct from taxable income any interest paid on home mortgages. This, in effect, is a major subsidy for homeowners (especially those who are upper-income) that is not available to renters.

MARKET MODELS

Housing policy researchers modeled the interaction of components of the housing market and submarkets, such as the market for low-cost housing. New filtering models, for example, dealt with the relationships among household demand, new construction, and changes in existing stock. Several studies by James Sweeney (1974), expanding on work done by Lowry, incorporated depreciation into the model and showed conditions under which filtering might or might not work to increase housing stock in low-quality submarkets.

Technological advances in the computer field ushered in a new method of investigating housing markets: the simulation model. These models were used to evaluate various housing policies and to determine the sensitivity of the estimated outcomes to alternative assumptions. The simulation approach entailed a researcher devising a model based on economic theory and statistical evidence, that is, mathematical functions that describe market behavior. The researcher then assigned alternative values—often from survey data—to the variables in the model and solved the model using a computer program. The validity of the model's equations was tested either by statistically estimating parameters based on historical data or by calibrating parameters so that the model simulated accurately the history of an actual urban housing market. Thus, housing market interactions were described in the equations of the model, and simulated, quantitative outcomes were estimated using alternative values of the variables as inputs. Perhaps the most influential of these models, developed by Frank de Leeuw and Raymond Struyk at The Urban Institute (1975), supported the desirability of new construction subsidies and filtering and cautioned about price inflation effects of demand-side housing allowances.

EXPERIMENTAL HOUSING ALLOWANCE PROGRAM

Another innovation in housing policy research was the first large-scale demonstration of a prospective policy, the Experimental Housing Allowance Program (EHAP), undertaken from 1972 to 1976 under the direction of a research team from Abt Associates. The 1970 Housing Act included authorization for large-scale experiments with a new type of demand-side subsidy—housing allowances—involving 15,000 to 20,000 families. The operative principle of housing allowances is consumer choice. Households receive a voucher for housing that they can "spend" on whatever housing they choose (within certain quality standards). There are many personal and social advantages to this approach. Less stigma is attached to housing allowances than to place-based housing subsidies, since participants are not "labeled" because of their residence as poor or as receiving assistance, and tenants enjoy a greater degree of independence. By allowing recipients to choose housing in any location, the program discourages concentration of poverty and enables those in areas not served by local housing authorities to receive housing assistance.

The main component of the EHAP was a full-scale test of the market impacts of a voucher program in two mid-sized metropolitan areas in which all eligible households could participate. Standard rents were estimated for each housing unit size for each locality, basically the same concept as the fair market rent schedules used by HUD for determining Section 8 rents. Eligible households were required to locate a unit of adequate quality. Upon doing so, the family received subsidy payments calculated as the difference between the estimated standard rent and 25 percent of their adjusted gross income. This program incorporated a fill-the-gap approach, that is, subsidies decreased as incomes rose. The difference between the housing allowance program and Section 8 for existing housing was that the allowance payment was given directly to the recipients, who were responsible for making their payments to the landlord. A household also had the liberty to choose a unit whose value was more or less than the FMR, and either supplement their subsidy or keep the difference, respectively.

The results of the EHAP were the following (Bradbury and Downs 1981). Of the 56 percent of eligible households that enrolled in the EHAP voucher program, 75 percent found or currently occupied adequate housing, resulting in a 42 percent participation rate (lower than expected). Because many of the participants continued to occupy their current units, there was limited improvement in housing quality, little effect on household mobility, and no rent inflation as a result of the program. Finally, the experiment showed that consumer-oriented programs were much simpler to administer than construction subsidies, leading to increased efficiency and lowered costs. Despite a consensus among policy researchers concerning the efficacy of housing allowances, the remaining criticism focused on their potential inflationary effects, especially in the short run in tight housing markets. This concern raised the possibility that demand-side policies might not be the best policy in all metropolitan market contexts.

Emerging Affordability Crisis

This period of housing policy experimentation and intellectual ferment in the 1970s occurred when the very nature of "the urban housing problem" was about to change dramatically. Central business district real estate booms increased the demand for building sites in the inner cities, putting pressure on the price of land for development. Rapid housing price and operating cost inflation, together with rising interest rates, worsened the prospects for potential homebuyers and developers. Policy researchers began to document that housing prices were increasing more rapidly than the prices of most other goods, while incomes were stagnating. As a result, the share of income spent on housing costs for both renters and homeowners rose steadily from 1972.

Evidence about the rising cost of credit and about inflating house prices and rents changed the focus of the policy debate from quality to affordability problems. Even though conditions in many lower-income urban neighborhoods remained depressed during the 1970s, the new threat to housing affordability touched a broader spectrum of American households than poor people, renters, and minorities. Indeed, after a quarter of a century of inexorable growth, rates of homeownership stalled. The government's seemingly convincing success (in reducing housing shortages) through massive, if often hidden, subsidies for the private construction of new single-family homes now seemed more transitory.

1980 TO 1995: MINIMALISM, PRIVATIZATION, AND DEVOLUTION IN HOUSING POLICY

Throughout the 1980s the nation witnessed continuing loss of low-cost rental stock, increasing rental affordability problems (especially among those with low incomes), and the emerging specter of homelessness. American Housing Survey data indicate that 483,000 units—over one-fourth of all that were built—were demolished each year from 1985 to 1989; 197,000 of these units were rentals. Conversion, upgrading, and temporary removal of units further reduced the supply of privately owned, low-cost housing. Between 1985 and 1989, 169,400 of all subsidized units were removed annually, 64,000 of them by demolition. Appropriations for HUD's subsidized housing programs fell more than 80 percent between 1978 and 1991 (inflation adjusted), and the number of new federally assisted housing units fell by 89 percent. The net result, as estimated by Phillip Clay in 1992, was that by 1993 the number of low-rent ($250 in 1974 dollars) apartments in both private and public sectors would have declined by 3.4 million (24 percent) since 1974.

Homelessness and Rental Affordability Squeeze

Average rental cost burdens escalated as modest-quality housing supply fell, and rents rose while incomes stagnated. According to the Bureau of Labor Statistics' revised rent index, real rents rose by 16 percent between 1981 and 1987, after having declined from 1967 to 1981. At the same time, poverty rates began to rise inexorably from the mid-1970s to the mid-1980s. As a result, by 1987 over 60 percent of low-income households paid more than half of their income on rent, and roughly one-third paid more than 70 percent of their income for housing.

Homelessness also rose to prominence as one of the country's most urgent problems. Martha Burt (e.g., 1992) provided the most comprehensive studies of homelessness, attributing it to the loss of low-cost units, the decreasing affordability of housing, rising poverty, and the growing deinstitutionalization of the mentally ill. According to the *Report of the National Housing Task Force*, in March 1988 there were 4.1 million more poor households than low-rent apartments at prices these households could afford. Although there is no generally agreed upon estimate of how many homeless there are (their living habits make them hard to find), all estimates show that homelessness is increasing and that at least a quarter of a million people are homeless on any given night.

Toothless Policy Responses

Following the recommendations of the President's Commission on Housing in 1982, the demand-side approach became the centerpiece of the Reagan administration's subsidized housing policy. The prevailing wisdom was that there were sufficient decent-quality units, but that they were no longer affordable to most low-income households. The "solution," therefore, would be demand-side policies that closed the affordability gap. In particular, Section 8 certificates were expanded and "vouchers"—coupons worth a certain amount of rental payment that could be applied to any available apartment—began to be issued on an experimental basis in the late 1980s (see lines D' and D'' in figure 5.1).

On the supply side of the housing market, the dual strategy of encouraging new construction of both units for sale to the nonpoor and subsidized units for rental to the poor was converted to a single track. President Reagan terminated all federal programs for new construction of subsidized housing and instituted a series of administrative changes that made it increasingly hard for existing public housing authorities to operate anything better than dilapidated warehouses for the poorest of the poor.

It is debatable whether this marked shrinking of the federal role in subsidized housing supply was stimulated more by ideology, popular opposition to supply-side options, weak HUD leadership, or policy research of the prior decade. Nonetheless, it is clear that production responsibilities were devolved to state and local governments and to the private for-profit and nonprofit sectors. The only new federal initiative related to subsidized housing production during the Reagan administration was the Low Income Housing Tax Credit, created under the Tax Reform Act of 1986, which provided tax breaks to developers who invested in housing for low-income households (see line C' in figure 5.1). "Public-private partnerships" and the growth of the nonprofit housing industry were hailed as furthering the move to divest the federal government of its role in housing policy.

The nonprofit housing industry emerged during the 1980s to partially fill the vacuum left by the withdrawal of the federal government from low-income housing construction. At this writing, there are an estimated 3,000 to 5,000 such organizations working nationwide.

Nonprofit production has been supported by public and private partnerships including state and local governments, banks, corporations, foundations, and religious institutions. Most of the corporate involvement since the early 1980s was motivated by the Low Income Housing Tax Credits.

The shift toward a demand-side federal housing strategy, coupled with locally tailored production options, was a logical response to the demonstrated shortcomings of past federal supply-side strategies and reflected a correct perception of the current rental affordability crisis. The clear shortcoming of the approach was its minimalist perspective: the nation "could not afford" to fully fund demand-side programs, it was argued. For example, despite the rise of voucher and Section 8 certification holders, by 1989 still only one-third of eligible households received any sort of federal housing assistance.

Legislative responses to the affordability crisis also represented mild palliatives in the form of the McKinney Act (1987) and the National Affordable Housing Act (1990). The McKinney Act provided direct support through HUD for emergency homeless shelters and other homeless assistance programs. Although the act's provisions were aimed at assisting the homeless, Congress never appropriated more than token funds, and the approach never addressed the prevention of homelessness.

The National Affordable Housing Act of 1990 established the HOME Investment Partnership Program, a block grant that allowed states and localities to carry out specially tailored housing strategies, and HOPE (Homeownership and Opportunity for People Everywhere), to create homeownership opportunities for tenants of public and assisted housing. The HOME program provided funds to state and local governments and nonprofit housing producers for a variety of programs, including rehabilitation, new construction, and rental assistance, if needed. Each community could establish its own policy priorities, subject to HUD approval of its Comprehensive Housing Assistance Strategy. As with the McKinney Act, resources seemed woefully inadequate compared to need. Appropriations for the HOME program were $1 billion; by comparison, at least an estimated $15 billion would be needed to eliminate rent burdens for all eligible households. The evaluation of the HOPE demonstration program indicated that the sale of public housing to tenants met with limited success. The majority of housing authorities had difficulty selling their housing; by the end of the program only about half of the units put on the market had been sold.

Homeownership Affordability and Developments in the Mortgage Market

Perhaps the most important housing policy emerging during this period was the rapid expansion of the secondary mortgage market due to innovation of mortgage-backed securities. In the secondary market, government-sponsored financial enterprises—the Federal National Mortgage Association (Fannie Mae) and the Federal Home Loan Mortgage Corporation (Freddie Mac)—purchase conventional mortgage loans originated privately by banks and savings and loans. The Government National Mortgage Association (Ginnie Mae) similarly purchases government-insured (FHA, VA) mortgages. Thereby, the lenders receive immediate repayment of their loan, and the secondary financial enterprises assume the risk of default. The funds are then available for the primary sector (banks and savings and loans) to lend again, thus increasing the credit available to homebuyers and housing developers.

Mortgage-backed securities extended the idea of the secondary market to another level. A portfolio of mortgages is assembled to secure bonds issued by Fannie Mae, Freddie Mac, or Ginnie Mae. Investors in these bonds are assured a return because of the repayment of the mortgages, and the risks of default on the mortgages are minimized by a diversified portfolio. By issuing these bonds, the secondary sector increases its funds available to purchase new mortgages from private lenders, and thereby further expands the supply of credit available to borrowers.

These innovations in housing finance, coupled with less-restrictive monetary policies, brought down mortgage interest rates from their peaks in the late 1970s. Indexes of homeownership cost peaked in 1982 and have fallen consistently since. Although younger renter households appear to be moving into homeownership at a slower rate than their cohorts a generation ago, by and large the threat of a homeownership affordability crisis has waned, and faith in the status quo of private, single-family construction has been reinvigorated.

Research Bucking Ideology

Much of the housing research during this period was iconoclastic. Most noteworthy was mounting scholarly disillusionment with the reputed benefits of the filtering process and the desirability of continued subsidy to homeowners through mortgage deductibility. The main underpinning was provided by Jerome Rothenberg and his colleagues

in *The Maze of Urban Housing Markets* (1991), a comprehensive theoretical model yielding new insights into housing problems and policy
solutions. They saw the market as an interrelated series of submarkets—each defined by common housing quality—among which
household demanders choose and builders and converters target for
supply. Within this framework, it became easier to comprehend why
housing problems such as affordability and homelessness arose, how
the filtering mechanism operated, and under what conditions alternative policies proved most efficacious.

Anthony Downs (1994), in particular, took the lead in showing how
single-family home construction in the suburbs contributed to waste
of agricultural land, burgeoning transportation problems, concentrations of low-income households in decaying center cities, and severe
inequities in tax bases among political jurisdictions within metropolitan areas. Other researchers looked at the budgetary costs and
economic equity and efficiency of mortgage interest deductibility, and
proposed capping the loan amount on which interest would be tax-
deductible. For example, the Joint Committee on Taxation estimated
that reducing the limit on qualified home mortgage debt to $300,000
would raise $1 billion in 1993 and $14.7 billion between 1993 and
1997. By comparison, the current estimated five-year cost of the Low
Income Housing Tax Credit is only $2.4 billion.

Thus far, this research has failed to generate any discernible impact
on public policy, because its implications buck dominant, commonly
held values. Individualism, as manifested in ownership of a single-
family home and in the ability to develop one's land in a manner of
one's own choosing, appears to overshadow counterarguments about
social efficiency and equity.

Yet, ideology need not necessarily constrain the impact of housing
research. One area in which recent research undoubtedly has, and is
likely to continue to have, influence concerns policies designed to use
housing not as an end in itself but as a means to enhancing tenants'
economic opportunities. The preeminent precedent here is James Rosenbaum's evaluations of the Gautreaux Program (1995), an initiative
that fulfills a court-mandated desegregation order by assisting Chicago public housing residents to move to low-poverty neighborhoods
through the use of counseling and Section 8 certificates. Rosenbaum's
evaluations were sufficiently positive to convince Congress to enact
the Moving To Opportunity demonstration in 1992, which is a broader
scale replication in five metropolitan areas, although subsequently
the program's funding was reduced. Other studies are now underway
that assess innovations in public housing that variously attempt to:

(1) provide comprehensive education, child care, and social services on site; (2) develop mixed-income projects; and/or (3) create escrow accounts for tenants' rents that help to accumulate downpayments for homes they eventually can buy. Results from such studies are likely to have strong impacts on program design, given the contemporary emphasis in political discourse on minimizing the dependency-creating impacts of all sorts of social policies.

LESSONS AND PROSPECTS

The role of housing policy researchers has varied over the past 50 years, at times being reactive and at others proactive, and providing more influence on some policy fronts than on others. Over the past two decades in particular, policy researchers have continually offered up-to-date documentation of housing conditions, and in this way have shaped the agenda. The impact of evaluations of specific policies has depended on whether the prevailing ideology of the period was congruent with the research conclusions. For example, from the late 1960s onward, housing researchers provided a strong intellectual rationale for switching focus from public housing and other supply-side strategies to demand-side strategies for helping poor renters. After a schizophrenic policy period in the 1970s when both approaches were tried, the demand-side approach was enshrined during the Reagan administration. Ironically, because of that administration's deemphasis of HUD in general, housing subsidy policies suffered cuts overall. Thus, many policy researchers applauded a change in housing policy emphasis while simultaneously decrying the contraction in the scale of policy in the face of mounting needs.

Commonly held values are also a constraint on the impact of policy research, which has become more uniformly critical with regard to policymakers' long-term emphasis on private construction and homeownership. Yet, it is questionable whether any policy impact is likely, given the American attraction to the suburbs and the "American Dream" of a single-family home.

If recent trends persist, there would be little reason to scale back expectations of homeownership. In 1992 mortgage interest rates fell below 8 percent for the first time in 20 years and remained so until early 1994. Combined with a deceleration in home price inflation, the aftertax annual cost of a representative starter home fell to a level last witnessed in the mid-1970s. Thus, prospects for returning homeownership rates to their historical levels, even among younger adults, appear bright at this writing.

Unfortunately, prospects appear considerably dimmer for rental households. The inflation-adjusted median income of renters in 1993 remained well below that of their cohorts in the 1960s and 1970s, falling back to its 1981 level after a brief recovery during the late 1980s. Monthly rental costs, on the other hand, have failed to decline significantly from their 1986 peak, despite weak economic growth. These two factors combined to produce in both 1992 and 1993 25-year highs in the median ratio of rents-to-incomes for renters. The specters of homelessness and of overcrowded families thus appear to cloud the horizon. Anticipated cuts in social welfare expenditures can only exacerbate these in the short run.

As for responses to these future prospects, it appears that the impact of housing policy research will continue to be constrained by yet another pervasive political tenet: federal deficit reduction and "HUD reinvention" that forces a minimalist, decentralized approach to new initiatives. At this writing, HUD has just submitted a legislative package to Congress that would dramatically reshape the nature of federal housing policy. The first provision in the HUD proposal is to consolidate 60 major HUD programs into three performance-based funds: a Community Opportunity Fund (similar to current Community Development Block Grants), an Affordable Housing Fund (comprising the current HOME, homeownership, HOPE, and homelessness assistance programs), and a Housing Certificate Fund (comprising all tenant- and site-based assisted housing programs). The second provision is to convert public housing to more market-based projects through: (1) deregulation of public housing authorities, including flexibility to demolish the worst projects; (2) modernization grants; (3) provisions of vouchers to current public housing residents; and (4) transition to market-based rents. The third provision is to create a government-owned Federal Housing Corporation that would transform the Federal Housing Administration into a more results-oriented, accountable, credit-enhancement operation. Although the fate of this proposal's particulars is in doubt, what seems clear is that the principles of reliance on market mechanisms, local flexibility, bureaucratic efficiencies, and budgetary downsizing will predominate.

Thus, the prospects for the foreseeable future are that federal housing policy will continue to be characterized fundamentally by minimalism, privatization, and devolution of planning and operational responsibility to states and localities. The critical challenge for housing policy researchers will be to help devise creative, locally responsive, resource-conserving initiatives that can better respond to the growing problems of rental affordability, homelessness, and the special needs of subpopulations. Whether the products of such research will have more or less influence at the state level than they have had at the federal level remains to be seen.

SUGGESTED READING

Apgar, William. 1990. "Which Housing Policy Is Best?" *Housing Policy Debate* 1(1):1–32.

Burt, Martha R. 1992. *Over the Edge: The Growth of Hopelessness in the 1980s.* New York and Washington, D.C.: Russell Sage Foundation and Urban Institute Press.

de Leeuw, Frank, Ann B. Schnare, and Raymond Struyk. 1976. "Housing." In *The Urban Predicament*, edited by William Gorham and Nathan Glazer. Washington, D.C.: Urban Institute Press.

DiPasquale, Denise, and Langley Keyes, eds. 1990. *Building Foundations.* Philadelphia: University of Pennsylvania Press.

Downs, Anthony. 1976. *Urban Problems and Prospects.* Chicago: Rand McNally College Publishing Co.

————. 1994. *New Visions for Metropolitan America.* Washington, D.C.: Brookings Institution.

Hartman, Chester W. 1975. *Housing and Social Policy.* Englewood Cliffs, N.J.: Prentice-Hall.

Hughes, James. 1991. "Clashing Demographics: Homeownership and Affordability Dilemmas." *Housing Policy Debate* 2(4):1215–50.

Joint Center for Housing Studies of Harvard University, The. 1994. *The State of the Nation's Housing.* Cambridge, Mass.: Author.

Kingsley, G. Thomas. 1991. "Housing Vouchers and America's Changing Housing Problems." In *Privatization and Its Alternatives*, edited by William T. Gormley, Jr. Madison: University of Wisconsin Press.

Nelson, Kathryn. 1994. "Whose Shortage of Affordable Housing?" *Housing Policy Debate* 5(4):401–42.

Quigley, John M. 1979. "What Have We Learned about Urban Housing Markets?" In *Current Issues in Urban Economics*, edited by Peter Mieszkowski and Mahlon Straszheim. Baltimore, Md.: Johns Hopkins University Press.

Report of the National Advisory Commission on Civil Disorders: Summary. 1968. New York: Bantam Books.

Rothenberg, Jerome, George Galster, Richard Butler, and John Pitkin. 1991. *The Maze of Urban Housing Markets.* Chicago: University of Chicago Press.

Schwartz, David, David Bartelt, Richard Ferlauto, Daniel Hoffman, and David Listokin. 1992. "A New Urban Housing Policy for the 1990s." *Journal of Urban Affairs* 14(3,4):239–62.
Shlay, Anne. 1993. "Family Self-Sufficiency and Housing." *Housing Policy Debate* 4(3):457–95.
Spence, Louis. 1993. "Rethinking the Social Role of Public Housing." *Housing Policy Debate* 4(3):355–68.
Stone, Michael E. 1990. *One Third of a Nation: A New Look at Housing Affordability in America.* Washington, D.C.: Economic Policy Institute.
U.S. Department of Housing and Urban Development. 1995. *HUD Reinvention: From Blueprint to Action.* Pub. no. HUD-1524-PA. Washington, D.C.: Author
Weicher, John C. 1979. "Urban Housing Policy." In *Current Issues in Urban Economics,* edited by Peter Mieszkowski and Mahlon Straszheim. Baltimore, Md.: Johns Hopkins University Press.

Other References

Anderson, Martin. 1964. *The Federal Bulldozer: A Critical Analysis of Urban Renewal, 1949–1962.* Cambridge, Mass.: MIT Press.
Barton, David, and Edgar Olson. 1976. "The Benefits and Costs of Public Housing in New York City." Madison: University of Wisconsin, Institute for Research on Poverty Discussion Paper.
Bradbury, Katherine L., and Anthony Downs, eds. 1981. *Do Housing Allowances Work?* Washington, D.C.: Brookings Institution.
Clay, Phillip L. 1992. "New Directions in Housing Policy for African-Americans." In *The Metropolis in Black and White: Place, Power and Polarization,* edited by George Galster and Edward Hill. Rutgers: State University of New Jersey, Center for Urban Policy Research.
deLeeuw, Frank. 1970. *Operating Costs in Public Housing: A Financial Crisis.* Washington, D.C.: The Urban Institute.
deLeeuw, Frank. 1976. "The Demand for Housing: A Review of Cross-Sectional Evidence." *Review of Economics and Statistics* 53:1–10.
deLeeuw, Frank, and Sam Leaman. 1972. "The Section 23 Leasing Program." In *The Economics of Federal Subsidies Programs.* Part 5: *Housing Subsidies.* U.S. Congress, Joint Economic Committee. Washington, D.C.: U.S. Government Printing Office.
deLeeuw, Frank, and Nkanta Ekanem. 1971. "The Supply of Rental Housing." *American Economic Review* 57:501–18.
deLeeuw, Frank, and Raymond Struyk. 1975. *The Web of Urban Housing.* Washington, D.C.: The Urban Institute.
Hanushek, Eric. 1982. "The Determinants in Housing Demand." In *Research in Urban Economics,* edited by J. Vernon Henderson. Greenwich, Conn.: JAI Press.

Lowry, Ira. 1960. "Filtering and Housing Standards: A Conceptual Analysis." *Land Economics* 36:362–70.

National Housing Task Force. 1988. *A Decent Place to Live: A Report of the National Housing Task Force.* Washington, D.C.: U.S. Government Printing Office.

Newman, Oscar. 1972. *Defensible Space: Crime Prevention through Urban Design.* New York: McMillan.

President's Commission on Housing. 1982. *The Report of the President's Commission on Housing.* Washington, D.C.: U.S. Government Printing Office.

Rainwater, Lee. 1970. *Behind Ghetto Walls: Black Families in a Federal Slum.* Chicago: Aldine.

Rosenbaum, James. 1995. "Changing the Geography of Opportunity by Expanding Residential Choice: Lessons from the Gautreaux Program." *Housing Policy Debate* 6,1:231–70.

Smolensky, Eugene. 1968. "Public Housing or Income Supplements—The Economics of Housing for the Poor." *Journal of the American Institute of Planners* 34:389–406.

Swan, Craig. 1973. "Housing Subsidies and Housing Starts." *American Real Estate and Urban Economics Association Journal* 1:119–40.

Sweeney, James. 1974. "A Commodity Hierarchy Model of the Rental Housing Market." *Journal of Urban Economics* 1:288–323.

Chapter Six

TRANSPORTATION AND LAND USE

William A. Hyman and G. Thomas Kingsley

Few phenomena of modern American metropolitan life have been more profound than suburbanization. Suburbs captured 77.9 million of the 103.4 million total population growth occurring in all of metropolitan America from 1950 to 1990. Not only did the number of people living in the suburbs increase dramatically, but from 1976 through 1986 the proportion of workers who both live and work in the suburbs grew even more rapidly. Two-thirds of recent employment growth occurred outside the central cities of the nation's largest metropolitan areas. There are now more jobs outside than inside the large cities of these regions. In the 1976–86 period, suburbs accounted for 120 percent of net job growth in manufacturing, while central cities suffered absolute losses in manufacturing employment.

Since World War II, nearly every problem of urbanized areas has somehow been tied directly or indirectly to the growth of the suburbs. According to conventional wisdom, a key part of the dynamic of the suburbanization process has been construction of highways. Better roads have made it possible for people to leave the central cities and realize the "American Dream" of owning a single family home while continuing to work in central cities. The conventional wisdom also recognizes that suburbanization has not occurred without great cost: congestion, pollution, unsightly commercial strips, and willy-nilly residential and business development that has gobbled up environmentally valuable land.

Transportation policy related to metropolitan land use has been implicit rather than explicit, and rather than actively attempting to shape urban form, has been passive in the face of larger, more powerful forces underlying decentralization. Furthermore, rarely can one point to policy studies or analyses as a cause of transportation decisions that intend to affect land use in the suburbs. Nor can one often point to instances of land-use policy studies that have directly affected transportation decisions. More likely, other factors besides social scientific research on interrelationships between transportation and land use have been the primary determinants of policy. These include: (1) frequently defining "the transportation problem" as involving national security (defense mobility during the Cold War and energy conservation after the oil embargo of 1973) instead of metropolitan concerns; (2) defining the problem as one of rush-hour congestion in city-suburb trips, wherein land use is assumed to be an independent variable; and (3) "pricing" urban highways by travel delays instead of congestion tolls, thereby not facing up to issues of efficient use.

Transportation planners and policymakers are not unaware of the connection between improvements in accessibility brought about by transportation and induced changes in land use. However, the direction of causality is empirically and theoretically ambiguous. When a major highway improvement results in substantially reduced travel time, often significant development follows. But just as often the seeds of the development were present before the transportation improvement. The development would have occurred anyway, and would have intensified the need for the transportation improvement. Theoretical models lead to contradictory implications regarding how transportation improvements would affect urban form, and thus have provided little help in clarifying causality. This lack of consensual intellectual foundation is an important reason for the relative impotence of policy research in this field.

In the period since World War II, transportation policymakers in the United States have not seen fit, for the most part, to use transportation as an instrument to influence land use. There are four reasons. First, the main focus of transportation has rarely been on the transportation–land use nexus. Second, the ambiguity concerning the direction of causality between transportation and land use has tended to undermine any temptation to use transportation as the primary urban growth management tool. Third, although there has been a temptation to view transportation as a strong lever for influencing development patterns, policymakers know that many other factors contribute more significantly to land use, particularly the underlying market forces encouraging decentralization. Among these factors are general population growth, expansion of specific industries in metropolitan areas, inexpensive middle-class housing, lower crime rates, and discomfort with blacks and other minorities in central cities. Fourth, policymakers have not been inclined to incur the wrath of developers, lenders, and others who profit from suburban growth.

A historical examination of transportation policy related to land use reveals that, with minor exceptions, transportation policy has done little to arrest the undesirable effects of suburban sprawl. Transportation policy in the post–World War II era has first and foremost been concerned with providing mobility. Viewed positively, this mobility-focused policy has played a supporting role in the decisions of individuals to populate the suburbs, get to work, shop, and visit friends, and for business in the suburbs to obtain needed inputs and sell goods and services. Viewed negatively, the inattention to unwanted land-use effects has undermined mobility of suburban life. Highway congestion, due in part to inefficient, low-density land-use patterns, has increased to nearly insufferable levels in many suburban areas. Accompanying environmental degradation of various sorts has followed. Recent legislation, however, requires transportation agencies to investigate the relationship between transportation, land use, and air quality. Policy research will contribute to and benefit from these investigations. With an improvement in the understanding of these relationships, decision makers will become better informed about the limits of policies intended to influence transportation and land use.

BUILDING THE INTERSTATE SYSTEM

From the end of World War II through the early 1960s, highway policy did not result from national policy studies or studies conducted by groups outside of government. Instead, a few important individuals in the Bureau of Public Roads and the American Association of State Highway Officials, working closely with the U.S. Congress and the president, shaped the most important federal policy.

During World War II, General Dwight Eisenhower had come to appreciate the importance of the German system of autobahns and subsequently championed a major national highway construction program in the United States as a keystone of enhancing the mobility of our armed forces. President Eisenhower and members of his administration also recognized the needs of growing civilian traffic, the problems of rising highway construction costs, and the relationship between the provision of new transportation facilities and the pace of national economic development.

At a meeting on April 12, 1954, Eisenhower reorganized federal road planning in the conviction that more automobiles would mean "greater convenience, greater happiness, and greater standards of living." "With our roads inadequate to handle an expanding industry," he said, "the results will be inflation and a disrupted economy." Eisenhower asserted that more than 60 million vehicles would soon jam the nation's roads, and it was necessary to embark on a major construction program to handle this traffic growth. Congress passed the Federal Aid Highway Act of 1956, which created the highway trust fund and authorized $25 billion over 12 years for a National System of Interstate and Defense Highways totaling 41,000 miles, including 6,100 in urban areas. These were to be financed with 90 percent federal funds and a 10 percent state or local match. Prior to 1956, there were only 480 miles of freeways completed or under construction in the 25 largest cities. By 1976, 7,400 miles of urban interstates were open to traffic after amendments to the Federal Aid Highway Act enlarged the system to 42,500 total miles and 8,600 urban miles.

Planning for the growth in traffic superseded land-use planning. By the time of the interstate highway program, the parkway design concept had become highly influential. The parkway design tradition sought to accommodate other urban development activities while providing multiple traffic lanes with a median divider. In contrast, the geometric design tradition emphasized designs that could serve heavier traffic at safe speeds in highly urbanized areas by stressing limited access via entrance/exit ramps. Inexorable traffic growth resulted in a continuous upscaling of urban highways from the 4 lanes at ground level typical of parkways to the 10-lane, sometimes sunken freeways with cloverleafs and overpasses.

Eisenhower's original concept for interstate highways was that they serve vital defense installations and be connectors between cities, not penetrate the cities. But the political coalition of state highway agencies, mayors, and city business leaders resulted in freeways plowing into most city centers. The apparent lack of concern for urban land use occurred partly because of the preeminence of engineers in policymaking roles. Engineers were primarily concerned with building roads, thereby improving accessibility and serving personal mobility needs, and they were convinced that they had public support. The posture of engineers was to be objective and untainted by politics, even though they frequently worked with politicians. Indeed, the public viewed highway engineers as competent experts acting in their interest, and politicians sought and relied upon their technical expertise and input.

Thus, a broad consensus generated the major highway construction program in the late 1950s and early 1960s. Even though the new urban freeways (including the beltways and the radial spokes from central cities to the suburbs) supported if not accelerated suburban development, the myopic focus on highway engineering dominated, uninformed by more holistic policy studies.

Evidence of the lack of policy studies and analyses that concentrated on the relationship between transportation and land use in the 1950s comes from Harvey Levine's *National Transportation Policy: A Study of Studies* (1978). Levine referenced over 600 studies and 1,000 articles published through 1977, including congressional hearings and books, and selected 36 for detailed evaluation. These 36 fell into four categories: (1) comprehensive transportation policy studies, (2) other major transportation policy studies, (3) contemporary studies receiving public exposure, and (4) miscellaneous transportation studies. Levine found that most studies conducted between World War II and the early 1960s were concerned with organizational issues regarding the federal government and economic regulation of various forms of transportation in terms of rates, entry and exit from markets, and so forth. Regulatory issues stemmed initially from seeking to restrain monopolists on the one hand, and, on the other hand, granting to common carriers some measure of protection from competition. In later years, especially in the 1970s, policy moved in the direction of reducing or eliminating regulation in favor of greater reliance on markets and competition.

The one major exception to the preceding generalization was the Doyle Report of 1961 (in Levine 1978), the first major national transportation policy study after World War II that addressed land-use issues at some length, although such issues again were secondary to other concerns. The Doyle Report was the result of a congressional recommendation for a study that would examine: (1) the need for regulation, (2) government assistance and user charges, (3) common ownership, (4) railroad consolidations and mergers, (5) railroad passenger service, and (6) additional regulatory and promotional matters. Along with many recommendations concerning these matters, the Doyle Report called for better coordination of federal programs, more support for local planning, and the undertaking of additional research in urban development. This call would soon be heeded.

DEFINING THE URBAN TRANSPORTATION PROBLEM

Numerous policy analysts asserted in the early 1960s that the most important economic problem that would confront the United States in the following 20 years would be the sweeping increase in urbani-

zation. Their common pronouncement proved to be influential. In
1962 President John F. Kennedy echoed this sentiment in an address
to Congress when he said, "Our national welfare requires the provision for good urban transportation with the proper use of private
vehicles and modern mass transport to help shape, as well as serve,
urban growth."

The Urban Transportation Problem, by Meyer, Kain, and Wohl
(1965), one of the most significant policy studies written in the post–
World War II period, was prepared in response to Kennedy's message
to Congress. Meyer, Kain, and Wohl felt that transportation improvements represented an indirect attack, at best, on the more basic problems of cities. Nevertheless, they acknowledged the reputed therapeutic value of urban transportation improvements because such
improvements constituted one facet of the general urban problem
on which there was some possibility of action, whereas other facets
were so complex and politically explosive as to defy easy analysis or
solution.

Meyer, Kain, and Wohl (1965) sought to test a number of hypotheses:
that urban transportation was in a "mess" and becoming worse; that
the decline in population and densities could be attributed to lack of
good mass transit; that rail transit was cheaper than mass transit and
still cheaper than automobile travel; and that the type of urban transportation was a key factor in shaping the aesthetic character and form
of the city. The study focused on rush-hour passenger movements;
this definition of the problem was to prove fundamental in minimizing attention to land-use responses to transportation policies.

In their 1965 study, Meyer, Kain, and Wohl concluded that decentralization of cities would have occurred with or without mass transit
and would continue. The potential influence of transportation policy
paled in comparison to the forces underlying decentralization and
suburbanization: technological change that resulted in decentralization of businesses and job opportunities, rising incomes that allowed
workers to live near the new jobs in the suburbs, and blurring of the
distinctions between living in the city versus the outer parts of a
metropolitan area. They argued that decentralization would change
the character of the urban transportation problem, since travel would
no longer be between central cities and suburbs, but between a home
and a job in the suburbs. Decentralization would lessen the fundamental urban transportation problem of moving people during rush
hours to and from areas of high population and workplace density.
They concluded that the quality of transportation had actually improved in the five years prior to 1965 due to suburbanization and

reciprical relationship

highway construction. They acknowledged the complementarity between the demand for urban transportation and the demand for suburban residential land. Nonetheless, by defining the urban transportation problem largely as rush-hour congestion on city-suburb trips, Meyer, Kain, and Wohl were able to cast the role of land use as an independent variable to which transportation demands and, ultimately, policy would respond.

FREEWAY REVOLT, ENVIRONMENTAL MOVEMENT, AND RISE OF PLANNING

In the mid-1960s, the freeway-induced destruction of inner-city neighborhoods, growing environmental awareness, and the concern with uncontrolled suburban development catalyzed a growing negative reaction to highway construction. After the passage of the Urban Relocation Assistance Act of 1962, the Transportation Act of 1966 (which provided for protection of public lands), the National Historic Preservation Act of 1966, the National Environmental Policy Act of 1969, and the Clean Air Act Amendment of 1970, planning and construction of highways became enormously complex. As a consequence, highway engineers became increasingly frustrated and their policy influence waned.

Some engineers, with encouragement from urban planners, began to turn toward construction of heavy and light rail, reserving freeway medians for transit, and creating a dense network of urban arterials serving both cars and buses. This new direction focused on a "system perspective" that placed as much importance on the design of entire urban transportation networks—including their interaction with land—as on the design of specific facilities.

Urban Renewal and Comprehensive, Coordinated, and Continuous Planning

By the late 1950s and early 1960s, poverty, crime, congestion, and racial problems in the cities began to capture public and political attention. Before 1950 most writers on urban problems saw the ills of urban life as stemming from high densities. In their view, the solution was to move city dwellers to less-crowded conditions. In the face of rapidly deteriorating urban centers in the early 1960s, stewards of the cities took a different tack and sought federal support for urban renewal. Big-city mayors supported revitalization of urban housing, community development, and, ironically, freeway construction. Rather than concentrating growth in the central cities, however, the result was to destroy the social cohesion of many poor and ethnic neighborhoods, and to accelerate suburbanization and sprawl. As the federal government established numerous grants-in-aid programs concerning housing, community development, and transportation, the interest in and need for planning and coordinating various federal aid programs grew, and the federal government imposed requirements on metropolitan areas for comprehensive planning.

A key provision of the Federal Aid Highway Act of 1962 was that federally aided transportation investments had to be based on a coordinated, comprehensive, and continuous planning process. Each metropolitan region was required to establish a Metropolitan Planning Organization (MPO) that would have the responsibility for this "3C" process. The "3C" process typically addressed such factors as economic development, population, land use, transportation facilities and travel patterns, financial resources, and social, economic, and environmental issues. The federal government did not show any preference for a particular land use, but merely encouraged land-use planning and the coordination of federal urban programs. Responsibility for implementation was left to state and local governments.

Planning reached its heyday in the 1970s. In fact, policymakers came to see planning as the vehicle through which to explore key policy issues. Many of the more sophisticated planning procedures of the period examined alternative investments and sought to make sense of the relationship between transportation and land use.

Many observers disparaged the 3C requirement as ineffectual, however. Suburbanization continued apace, more highways were built, and little apparently could be done through planning to shape urban form or thwart decentralization. Declining average densities of metropolitan regions accompanied the inexorable growth in automobile ownership and travel. Mass transit could not compete effectively with automobiles, especially in light of inexpensive gasoline, lack of growth management policy, and the preferences of increasing numbers of residents and businesses to locate in the suburbs. But, 3C planning was doomed by a more fundamental factor. As Alan Altshuler, J. P. Womack, and J. R. Pucher later wrote in The Urban Transportation System (1979), no public consensus ever evolved that high-density development should be the outcome of transportation and land-use policy decisions. Absent such a consensual goal, planning often proved ad hoc, piecemeal, and inconsistent.

Frustrations of Land-Use Theories and Modeling

With the establishment of the 3C process, some areas began to use urban land-use models to help guide their planning. Models that sought to capture the key relationships among transportation, housing, and land use originally emerged from analysts as the interstate highway program was getting underway. These models extended to the urban context the theory that von Thunen developed in the early 19th century to explain agricultural activity, rents, and land-use patterns. Von Thunen's central claim was that land devoted to agriculture decreased in intensity with distance from market centers, due to transportation costs (see discussion in Isard 1960). The contemporary models took two forms.

The first form appeared in the early 1960s, and involved mathematical economic analysis. These models could be used to explain how economic rents paid for land were affected by such factors as commuting costs, size of lot, consumer preferences for housing, and income. There was controversy over whether this approach, referred to as the "new urban economics," could contribute meaningfully to urban public policy. There was concern that this endeavor attracted too many urban economists away from policy to theoretical investigations. Critics charged that too many simplifying assumptions had to be made to derive mathematical solutions, and that such solutions thus would provide little insight. Defenders of the "new urban economics" rebutted that, despite the complexity of urban systems, these models produced results of considerable interest and realism, with relatively little input and effort.

Another class of land-use and transportation models arose almost simultaneously and relied upon simulation. Many planners and policymakers looked more favorably on these models because they were more realistic and had more policy handles. One of the earliest, most widely applied, and best known is the Lowry Model, developed in the early 1960s and named for its developer, Ira Lowry (1964). Forecasts of basic employment (e.g., in manufacturing) in this model drive predictions of the location of residences and of population-serving (nonbasic) employment. Population-serving businesses sell goods and services that are purchased often, typically by residences. When residences decentralize, such businesses tend to decentralize as well.

In the Lowry model, the distance between the zone and important workplaces for both basic and service industries and the amount of land available for development determine the number of residences in each zone, based on a gravity model. The principle underlying the gravity model is that the attraction between places of economic activity is directly related to quantity of economic activity in each place and is inversely proportional to the square of the distance between them, analogous to Newton's second law of physics.

Reflecting on these developments in their policy study, *Autos, Transit, and Cities*, Meyer and Gómez-Ibáñez (1981) expressed the frustration many policymakers have experienced in applying land-use theory and simulation modeling to transportation planning and the management of urban form. This frustration has arisen principally because the central paradigms concerning residential and business location have yielded different predictions about the consequences of transportation policy. The authors explained that the model of residential location assumes a city center where a fixed number of workers are employed, and reduces the residential decision to determining how far from the city center one should live. Transportation improvements lower the travel time costs of living farther from the city, and thus encourage household decentralization. These changes will affect the price of land: residential land close to the city center will decrease in price relative to residential land farther out. This, in turn, encourages still more businesses to locate near the city center.

In contrast to the residential location model, Meyer and Gómez-Ibáñez (1981) explained that in the standard business location model, the number and location of jobs are not assumed to be fixed. Firms in the urban center compete with firms in the suburbs and other urban areas for sales and profits. A change in city-suburb commuting costs changes the competitive advantage of firms in relationship to one another and can affect business location decisions and levels of employment. According to Meyer and Gómez-Ibáñez, business location theory posits that a transportation change alters the real incomes of those employed in the city center and, in turn, the wages an employer needs to pay to attract workers. A reduction in commuting cost would reduce wages required, thus improving the competitive position of a central city firm in relation to suburban ones.

If everyone's income were to remain the same, a reduction in commuter costs would reduce rents for residential land near a central city business district, as explained by the residential location model. Thus, business location or expansion in the core area would cost less. But the effect of the previously mentioned reduction in wages is predicted to yield the opposite effect of the residential location model. Decreased incomes make moving into suburban housing less affordable, but at the same time cause people to lower the value they place on travel time, which tends to encourage longer commutes. Meyer and Gómez-Ibáñez (1981) concluded that, on balance, the constraint of lower incomes inhibiting moves to the suburbs is stronger than the impetus of lower travel-time costs. This means that demands for central city sites should rise, bidding up land prices and reducing the competitiveness of businesses located there. Such contradictory predictions from land-use theories acted as roadblocks to their more widespread use by policymakers. This is a case where a muddled, underdeveloped intellectual framework impeded the practical implementation of transportation policy in the context of comprehensive land-use planning.

Many of the policy studies of the early 1970s took up the issue of the relationship between transportation and land use, concurrent with the increased attention given to planning and modeling. The *1972 National Transportation Report* (U.S. Department of Transportation, 1972), for example, acknowledged that rapid urbanization was a cause of many types of problems the nation would ultimately have to address. This report further recognized that the provision of adequate transportation facilities could probably not match the pace of development of land at urban densities. Even so, the report bemoaned that transportation had been reactive rather than proactive with respect to urban development. For example, the report charged that transportation systems had been designed mainly to meet long-term travel forecasts based on past trends rather than projections derived from purposive, planned development, and that little attention had been given to the feedback between providing transportation facilities and subsequent urban development. This study claimed that, on the whole, urban transportation systems operated reasonably well in spite of their complexity and the diversity of travelers and uses, but that the systems were becoming congested during peak hours, the choice of transportation mode was too limited, there were undesirable environmental effects, and too often transportation facilities were built without attempting to foster desirable development patterns. Nevertheless, without a solid intellectual foundation for clarifying the relationships between transportation and land use, such complaints and admonitions largely fell on the deaf ears of policymakers.

TRANSPORTATION POLICY IN THE AFTERMATH OF THE OIL CRISIS

As a result of the Arab-Israeli War of 1973 and subsequent embargoes imposed by the Organization of Petroleum Exporting Countries

(OPEC), energy conservation emerged as an issue every bit as important as protecting the environment. Policy analysts could not ignore direct energy consumption by transportation and the indirect effects on energy consumption through inefficient land-use patterns. An entirely new perception of "the transportation problem" was foisted upon policymakers and the public by unforeseen, uncontrollable international events.

The 1977 study entitled *National Transportation Trends and Choices* was conducted in the aftermath of the OPEC oil embargo, and so was preoccupied with the issue of energy conservation. The study report concluded that the transport system could not easily absorb a petroleum shortage of more than 10 percent, and noted that emergency rationing plans were under development. It called for a comprehensive approach to improve the energy efficiency of the transportation system, including demand-management actions. Policies for creating more energy-efficient land-use patterns were not promoted, however. The study was completed during the end of Ford's term as president, and was withdrawn from circulation as Carter assumed the presidency, so it had little influence beyond a handful of people who saw early copies of it.

National Transportation Policies through the Year 2000, the 1979 study of the National Transportation Policy Study Commission (NTPSC), came close on the heels of *Transportation Trends and Choices*, but reflected new national concerns. The NTPSC study occurred at a time of peak interest in the deregulation and regulatory reform of the railroads, airlines, and intercity bus industry. The NTPSC concluded that an appropriate mix of transportation was best achieved by nurturing an environment that permitted the free choice of consumers and shippers, and in which prices reflected both monetary and nonmonetary costs. Competition, reducing governmental interference, and suitable pricing mechanisms were deemed paramount. References to metropolitan land-use planning and the interconnections with transportation were almost nonexistent.

In contrast to the two policy studies just cited, a highly influential study in terms of accentuating public concern about uncontrolled urban development was *The Costs of Sprawl*, prepared by the Real Estate Research Corporation (1974). This study produced detailed estimates of the energy, environmental, capital, and operating costs associated with six hypothetical new communities of varied density and community design. In comparison to low-density development, high-density development was determined to consume 44 percent less energy, to result in 45 percent less air pollution, and to lessen capital requirements for infrastructure.

Altshuler and colleagues' previously mentioned 1979 policy study on urban transportation systems was written partly in response to *The Costs of Sprawl*. It was a policy study that refocused transportation issues on urban issues and included a lengthy discussion of the case against urban sprawl. The authors contended that urban sprawl involves the prodigal conversion of land to transportation from agricultural and other vital life-supporting uses (such as forest and wetland), is wasteful of energy, is economically inefficient, is environmentally harmful, imposes hardship on those without ready access to cars, limits access to employment by the poor (especially the black poor), and has accentuated class and race segregation.

As a counterpoint to the critique of urban sprawl, Altshuler et al. (1979) described the defense of market dominance. They explored at some length virtually every assertion of the critics of sprawl and concluded that the jury was still out on whether the net effect of sprawl was deleterious. Altshuler et al. also concluded that: there were few circumstances in which transportation could have a significant impact on metropolitan land development; total cessation of highway construction would have virtually no impact on land development for years to come; and mass transit improvements could enhance only modestly the relative accessibility of locations served. Such highly respected skepticism about the efficacy of transportation policy and the undesirability of free-market outcomes did not provoke widespread enthusiasm to employ transportation as a tool of land-use planning.

EMPHASIS ON EQUITY VERSUS EFFICIENCY: 1970S AND 1980S

With new highway construction costs so high in urban areas and environmental opposition so great, policymakers in many parts of the country no longer could look to highway construction as a panacea for congestion. But policymakers were equally skeptical of the ability of the marketplace, including congestion-pricing policies, to provide rational signals to metropolitan households concerning residential and job location, automobile ownership, and the type of transportation to take to work. So far, it has been considered more politically expedient to tax each person in terms of congestion delay rather than to raise the gasoline tax a few pennies, let alone impose congestion pricing charges or increases in parking costs amounting to several dollars per day.

Curiously, since World War II, scarce transportation capacity in urban areas has been rationed through congestion, not by prices, as occurs for most other commodities and services. Public and political acceptance of a significant amount of congestion has been among the most important implicit national policies affecting land use. There has been a total unwillingness of the body politic to price urban transportation so that it reflects the true social costs. Imposing congestion pricing has long been acknowledged by modelers of transportation and land use as one of the single most effective things government could do to reduce sprawl and retard the decentralization of metropolitan areas. In place of a sensible pricing policy advocated by economists, and by many environmental groups, congestion delay was and continues to be the de facto cost of urban travel.

This implicit policy of "pricing" use of transportation by imposing time delays of congestion has further constrained the potential role of social scientific policy analyses in the field. Social science has always been weakest when it comes to conducting positive analyses of equity issues, as opposed to efficiency issues.

ERA OF LIMITS

In the 1980s and 1990s, scarcity of federal funds due to enormous budget deficits, shortage of highway capacity, and limited ability of the environment to absorb additional pollution became the most important determinants of transportation and land-use decisions. The "era of limits" entered the public consciousness as far back as the 1960s with the publication of Paul Ehrlic's *Population Bomb* (1968), and became the focus of much environmental debate when *Limits to Growth* was published in the 1970s (Meadows, et al., 1972). However, the issue of scarcity did not fully affect transportation decision making until the late 1980s. At that point, the public was willing neither to tax nor to spend significantly more on behalf of expanding transportation, although transportation fared well in comparison to other federal discretionary programs, most of which were cut back. In addition, environmental laws and regulations and resistance of citizens to highway construction in their backyard posed major obstacles to road building. Public sentiment shifted toward a more efficient use of existing transportation facilities and, importantly, a recognition that efficiencies in transportation were linked to efficiencies in land use. Once again, a shifting of public consensus about the definition of the problem spawned a public policy response; policy research provided little impetus to this shift. Indirectly, however, this shift provided more leverage for the subsequent exercising of power by policy researchers.

During the 1980s and 1990s the tools of economists and operations research experts have been applied with increasing frequency in such areas as capital budgeting and resource allocation, especially in the realm of pavement and bridge management systems. Indeed, it might be argued that professionals with an economic and operations research orientation now have a major influence on the process of allocating scarce resources, much as economists did in bringing about transportation regulatory reform in the 1970s. Although regulatory reform had little impact on land use, improved methods for allocating scarce funds among capital improvements, operational enhancements, maintenance, and demand management strategies may prove to have some indirect effect on land-use decisions in urban areas capable of developing clear, politically acceptable land-use goals, objectives, and policies.

Some metropolitan areas, such as Seattle, Madison (Wis.), and Washington, D.C., have developed vision plans that provide a policy framework for managing transportation, land-use, economic development, and environmental enhancement. When policies in such plans shape decisions concerning the allocation of limited funds among capital, operational, maintenance, and demand management projects, there is a real possibility of affecting land use, if only marginally.

Improved modeling is also helping to inform policy decisions in this era of limits. In Washington County, Oregon, under a national demonstration project entitled "Land Use, Transportation, Air Quality Connection," the predictive power of traditional transportation models was increased by including variables describing employment density and pedestrian friendliness. These changes enabled planners and policymakers to explore transportation alternatives that can satisfy growth management objectives.

The clearest manifestation of the shifting public perception of the transportation problem was passage of the 1991 Intermodal Surface Transportation Efficiency Act (ISTEA). It marked the end of the interstate highway construction era and confronted head-on the scarcity of funds, limited highway capacity, and the stress on the environment of having to absorb excessive pollution. The ISTEA emphasized maintaining existing facilities instead of building new ones, achieving operational efficiencies to make the best use of existing facilities, using the most efficient and effective mix of transport modes in each circumstance, and ensuring compliance with the pollution standards of the Clean Air Act and its amendments. More particularly, the ISTEA provided for unprecedented flexibility in the use of highway funds for mass transit and vice versa, imposed planning procedures that require states and metropolitan planning organizations to consider the impacts of transportation actions on land use, established a congestion management and air quality program requiring that transportation actions be consistent with efforts to attain air quality standards, and mandated the use of management systems that can improve planning and capital budgeting.

The ISTEA legislation was also future-oriented, with a major emphasis on advanced technology, including high speed rail, Intelligent Vehicle Highway Systems (IVHS), and telecommuting. Just as automobile technology in the past had a profound influence on urban form, technology being developed for the 21st century could have equally profound positive and negative effects on land use, whose net result is unpredictable. IVHS, by helping highways to handle the projected doubling of traffic in the next 20 to 30 years, will support suburbanization and decentralization trends. Automated highway systems and magnetic levitation trains in major corridors could stimulate major development and land-use changes in localized areas by providing significant improvements in accessibility. On the other hand, telecommuting may allow significant numbers of would-be commuters to stay at home. The accompanying revolution in digital communications and the construction of a digital information infrastructure could potentially dampen shopping at malls in favor of catalog and television/telephone shopping. As a result, new mall construction would not be as attractive as in the past, and some malls might even be forced to close. Land-use implications may be far-reaching.

The ISTEA brought about a resurgence in comprehensive planning after a long hiatus that stretched from the Reagan years through the first part of the Bush administration. Accompanying the dramatic changes instigated by ISTEA has been a sharp increase in transportation policy research. One possible consequence, though it will not be fully manifest for a number of years, is that the relationship between transportation and land-use effects will become better understood. Consequently, transportation land-use policy, whether exerted through planning, programming, legislation, or regulation, may become more effective than it has been in the past, and the role of the policy researcher in this field may be strengthened.

This windfall of the ISTEA as it relates to the connection between land use and transportation policy may be shortlived, however. Planning, especially federal planning laws and regulations, bespeaks of centralized control. The public sentiment of the 1990s clearly favors a reduced role for the federal government, and Congress could easily soften or revoke ISTEA. Local decision making and market forces have nearly always held sway in the land-use arena. For as long as ISTEA remains fully in force, it will foster a better understanding of how growth management options affect transportation and land use. Local policies and economic conditions will ultimately determine land-use changes. Transportation will be an explicit instrument of those changes only where there is political consensus and the resultant policies do not run counter to stronger economic forces.

SUGGESTED READING

Alonso, W. 1964. *Location and Land Use—Toward a General Theory of Land Rent*. Cambridge, Mass.: Harvard University Press.

Altshuler, Alan, J.P. Womack, and J.R. Pucher. 1979. *The Urban Transportation System: Politics and Policy Innovation*. Cambridge, Mass.: MIT Press.

American Association of State Highway and Transportation Officials. 1991. *The States and the Interstates*. Washington, D.C.: Author.

Brand, Daniel. 1991. "Research Needs for Analyzing the Impacts of Transportation Options on Urban Form and the Environment." In *Transportation, Urban Form, and the Environment* (pp. 101–16). TRB Special Report 231. Washington, D.C.: Transportation Research Board.

Cambridge Systematics, Inc., Calthorpe Associates, and Parsons Quade Brinkerhoff and Douglas. 1992. "Making the Land Use, Transportation, Air Quality Connection: The LUTRAQ Alternative/Analysis of Alternatives." Interim Report prepared for the 1,000 Friends of Oregon. Washington, D.C.: Cambridge Systematics, Inc.

Deakin, Elizabeth A. 1991. "Jobs, Housing, and Transportation: Theory and Evidence on Interactions between Land Use and Transportation." In *Transportation, Urban Form, and the Environment*. TRB Special Report 231. Washington, D.C.: Transportation Research Board.

Ehrlich, Paul R. 1968. *The Population Bomb*. New York: Ballantine.

Frieden, Bernard J., and Lynne B. Sagalyn. 1992. *How America Rebuilds Cities*. Cambridge, Mass.: MIT Press.

Isard, Walter. 1960. *Methods of Regional Analysis: An Introduction to Regional Science.* New York: John Wiley and Sons, Inc.

Kemp, Michael A., and Melvyn D. Cheslow. 1976. "Transportation." In *The Urban Predicament,* edited by William Gorham and Nathan Glazer. Washington, D.C.: Urban Institute Press.

Knight, R.L. 1980. "The Impact of Rail Transit on Land Use: Evidence and a Change of Perspective." *Transportation* 9(1):3–16.

Lee, D.B., Jr. 1973. "Requiem for Large Scale Models." *Journal of the American Institute of Planners* 39(3):163–78.

Levine, Harvey A. 1978. *National Transportation Policy: A Study of Studies.* Lexington, Mass.: Lexington Books.

Lowry, Ira S. 1964. *A Model of Metropolis.* Santa Monica, Calif.: RAND Publication Co.

Meadows, Donella H., Dennis L. Meadows, Jorgen Randers, and William W. Behrens II. 1972. *The Limits to Growth.* London: Universe Books.

Meyer, John R., and José A. Gómez-Ibáñez. 1981. *Autos, Transit, and Cities.* Cambridge, Mass.: Harvard University Press.

Meyer, J.R., J.F. Kain, and M. Wohl. 1965. *The Urban Transportation Problem.* Cambridge, Mass.: Harvard University Press.

National Transportation Policy Study Commission. 1979. *National Transportation Policies Through the Year 2000.* Washington, D.C.: U.S. Government Printing Office.

North, D.C. 1955. "Location Theory and Regional Economic Growth." *Journal of Political Economy* 63(3):243–58.

Papageorgiou, George J., ed. 1976. *Mathematical Land Use Theory* (pp. 3–27). Lexington, Mass.: Lexington Books.

Real Estate Research Corporation. 1974. *The Costs of Sprawl: Environmental and Economic Costs of Alternative Residential Development Patterns at the Urban Fringe.* Prepared for the Council on Environmental Quality, the Department of Housing and Urban Development, and the Environmental Protection Agency. Washington, D.C.: U.S. Government Printing Office. April.

Smolensky, Eugene T., Nicolaus Tideman, and Donald Nichols. 1972. "Waiting Time as a Congestion Charge." In *Public Prices for Public Products.* Washington, D.C.: Urban Institute Press.

U.S. Department of Transportation. 1977. *National Transportation Trends and Choices.* Washington, D.C.: U.S. Government Printing Office. January.

———. 1972. *National Transportation Report.* Washington, D.C.: U.S. Government Printing Office. July.

Warren, William D. 1993. "A Transportation View of the Morphology of Cities." *Transportation Quarterly* 47(3, July):368.

Wegner, M. 1994. "Operational Urban Models: State of the Art." *Journal of the American Planning Association* 60(1):17–29.

Wegner, M., R.L Mackett, and D.C. Simmonds. 1991. "One City, Three Models: Comparison of Land Use/Transport Policy Simulation Models for Dortmund." *Transport Reviews* 11:107–29.

Chapter Seven

EDUCATION

Paul T. Hill

Research influences urban education, but not always for the better and seldom in the ways scholars anticipate. Big-city school systems are so complex and so susceptible to influence from many directions, that many findings researchers consider valid and important have no direct or predictable impact. In fact, research is used as a weapon in litigation and interest group struggles as often as it is used as an objective source of evidence and ideas. This is especially true in urban education, which is driven more often by political trends and lawsuits than by rational problem solving.

These are negative conclusions, especially from one who has made a career in the field, but they reflect the realities of urban public education. The demands on big-city school systems are so diverse and subject to such abrupt and profound changes that research often lags behind the coping behavior of city superintendents, principals, and teachers. Furthermore, the control of urban education is so fragmented and so driven by crises and scandals that the demand for objective analysis and hard data is strictly limited.

As in any other area of inquiry, research on urban education has its professional and methodological problems—research questions are sometimes poorly defined, methods poorly matched to the questions being investigated, and results poorly reported. No doubt, the field would be more influential if it could attract a better class of researcher. But what it lacks most is a well-defined policymaking audience. In urban education, there is no small set of decision makers who could, if persuaded by a research finding, act on it decisively. Although many actors take positions and make demands, none of these individuals, not even superintendents and school boards, can assuredly determine what happens in schools. Educational policymaking takes place through infinitely complex interactions of demands, needs, and information, rather than through authoritative decision making and hierarchical implementation.

Much that is wrong with educational policy research could be improved by the discovery of an authoritative, rational policymaker. However, as this chapter explains, no such event is likely. There are critical events and forums that use research-based evidence, but these are unpredictable and often difficult to influence. Lawsuits introduce an authoritative decision maker, the judge, but his or her decisions are driven by legal doctrines and by litigants' views of the relevance and meaning of research. Teachers' union contract negotiations often decide more issues than any other forum, but they are strongly driven by the economic interests of a particular group, and not highly receptive to research evidence.

In such an environment, researchers sometimes have great difficulty being heard, and are often forced to target their work toward a particular audience that might, if receptive at all, use the results to further its own ends. My own research has followed that course, and has been targeted to business and political leaders who could, if they take a serious interest in education, countervail the influence of entrenched provider groups, especially school administrators and teachers' unions. However, researchers often guarantee that their results will be misused, by glossing over issues that might get them in trouble with important groups or by exaggerating the importance of their own findings.

As this chapter demonstrates, people attempting to improve urban education encounter many obstacles. Superintendents, principals, teachers, and researchers are all preoccupied with conflicts among adult groups. The motto of many urban school systems, "Putting Children First," expresses a noble aspiration. But, in truth, politics—of labor, neighborhoods, ideology, and race—usually comes first. Urban school systems are therefore often harsh and hostile places for adults, but the people who suffer most are the children on whose behalf the whole enterprise is supposedly run.

This chapter's discussion is organized into three parts. I first provide an overview of educational policymaking in big cities that explains why policy research is so seldom directly influential; second, I review the connection between research and policy in five key areas: school desegregation, school finance, design and evaluation of federal programs, testing and accountability, and school effectiveness; and third, I analyze ways in which research might have a more consistently constructive effect on future educational policy.

ENVIRONMENT FOR URBAN EDUCATIONAL
POLICY RESEARCH

Urban education is primarily minority education. African-American children constitute more than half the student populations in most of the nation's largest school districts. Combined with Hispanic children and non-Hispanic immigrants, minority group children are the majority in all of the 10 largest urban districts. Big-city students are also more likely to be low-income and to come from single-parent homes than students in other school systems. Although some small-town and suburban districts also serve large numbers of African-American and Hispanic children, those students are much more likely than urban students to come from intact homes and to enjoy nonpoverty incomes.

Urban students also live the most stressful lives outside of school. Compared to majority and minority students from outside center cities, urban students are more likely to suffer health problems such as asthma and uncorrected vision and hearing problems, they change residences frequently, they live apart from their parents for extended periods, they experience the death of close relatives, and they endure crime and violence.

The school systems serving big-city students are also under duress. Once-excellent facilities built near the end of the 19th century are still in use, many suffering from decades of neglect. School boards, once islands of stability and forums for the best-educated and most civic-minded of citizens, are now staging areas for guerrilla warfare by the politically ambitious. Unionized teachers, following decades of bargaining in which school boards made concessions on work rules rather than wage demands, resist any attempt to adapt school programs to new needs.

After a period of enrollment declines due to middle-class flight from city schools, enrollments in many urban areas are growing dramatically due to immigration. Since the late 1980s, New York, Los Angeles, Chicago, and Miami have collectively added nearly 100,000 new students annually who are either foreign-born or children of immigrants.

As school enrollments rise, city budgets fall. New York, Chicago, and Los Angeles have made crippling midyear cuts in school budgets in each of the last three years. Last year's cuts in Los Angeles amounted to approximately $240 million from a general fund budget of $2.9 billion, and this year's cuts should be about as large. According to estimates from consultants Booz, Allen and Hamilton, Chicago faces continuous deficits for most of this decade, which are projected to rise to over $500 million in the 1997–98 school year.

It is hard to imagine how any organization could provide consistently good services in this environment. But even if funding were restored and existing programs rebuilt, schools would not be equipped to meet the needs of their new populations. Schools would still not be effective for immigrants or for native-born minority students, whom the schools were failing long before the present crisis.

Until the 1950s, big-city schools were among the best in the country and were the source of America's most successful business leaders, public officials, and scholars. Such past glories are part of the burden that urban schools now must bear. The middle-class families who produced those successful students have gone to the suburbs and have been replaced by poor African-Americans and Hispanics—many of whom have migrated from the rural U.S. South, the Caribbean, or Central America. High schools whose graduates reliably went on to become leaders in science, law, and medicine now graduate fewer than half the students who enter ninth grade.

People who taught in the schools when they were the most advanced and admired in the country, or who attended the schools themselves before the dramatic change in student populations, are acutely conscious of the schools' decline. Whatever their personal values and motivations for becoming teachers, they are confused and upset by the troubles that "those children" have brought to their schools. In some cases "those children" come from racial and class backgrounds that make them less motivated and prepared for education than their predecessors in the same schools. In other cases, school children are also recent immigrants, many of whom do not speak English and have had little prior schooling in their home countries. Many families, whether immigrant or native-born poor, make frequent residential moves that force children to transfer from one school to another. The result is that schools in poor areas of cities often have to teach a constantly shifting population. In New York, Miami, and Los Angeles, for example, many schools experience an annual student turnover rate in excess of 100 percent.

To meet varied and shifting needs, urban public school systems need to be flexible and diverse, but most are the opposite. Unfortunately, most big city systems are inflexible, due to a combination of mandates and past commitments including court orders, federal and state regulations, and union contracts.

Until the 1960s, elementary and secondary education was a community function. It was carried on locally with little attention from the states and none from the federal government. Leaders of government were seldom concerned about educational operations, costs, or outcomes, and were never held accountable for schools' success. Schools were funded by local government and overseen by locally elected boards of education, and they were regarded as unique institutions in which professionals hired by parents and community elders cared for the young. Ideas about education came from the writings of scholars such as John Dewey. Though some ideas gained national attention, they influenced instruction by persuading teachers, not by inspiring new laws, programs, or court cases.

Education did not become a focus for national policy debate until the late 1950s and 1960s. The U.S. Supreme Court's 1954 decision in *Brown v. Topeka Board of Education* established that a national policymaking body could set the terms under which schools operated nationwide. President Eisenhower's action to enforce the *Brown* rulings in Little Rock, Arkansas, made it clear that the national government could and would override local educational policy. As later sections of this chapter show, the development of federal interest in education exacerbated the fragmentation of school policymaking.

Other domestic policy areas such as health care financing are driven by mandates and interest group politics. But education is far more fragmented and susceptible to politicization than most. Unlike health care, welfare, urban development, or public housing, education is not driven by a national funding program. Although there are federal grant-in-aid programs in education, the funds dispensed are small, currently amounting to less than 6 percent of total federal, state, and local spending on elementary and secondary education, and the programs they support are add-ons to regular local instructional services. The federal government did not create the elementary and secondary education system, and its regulatory powers are weak. Even the state governments, to which the U.S. Constitution assigns primary responsibility for elementary and secondary education, have strictly limited powers. Until the 1980s, states provided far less than half the funds for schools, and the lion's share was raised from local property taxes. Now that most state governments have assumed responsibility for school funding, the potential for state influence has grown. But long traditions of local district autonomy and deference to classroom teachers limit the potential influence of official government policy. Teacher union contracts also define so much of what can be done within schools that state officials have little direct influence over local educational practice.

Finally, teaching is intensely personal and intimate. Public policies can determine who is allowed to teach, can require teachers to cover some subjects and avoid others, and can create penalties for unethical or abusive behavior. But they cannot control in detail what teachers do in their classrooms—whether they are imaginative or wooden, logical or scattered, caring or cold. Policy can, in short, constrain teachers from being negligent or abusive but cannot ensure that they will teach effectively.

As the following sections illustrate, policies developed in the belief that government actions have predictable effects usually lead to surprises, and often to disaster. Moreover, since policy is a blunt and imprecise instrument for improving education, so too is policy research.

HOW RESEARCH AFFECTS POLICY AND HOW BOTH AFFECT EDUCATION

This section reviews the connection between research and policy in five key areas: school desegregation, school finance, design and evaluation of federal programs, testing and accountability, and school effectiveness.

School Desegregation

When the Supreme Court held school segregation unconstitutional, it reflected a broad societal trend in the understanding of social justice. Black Americans' loyal and competent service in World War II and President Harry S Truman's subsequent decision to integrate the Army set the stage for a serious rethinking of American race relations. Although southern states still required racial segregation in public facilities in 1954, vast numbers of Americans were uncomfortable about forced segregation. In the *Brown* decision, the Supreme Court reflected and advanced the new national sensibility by establishing a clear doctrine that served as the premise for many subsequent policy developments: that separate public facilities were inherently unequal. The justices cited a piece of social science research—psychologist Kenneth Clark's finding that black children chose to play with white dolls—to supplement their legal and moral arguments and to illustrate the harmful effects of segregation. However, there is no reason to think that this small and little-known study carried much weight in the Court's construction of a major landmark in constitutional law.

In the decades after the *Brown* case, its principles were applied to many new situations. Research played an important role in this process. Researchers illustrated that northern school systems were as segregated as southern ones. This was not because of policies of racial separation, but because school enrollments followed housing patterns, which were segregated. These findings led to new policies and legal doctrines banning school segregation however it occurred, whether through the deliberate actions of public officials or through the actions of markets. Throughout the 1960s and 1970s, researchers continually found new ways in which public schools treated the races unequally. Black students were found to attend worse-funded schools with less well-trained teachers, to be assigned to all-black classes within racially mixed schools, and to be given less encouragement by teachers in desegregated classrooms. All these findings led to lawsuits or enforcement actions by federal civil rights agencies.

In the early 1980s, civil rights lawyers used evidence of lower average educational achievement among blacks to argue that disparate outcomes are themselves evidence of discrimination. Although that principle was never enacted into law, it had a profound effect on local school administrators, who began trying to equalize black and white students' educational outcomes.

The most recent application of the *Brown* principle, the attack on "tracking," has been heavily influenced by research. Tracking is the practice of assigning students to different courses of study depending on their perceived academic ability and speed of learning. In the mid-1980s, Jeannie Oakes (1985) published a book, *Keeping Track*, showing that low-income and minority group high school students were much more likely than white and higher-income students to be assigned to remedial or "dumbed down" courses of study that did not prepare them for higher education or challenging, high-paying jobs. The result was that many disadvantaged students were never taught algebra, English literature, world history, or laboratory sciences. Tracking deprived students of important life opportunities. It also flew in the face of other recent research showing that lower-achieving students tried harder and learned more when exposed to challenging materials than when assigned repetitious drill and practice on basic skills. As a result, undemanding remedial and "general" tracks were abolished in many states and localities, and vastly greater numbers of students were taught the high school curriculum traditionally available to middle-class students.

Like other desegregation efforts, elimination of tracking can be pursued to extremes that vitiate its effects. Some local school boards have construed elimination of tracking to require them to ignore all distinctions between highly prepared and poorly prepared students and between fast and slow learners, and to require teachers to instruct all together. In the name of de-tracking, some school boards have eliminated advanced courses for students able to master college-level material. These actions go far beyond the research evidence, which shows that many students who could learn core high school materials had been tracked out of them. The evidence did not show that all students could learn best in courses paced to slower learners, or that accelerated classes for the gifted harmed other students. As a result of extreme antitracking policies, academically ambitious minority students in some cities have complained about their lost opportunities, and some able higher-income students are leaving for private schools.

Unfortunately, research has not always helped desegregation policies to succeed. Although research could identify and guide policymakers toward eliminating discrimination, nothing could ensure that students would continue attending desegregated schools. "White flight" is the popular name for desertion of city schools by advantaged students, including the children of the growing black middle class. In the 1970s and 1980s, vast numbers of such students left desegregated city schools in favor of suburban public and private schools. The result, creation of predominantly low-income and minority school populations in virtually all the big cities, has led to many of the problems discussed previously. Some researchers have documented the phenomenon of white flight, but few have been willing to link it directly to desegregation or to consider the implications of continued efforts to eradicate distinctions among students whenever they occur in schools.

School desegregation was based on a constitutional principle reflecting a strong national consensus that government institutions must not discriminate on the basis of race. Once that principle was established, many advocates and researchers claimed that racially integrated schools were also more effective. Research on the effectiveness of school desegregation shows mixed results, however. Robert Crain, for example, has shown that minority students who attend classes with white students have better outcomes (e.g., test scores, persistence in school, course completion, college attendance) than in segregated schooling, and at no apparent cost to their white schoolmates. But these findings come from situations in which desegregation was genuine and stable. They clearly do not apply to students of any race who have endured turbulent years of racial tension and turnover of schools from predominantly white to all black.

Some African-American educators have concluded that desegregation had a definite downside for black students, in that it removed students from community schools where teachers and parents were often lifetime acquaintances and former schoolmates, and where students and teachers attended the same churches and lived in the same neighborhoods. Desegregation, which was typically accomplished by moving black students into formerly all-white schools, broke these community bonds. After desegregation, some black educators claim, black parents saw schools as white institutions, unpredictable and geographically and emotionally distant. No formal research has been conducted to test the implications of this phenomenon, but much of the school effectiveness research, discussed at the end of this section, focuses on the need to strengthen urban schools by linking them once again to the broader community.

School desegregation is such an emotional topic, so clouded in fears of racism (and fears of being thought racist), that we may never know exactly how it affected the students involved. New research by David Grissmer and Sheila Kirby of RAND suggests that African-American students are, on average, staying in school longer now than before the 1950s, are more likely to take algebra and challenging academic subjects, and have higher scores on Army admissions tests. These benefits, however, probably do not extend to big-city students, especially those in areas of concentrated poverty. For urban students, educators and researchers still have not found a way to ensure that an end to official racial discrimination leads to an end to race-linked disadvantages in education.

School Finance

Concern over equal funding of schools can be seen as another legacy of the *Brown* decision. Researchers have stimulated lawsuits and provided data for litigants. Their efforts have helped promote an overall increase in school spending, but have not succeeded in equalizing funding of schools in rich and poor areas.

In the late 1960s, Arthur Wise (1968) wrote a book documenting the vast inequalities in educational spending between rich and poor areas of many states. He argued that these inequalities demonstrated a violation of the Constitution's guarantee of equal treatment under the law, and recommended litigation on behalf of students in poor areas.

Within only a few years, lawsuits in many states produced court orders requiring states to equalize their systems of school finance. Most states relied on local property taxes to pay for schools. School systems in areas with valuable business or industrial facilities could raise a great deal more money from property taxes than districts that contained only small homes and businesses. The court orders required state governments to equalize total funding by allocating disproportionate amounts of state money to the poorer areas.

School finance equity litigation continues to this day, even in states such as California and Texas, where past lawsuits have led to court-ordered equalization. As Stephen Carroll and others have shown, state legislatures find it extremely difficult to allocate state funds preferentially to poorer areas. State financing schemes that favor poorer areas are enacted and stay on the books, but subsequent legislatures enact special programs favoring richer areas, and ultimately produce rough equality in state funding for school districts. Rich areas also find it easy to raise local taxes and keep spending well ahead of targets set by state planners.

Since the 1960s, when the first lawsuits inspired by Wise's book were heard, state funding has grown from less than 20 percent to more than 50 percent of total school spending nationwide. Some states such as California have assumed nearly full responsibility for school funding. Yet, as Jonathan Kozol (1992) has shown in *Savage Inequalities*, total spending in rich and poor areas is still vastly unequal.

This is one area where research has had a definite effect: documentation of school finance inequalities still feeds a nonprofit and pro bono litigation industry in many states. Even though equalization seldom lasts long, such litigation persists because it is a good way to increase education's share of the state budget.

In recent years state school finance litigation has also created leverage regarding nonfinancial aspects of state educational policy. In states such as Kentucky, New Jersey, and Alabama, school finance lawsuits have led to court-ordered reforms in all aspects of the state school system, including curriculum, teacher training, and testing. Because low-spending districts often have more poor and minority students and lower test scores, litigators can use school finance inequality as an opening wedge for ambitious reforms of all aspects of education. It remains to be seen whether courts—and the litigators and researchers who have drawn them into substantive education reform—know how to use this broad reform authority effectively.

Ironically, researchers have paid little attention to another aspect of inequality—within-district differences in per pupil spending. Actual per pupil spending varies dramatically within urban districts, owing to teachers' union contract provisions about teacher assignments. In most cities, senior teachers can choose where they teach, and most prefer schools in safer, less-demanding middle-class schools. Schools in the poorer areas of cities are often staffed by junior teachers waiting for their chance to transfer out, and by teachers on "provisional certification" due to incomplete training or low test scores. Because senior teachers make more than twice as much as beginners, actual school spending can be as much as twice as high in middle-class schools as in poor ones. These spending practices may have as great an effect on children as do interdistrict inequalities. Researchers and litigators have not teamed up to attack inequities in per pupil spending, possibly because legal action would inevitably involve the influential teachers' unions.

Research on the effects of school spending has produced highly equivocal results. Since the celebrated report by James Coleman in 1966, researchers have found over and over again that aggregate school spending is not closely correlated with student outcomes. There may be floors below which school spending cannot fall without affecting student outcomes, but within a broad range of variation, school spending does not drive results. Subsequent studies by Coleman confirmed the common-sense proposition that aggregate spending matters less than what is done with the money. He showed how low-spending parochial schools often provide a richer academic experience than better-funded public schools.

The field has produced few comparably illuminating findings. The greatest weakness of research on effects of school spending is that the methods used have assumed that the same amount of money is spent on every student in a district. Since that assumption is manifestly false, and since within-district variations in student performance are usually as great as between-distinct differences, it is not surprising that researchers have failed to link spending and student outcomes. The research has, as a result, failed to direct policymakers' attention to two serious problems: first, that some low-spending districts simply cannot mount quality instructional programs, and second, that within-district differences in spending exacerbate the educational disadvantages of minority students living in the poorest neighborhoods.

From Wise to Kozol, researchers have focused on interdistrict spending differences, on which data are most readily available, and on which litigation is easiest to initiate. But school finance research is unlikely to produce educational benefits until it focuses on the tougher problems of within-district spending inequalities and variations in the ways money is used.

Design and Evaluation of Federal Programs

Until 1964, the only consistent focus for federal educational policy was racial justice. However, President Lyndon Johnson's Great Society made schools part of government. By offering federal funds to virtually every school district, the Elementary and Secondary Education Act (ESEA) of 1965 made the federal government a force in education. Although Johnson's original intention was simply to raise educational spending, the logic of national politics quickly transformed the ESEA from a revenue-sharing program into a directive federal program. Charges of federal meddling in local affairs led the drafters and early implementers of the ESEA to explain it as a source of extra funds to help localities improve schooling for the lowest-income children.

Trapped between members of Congress who would not support a program that neglected private Catholic schools, and others who would not support a program that breached the separation of church and state, the drafters targeted the ESEA to individual children, who could benefit whether they attended public or private school. To ensure that funds were used on education and not diverted by local authorities into tax relief or spending on other public services, drafters required recipient school systems to maintain their previous spending on schools, and to refrain from supporting formerly local programs with federal funds.

Research had virtually nothing to do with establishing the need for the ESEA or designing its provisions. Once the law was enacted, administrators in the U.S. Office of Education searched for an academic or theoretical premise that could guide decisions about federal regulation and oversight. They quickly settled on the concept of "compensatory education," then recently formulated by Benjamin Bloom of the University of Chicago. Bloom's research had convinced him that virtually all children could learn ordinary academic subjects, but that variations in prior experience and personality led some students to learn more rapidly than others. Bloom argued that schooling should take account of students' different learning rates and give every student the amount of instruction necessary for him or her to master the material. Schools could be organized to provide standard introductions to key material, and then individual students could receive "compensatory education" to permit each to develop mastery. Bloom's ideas fit the ESEA perfectly and established the need for a program that supplemented regular class instruction and targeted individual students.

It was thus political and administrative imperatives, not research, that drove ESEA. Within two years after the ESEA's enactment, poverty groups complained that funds were being diverted from services to poor students into activities that benefited more privileged students. The result was a new set of regulations requiring school districts to demonstrate that ESEA funds were used only for low-income students, and that the services purchased by ESEA funds could not benefit others. Federal administrators developed a compelling rationale for these requirements: regular school programs are adequate for most students but due to poverty, racial discrimination, or the failure of schools to take account of distinctive learning styles, some students need "something extra." By the early 1970s, Bloom's ideas about compensatory education were transformed into a complex regulatory and funding system.

Although the ESEA never comprised more than 7 percent of local expenditures on elementary and secondary education, it had a profound effect on local school policies. Local superintendents and administrators accepted responsibility for guaranteeing that the new money would keep coming. Wanting to ensure that federal funds would be administered by local people who shared the goals of ESEA, the federal Department of Health, Education & Welfare required localities to set up special units to manage the expenditure of ESEA funds. Federal officials also began monitoring localities' compliance with federal requirements, and stopped the flow of grant funds to noncompliant districts.

The result, after less than five years, was a profound change in the mission and structure of local school districts. Federal administrative set-asides allowed school system central offices to become much larger, and requirements for special administrative units made school systems more divided and complex. Federal support for state departments of education greatly increased the size and variety of the state oversight offices to which local administrators had to answer.

In political terms, the ESEA was a highly successful statute. Local educators were happy to get the funds. Advocacy groups for the poor saw it both as a way to improve disadvantaged children's education and as a source of new job opportunities for low-income parents who worked in schools as teachers' aides, counselors, and parent relations specialists. Members of Congress and state legislators appreciated the fact that the ESEA distributed money to virtually every locality. Congress steadily increased ESEA funding and enacted new programs, essentially patterned on ESEA, for newly defined beneficiary groups.

One novel provision of the ESEA was its evaluation requirement. The national Office of Education and the state and local education agencies that received ESEA money were to evaluate the program's effects on children and publish the results. The author of the evaluation provision, Senator Robert F. Kennedy of New York, intended evaluation results to be used primarily at the local level, enabling parents to hold teachers and principals accountable for their children's progress. However, the amounts of money available for evaluation—0.5 percent of the $1 billion appropriated annually in the early days of ESEA—were so large that they eventually supported an ambitious set of studies to assess the performance of ESEA at the national and state, as well as the local, levels.

Lavish funding, and the opportunity to conduct sophisticated analyses of vast files of demographic and test score data, attracted the best talent to the national-level evaluation of ESEA. However, differences among local programs—regarding who received services, in what subjects, and for how long—defeated most efforts to estimate national-level effects of ESEA. Evaluators could not say for certain whether or not the program had any effects on students. Research findings had few clear implications for policy, but they did affect policy indirectly. Hoping to get better evaluation results, national program administrators began in the early 1970s to tighten regulations about who could receive services funded by the ESEA and what the services could be.

The enactment of new federal and state categorical grant programs to improve services to individuals with disabilities, promote desegregation, and support bilingual education added to the complexity of federal-state-local relationships. Between 1965 and 1975, education changed from a local activity largely controlled by professionals to a government enterprise based on regulation, judicial interpretation of rules, specialization of function, hierarchical oversight, and explicit use of rewards and sanctions.

Despite the fact that federal program evaluation remained the best-funded area of educational policy research, the field had lost its luster by the early 1980s. Researchers from the top universities had tired of repetitious examinations of the same programs, and some were frustrated that congressional decisions on the program made little use of their findings. Some researchers were also concerned that the proliferation of federal and state programs built on the ESEA model was destroying the effectiveness of recipient schools.

In 1980 a number of researchers started trying to look beyond the evaluation of specific programs to the evaluation of the underlying policies that the programs had in common. Several reports documented how the proliferation of ESEA-style programs had changed schools, especially in the big cities. The populations served by the ESEA and similar programs that followed it were concentrated in the cities, due largely to the post–World War II migration of rural blacks and Puerto Ricans. City school systems therefore had proportionately larger federal grants, and had to build a wider array of separate administrative structures, than did rural and small-town districts. City public schools also experienced two other events that led to greater formalization and complexity. The first was the growth of industrial-style teachers' unions, which demanded increasingly complex and explicit contracts about teacher working conditions, tenure, pay, and promotion. The second event was the increase in educational litigation. This was initiated by parents and public interest groups eager to establish the rights of disadvantaged children and children with disabilities to instructional services that met their individual needs.

As Jane Hannaway (1993) and others found, the result of these events was nothing less than a revolution in the jobs and career demands of educators. School superintendents became responsible for managing relations with federal inspectors and acting as defendants in lawsuits. A new class of local administrators emerged, people paid from federal funds and acting to ensure that the local system complied with federal program requirements. School principals became responsible for managing an array of separate programs within their schools, ensuring that teachers paid from one program did not instruct students eligible for another program. Teachers also became specialized, some responsible for regular classroom instruction and others for delivering supplements that only certain students could receive.

Urban elementary schools had changed dramatically, from simple organizations of teachers—each responsible for a group of students—to holding companies for a variety of discrete programs. As state and local school boards imitated the federal model, children were pulled out of their regular classrooms to participate in a wide array of specialized programs. These included remedial reading and mathematics, individual training and therapy for children with handicaps, ethnic awareness and self-esteem programs for minority group children, and "enrichment" courses and field trips for gifted and talented children. Students spent time with a variety of specialists, and were often pulled out of regular instructional sessions to receive supplementary instruction in the same subject.

Researchers documented one clear effect of the proliferation of federal programs—that no single person in a school was responsible for a student's progress. The personal bond between teacher and student was broken, and many children became labeled as recipients of certain services or holders of certain rights. Special programs for dropout prevention and school safety relieved teachers of responsibility for the environment of the school outside their classrooms. Teacher union contracts spelled out an increasingly restrictive vision of what teachers were and were not required to do.

Few schools escaped these changes. Even suburban schools with few disadvantaged students and small federal grants followed the pattern of establishing many separate programs. High schools, which were traditionally divided into departments for English, mathematics, and science, became further divided into many specialized programs. The "shopping mall high school," offering students a rich sampler of alternative courses, became the norm.

Although the problems caused by this fragmentation of schooling have been well understood for nearly 15 years, the pattern has proven extremely difficult to change. Today's educational reform efforts, including magnet schools, site-based management choice, and charters for highly integrated specialty schools, are all intended as remedies for school fragmentation. Likewise are efforts to amend the ESEA to allow whole schools, not individual students, to benefit from federal funds. But the institutional weakness of public schools in general, and of big city schools in particular, can be traced directly to policies that changed schools from community institutions into government agencies.

Research had only a small part in creating those policies and in documenting the problems they caused. Research findings that fit the agendas of well-organized interest groups, especially the civil rights community, reliably led to new rules and tighter enforcement. Findings that documented the adverse effects of the proliferation of federal programs fit into no one's advocacy agenda. The policy response was therefore much slower, taking more than a decade to make real changes in federal program strategies.

Testing and Accountability

Student achievement testing is a technology whose use has grown beyond the intentions of the researchers who developed it. Originally designed to help select applicants for jobs, academic institutions, and the armed services, achievement testing tries to estimate knowledge or predict performance based on a small sample of a person's behavior, and to provide valid interpersonal comparisons. It requires relatively little of the test-taker's time and produces numerical scores quickly and at low cost.

The statisticians and mental measurement experts who developed student achievement testing are comfortable with its role as a predictive tool in identifying applicants most likely to succeed in college or best prepared to enter certain jobs or military specialties. They also regard testing as a good aid to instruction—a tool to supplement teachers' impressions of student performance—and a source of public information about trends in students' knowledge and performance. Test developers, however, are much less certain about the value of their own technology as a definitive measure of anyone's performance or ability. They know that some people do not test well and that individuals' scores can vary widely from one testing episode to another.

Most test developers also know that test scores can be strongly affected by coaching and practice. They are, therefore, cautious about any potential use of scores as the sole criterion for student admissions or promotion, or as the sole basis on which educators will be rewarded or punished for performance.

However, testing has proven to be a magnet for policy entrepreneurs. The prospect of obtaining simple measures of student, teacher, school, and system performance has proven irresistible. Despite test-makers' cautions, many policymakers have tried to use tests as the definitive instrument of policy. Test-driven policy has many forms: student competency tests that students must pass before graduation, regardless of their performance on other measures; systemwide improvement mandates that require average student test scores to rise by a fixed amount in a specific amount of time; and school accountability measures that reward or punish teachers on the basis of average student test scores. All such policies share one assumption—that measuring an outcome will motivate teachers and principals to improve it.

The assumption that measurement leads to improvement dominated policymaking in many states in the late 1980s. These states created new testing programs linked to promotion and graduation requirements, but did not increase state funding for school improvement. One state's highly touted omnibus education reform bill was drafted by legislative staff members who were instructed to find every plausible new initiative that would not cost the state money. The result, in many states, is what Michael Fix of The Urban Institute has called "aspirational legislation": statutes that established goals for schools and students without considering whether the goals could be met or what changes in the schools were implied.

Test developers did not encourage "aspirational legislation," and they and other researchers were quick to point out its costs. In many districts, the curriculum was narrowed to focus student attention on materials covered by the tests; many students were deprived of more ambitious instruction while their slower classmates were drilled in practice items and test-taking strategies. As predicted, test scores in many districts rose. But as Daniel Koretz has shown, many of the gains were specific to the particular tests used. Apparent gains on one test disappeared when students were given another differently designed but equally valid test on the same material.

Researchers' criticism has slowed the rush toward test-based policy but has not stopped it. For many policymakers and influential laymen, the idea that schools can be improved simply through testing is irresistible. Few understand that tests cover narrow samples of what students need to learn, or that testing the full array of necessary knowledge would demand most of the time now used for instruction.

Researchers who have developed testing technology face the scientist's quandary: the best results are the ones most likely to be misused. Though current state and federal policy proposals are less blatantly test-based than those prevalent in the late 1980s, many proposed federal and state programs still make teachers and principals responsible for test scores above all else. Despite the dangers of overreliance on testing, policymakers are irresistibly attracted to any simple, cheap measure of program outcomes, and they are likely to continue using the existing forms of student testing until something better comes along.

Some testing experts are working to develop new forms of student assessment that mirror the real goals of instruction more closely than existing assessment instruments, and enhance rather than compete with the instructional process itself. The search for "authentic assessment" (testing that taps all the elements of knowledge that students are supposed to master, and allows students to demonstrate knowledge through realistic tasks) has just begun.

Notwithstanding the rudimentary state of the "authentic testing" technology, many federal and state policies are being formulated on the assumption that richer, fairer, and more efficient testing is possible. New, comprehensive education reform laws in the states of Kentucky, Washington, Oregon, and Ohio, and proposed reforms in states such as Alabama and Tennessee, assume that "authentic tests" are available now or will be soon. Federal evaluation requirements for vocational education are also based on "authentic testing."

If "authentic" testing proves possible soon, new and proposed designs for federal and state education policies might work as intended. But those who advocate test-driven policies are gambling on extremely fast development of an unprecedented capability. Like the advocates of new defense systems who frequently assume that an airplane or missile that can be imagined can be readily produced, advocates of test-based policy may be in for years of unexpected costs and disappointing results.

School Effectiveness

Research on effective schools comes from a totally different research tradition than the test-based policy just discussed. Unlike test-based policy, which assumes that schools perform in response to externally mandated performance standards and the pressures of rewards and penalties administered by public authorities, effective schools research emphasizes the importance of school staff collaboration in light of a school-specific mission.

Effective schools research started in the mid-1970s, when Ronald Edmonds compared a number of effective and ineffective schools serving minority students. He identified several features that distinguished the two types of schools, including clear goals for what students were to learn, concentration of staff and student effort on learning, strong instructional leadership by the principal, and habits of collaboration and sharing among teachers. Many subsequent studies found similar differences between effective and ineffective schools. At about the same time, other studies showed how state and federal categorical programs could cause fragmentation of school staff effort and a focus on regulatory compliance rather than on instruction.

Since the late 1970s, many prominent researchers have concentrated on finding ways to reduce the adverse effects of regulation and compliance pressures on school effectiveness. These efforts have gone in two directions: some have studied schools that have retained their instructional focus and coherency despite the prevalence of regulation; others have considered possible changes in school system governance that would reduce the forces of fragmentation. The former line of research has produced significant practical guidance for teachers and principals seeking to overcome the effects of regulation on their schools. It has also encouraged foundations to fund many innovative educators on grounds that external support provides a warrant for a school's developing a distinctive approach to instruction, regardless of regulatory pressures. This school-focused research, however, leads to a consistently negative conclusion: principals and teachers can overcome the fragmenting effects of regulation only if they are able to assume the personal risks of being found out of compliance or if they can find a foundation grant or other warrant for being different.

These findings have inspired the second line of research—that of alternative governance systems for public school systems. The guiding premise of this research is that the compliance demands on teachers and principals have become counterproductive. Policymakers and interest groups are ultimately frustrated in their efforts to improve schools through regulations, court orders, and special program requirements for different classes of students. This is because, as discussed earlier, schools' compliance responses reduce the quality and flexibility of instruction. Consistent with this premise, some researchers have argued that the key to school improvement is to find new ways of using public funds to support schools.

This argument was first made in the mid- and late 1970s by critics of federal programs, including Paul Berman and Milbrey McLaughlin, Jane Hannaway, Lee Sproul, John Coons, and myself. However, concern about the consequences of governance for school effectiveness did not receive serious attention until the late 1980s and early 1990s, when John Chubb and Terry Moe (1992) published *Politics, Markets, and America's Schools*. They argued that democratic government inevitably imposes harmful bureaucratic constraints and that the only way to have effective schools is to remove them from public control. Chubb and Moe proposed that public school systems be abolished and that all children receive public scholarship funds, which their parents could use to pay tuition in any accredited school. They argued that such public tuition subsidies would create a strong demand for good schools, which entrepreneurs would rush to satisfy. The result, they predicted, would be a system of privately run schools that would be forced by competition to be efficient, effective, and responsive to community needs.

The "educational choice" proposal originated with economist Milton Friedman and was promoted in the early 1970s by the U.S. Office of Economic Opportunity. But it was Chubb and Moe, in the late 1980s, who made the case for "choice" clearly and dramatically. They gained strong supporters among business leaders, who instinctively believed in the superiority of market solutions, and among many minority parents, who were convinced that public schools were not working for their children. Catholic school advocates also supported "choice" in the hope that it would lead to public subsidies for financially struggling parochial schools. President Bush proposed to use federal program funds as the foundation for tuition subsidies, and "choice" initiatives appeared on election ballots in several states.

Despite widespread disillusionment about public education, to date "choice" proposals have consistently met defeat at the national level and seldom pass at the state level. The public apparently accepts researchers' criticisms of public education, but regards the "choice" prescription as extreme or premature. Many "choice" supporters have been sobered by the fear that it would create competition for admission to the most admired schools, but would do little to increase the supply of good schools. If that were to happen, the majority of students, especially "problem" students whom sought-after schools have no need to admit, would derive no benefit from choice.

The search for governance alternatives that will let schools become simpler and more accountable enterprises continues. In this search, researchers are in an unaccustomed position of leadership. University of Minnesota researchers Joseph Nathan, Ted Kolderie, and John Brandl formulated the concept of "charter schools" and successfully pressed for its adoption by the Minnesota Legislature. Charter school laws, which have been enacted in several states, allow small numbers of schools to secede from public school systems yet continue to receive public funds. They operate as independent enterprises constrained only by the terms of a publicly granted charter or license. Some researchers have proposed making charter schools universal: public school boards would stop operating schools entirely, and would help schools by entering into contracts with a variety of organizations including teacher guilds, universities, nonprofit organizations, foundations, and profit-making firms.

An all-charter system would create positive performance incentives for school staffs and ensure that public funds are spent where they count, at the school level. A school would need to attract students to survive. It would therefore have to offer a distinctive curriculum, social climate, or extracurricular program to entice parents and students. This would encourage a number of behaviors that "effective schools" advocates have tried to create in public school staffs. School staffs would have a strong incentive to articulate a mission for the school and to ensure that all elements of the school contribute to its attainment. The mission would also have to be easily explained to parents (i.e., it must be focused on what children will experience in school and what they will be able to do upon leaving it, not on subtleties of educational technique that may matter only to professionals).

The demands of economic survival would also make teachers concerned about the performance of the school as a whole. Teachers would therefore have strong incentives to help one another, to identify weaknesses, and to ensure that variations in teacher performance did not harm the school's ultimate product and reputation. Schools could also spend more on teachers. Because the local central administration would be reduced to a contracting agency, more money—perhaps as much as a third more—would come to the school level.

Whether these proposals for the redesign of public education will ever be implemented, and how they will work in the real world, remain to be seen. Proposals for more autonomous and entrepreneurial schools run directly against the trend toward test-based accountability—which would standardize curriculum and instruction to ensure that all students have equal chances of passing government-mandated tests. Although many federal and state policy proposals endorse both test-based accountability and "effective schools" principles, the two objectives may not be compatible in practice. In the past, highly prescriptive requirements linked to strong penalties have led to standardization of "safe" practices and corresponding reductions in problem-solving and adaptation at the school level.

School effectiveness research and test-based accountability derive from very different conceptions of the public school. The former assumes that a school is a professional organization whose success or failure depends on the ability of the staff to understand students' needs and to use on-site expertise to meet those needs. The latter assumes that a school is a government agency whose success depends on the clarity of goals and the strength of incentives for diligent work toward these goals. Whether these assumptions, and the policy prescriptions that follow from them, will complement or oppose one another, remains to be seen. Unfortunately, with few exceptions, the recent history of research as a guide to public education policy is not encouraging. The most likely scenario is that policies consistent with "school effectiveness" principles will be enacted separately from policies establishing test-based accountability. If that is so, and no effort is made to consider how the two policy principles can operate in concert, urban public schools will be forced to cope with yet another set of contradictory mandates.

IMPLICATIONS FOR FUTURE RESEARCH AND POLICY

In a field as politicized and chaotic as urban education, it is inevitable that research will be used as a tool by contending sides. Even when

research is used by the sponsors of policy initiatives, its ultimate
effect on events is impossible to predict. New initiatives are continually eclipsing older ones, and policies that have endured for a long
time can often be compromised or cut back in implementation.

Even when a policy is motivated by a research finding, it is seldom
pursued as the researchers imagined or intended. Most social science
research estimates the effects of a particular variable on another variable, on the assumption that all other relevant factors remain constant. But other factors never remain constant. Too many diverse
groups have stakes in education, and all constantly press for changes
favorable to themselves. Administrators and policymakers who just
want to do a good job are faced with the need to make changes in a
system while it is in full-scale operation—a feat not unlike changing
a tire while the car is proceeding at full speed. The uses of research
are therefore often surprising, sometimes perverse, and usually disappointing.

None of these conclusions are meant to suggest that researchers
should abandon their profession. Policymakers will use any information they can get. Social science research has the advantage of methodological discipline and full disclosure of methods and results. Even
if policies are never quite right, the processes of program evaluation,
abandonment, and search for alternatives are likely to be more efficient
if guided by good information.

Researchers should, however, take some care to ensure that their
results are used as appropriately as possible. This means taking some
account of the motives and tactics of policy entrepreneurs and interest
group advocates. Researchers should understand that any finding indicating a denial of equal opportunity will lead to litigation and new
policy mandates. No one can justifiably be surprised when corrective
policies are harsh or when judges or legislators add new mandates
without adding the resources needed to carry them out. Nor can researchers expect extremely complex schemes to hold together; policy
ideas that require unprecedented commitments of time, funds, and
administrative resources are simply not going to be implemented as
designed.

As this is written, the futility of complex reform schemes is being
demonstrated again, in the collapse of the Clinton administration's
effort to align the public education system via material goals, standards, and curricula. This effort reached its high water mark in early
1994, when the administration's *Goals 2000: Educating America Act*
created a national board to approve educational content standards and
encouraged every state to align its educational system with the national
effort. Scarcely a year later, however, national standards and devel-

opment efforts are under attack from the Republicans in Congress and from a coalition of conservative intellectuals and the religious right. The federal presence in kindergarten through twelfth-grade education is likely to shrink precipitously over the next five years, as funding is cut and categorical program regulations are eliminated.

In the future, as in the past, the market for social science research on urban educational policy will be highly decentralized. Researchers can seldom be sure who will use their results, or to what ends. If researchers want to have a definite and constructive influence on urban educational policy, they have two alternatives. The first is to report results so narrowly that they can be applied only to a limited range of situations. The second is to embed the reporting of particular results into a broader analysis of how they might be used or misused. As an example of the former, Oakes' (1985) findings about tracking in high schools might have been applied narrowly to schools that kept minority students out of regular high school classes, and not generalized to every situation in which students of different aptitude are placed in classes teaching the same material but at different paces. An example of embedding the reporting of particular results into a broader analysis is research that draws the connection between factors leading to school effectiveness and the reform of the governance system. Two examples of such research, one by myself and one by Joan Lipsitz, considered how a particular phenomenon—a school with a clear mission, dedication to high standards, and strong norms of cooperation among faculty members—occurred and what forces facilitated or impeded it. Such analysis led to prescriptions about changes in the broad governance system.

Litigators and policymakers are still free to misunderstand research results and prescribe overly narrow interventions. But nobody wants to pursue a futile line of action. If research can explain how undesirable outcomes occur and how they are embedded in the structures and incentives of public education, policymakers are far more likely to understand and use real points of leverage for change. Likewise, if researchers are able to formulate alternative lines of action and explain how they will operate in the real world, policymakers are likely to make far better choices.

SUGGESTED READING

Chubb, John A., and Terry E. Moe. 1992. *Politics, Markets, and America's Schools*. Washington, D.C.: Brookings Institution.

Coleman, James. 1966. *Equality of Educational Opportunity.* Washington, D.C.: U.S. Government Printing Office.

Farcas, Steve. 1993. *Divided Within, Besieged Without.* New York: Public Agenda Foundation.

Grissmer, David, and Sheila N. Kirby. 1995. *Student Achievement and the Changing American Family.* Santa Monica, Calif.: RAND.

Hannaway, Jane. 1993. "Political Pressure and Decentralization in Organizations: The Case of School Districts." *Sociology of Education* 66(3):147–63.

Hanushek, Eric A. 1991. "When School Finance Reform May Not Be Good Policy." *Harvard Journal on Legislation* 28(2).

Hill, Paul T. 1992. "Urban Education." In *Urban America: Policy Choices for Los Angeles and the Nation,* edited by J.B. Steinberg, D.W. Lyon, and Mary Vaiana. Santa Monica, Calif.: RAND.

Hill, Paul T., Gail Foster, and Tamar Gendler. 1991. *High Schools with Character.* Santa Monica, Calif.: RAND.

Johnson, S.M. 1984. *Teacher Unions in Schools.* Philadelphia: Temple University Press.

Kearns, David T., and Denis Doyle. 1988. *Winning the Brain Race.* San Francisco: Institute for Contemporary Studies Press.

Kirp, D., and D. Jensen. 1986. *School Days, Rule Days.* London: Falmer Press.

Kozol, Jonathan. 1992. *Savage Inequalities: Children in America's Schools.* New York: Harper Perennial.

Lipsitz, Joan. 1983. *Successful Schools for Young Adolescents.* New Brunswick, N.J.: Transaction Press.

Oakes, Jeannie. 1985. *Keeping Track.* New Haven, Conn.: Yale University Press.

Ravitch, Diane. 1983. *The Troubled Crusade: American Education, 1945– 1980.* New York: Basic Books.

Rosenholtz, S.J. 1984. "Effective Schools: Interpreting the Evidence." *American Journal of Education* 93(3):352–88.

Rotberg, Iris C., and James Harvey. 1993. *Federal Policy Options for Improving the Education of Low-Income Students.* Santa Monica, Calif.: RAND Institute for Education and Training.

Shanker, Albert. 1990. "A Proposal for Using Incentives to Restructure Our Public Schools." *Phi Delta Kappan* 71(5):344–57.

Sizer, Theodore. 1984. *Horace's Compromise: The Dilemma of the American High School.* Boston: Houghton-Mifflin.

Tyack, David. 1974. *The One Best System: A History of American Urban Education.* Cambridge, Mass.: Harvard University Press.

————. 1990. "Restructuring in Historical Perspective: Tinkering toward Utopia." *Teachers College Record* 92(2):170–91.

Wise, Arthur E. 1968. *Rich Schools Poor Schools.* Chicago: University of Chicago Press.

————. 1979. *Legislated Learning.* Berkeley, Calif.: University of California Press.

Chapter Eight

DRUG ABUSE

Adele Harrell

Drugs and crime have occupied a dominant position in U.S. domestic policy for much of the past 30 years. In successive waves, use of marijuana, heroin, and cocaine has experienced renewed popularity, creating public alarm and vastly increased public commitments to drug control. Drug enforcement, treatment, and prevention have become booming industries. By the early 1990s public drug control expenditures reached record levels, as did the number and size of federal, state, and local agencies engaged in efforts to control illicit drugs. The 1992 National Drug Control Strategy listed over 40 federal agencies, offices, or programs engaged in drug control, and projected a federal drug budget of $12.7 billion for 1993.

Drug policy has been far from consistent across time. Periods in which policies emphasized efforts to punish, incapacitate, and deter drug users and sellers through law enforcement have alternated with periods in which policies focused on treatment of addicts and prevention efforts, coupled with proposals to differentiate between drugs on the basis of their dangerousness. Throughout, there has been intense debate over the effectiveness and fairness of antidrug laws and enforcement strategies.

INDIVIDUAL RIGHTS VERSUS THE COMMON GOOD

The struggle to develop coherent, effective policies has highlighted deep divisions in American views of the role of government. In the realm of drug policy, individual rights to make controversial or unpopular choices in "the pursuit of happiness" come into conflict with the responsibility of government to protect citizens from threats to public safety and health. To the extent that drug use is viewed as a personal decision without public costs or implications, it is defended as an individual right. To the extent that drug use results in threats to public safety and health, the public demands government intervention to protect the common good. Analogies between illegal drugs and legal drugs such as alcohol and nicotine contribute to the unease over where to draw the line on psychoactive substances.

Current drug policy has its roots in the 1960s. On college campuses, marijuana became a symbol of protest against the war in Vietnam and the "establishment." By the 1970s use of illicit drugs, particularly marijuana and cocaine, became associated with the life styles of upwardly mobile college students and movie stars. Tolerance for marijuana use grew. Laws reducing penalties for possession of small amounts of marijuana were passed in 28 states; and cocaine was perceived, even by White House experts, as a relatively benign drug. At the same time, an upsurge in heroin use, a legacy of the war in Vietnam, was viewed with far less tolerance and met with a strong law enforcement response.

In the 1980s the prevalence of marijuana and cocaine use declined dramatically, led by the aging of the 1960s' generation of college users, the increasingly obvious problems that resulted from sustained cocaine use, and a renewed emphasis on restrictive drug policies. Unfortunately, the reduction in the overall number of users was more than offset by the advent of crack in the mid-1980s. Crack—a highly addictive, inexpensive version of cocaine, which was still perceived by many as a glamour drug—was introduced to a whole new class of less-affluent users at the very time when drug popularity was waning among middle-class, casual users. The marketing of small quantities of cheap cocaine took place on the street corners in inner-city neighborhoods. It brought with it unprecedented violence because of a public and poorly regulated retail distribution system and an upsurge in addicts experiencing serious social and medical problems.

By the 1980s, tolerance toward drugs evaporated and the focus turned to controlling drug use. The goals of policy were clear: zero tolerance for use, elimination of the supply of drugs from the market through interdiction and crop eradication, and deterrence or incapacitation of drug users and dealers through stepped-up enforcement and penalties. Stiffer drug laws, heightened street enforcement, and mandatory sentences were put in place at the state and federal levels.

A critical look at this history suggests that class divisions have played a major role in shaping public opinion about the appropriate balance between individual rights and public responsibilities. The "rights" side of the argument gains acceptance when drug use is popular among middle-class Americans, and loses ground when drug use is seen as a custom of minority groups and the poor. The middle class has greater political and social power to define what behaviors are considered appropriate and customary, and to define the range of harms demanding public control. Drug use is viewed as deviant and criminal when it is something that "good, upstanding citizens like us do not do." These values, as defined by the middle class, are generally those embodied in the law and enforced through the exercise of formal and informal social control.

In contrast, minority groups and the poor have less influence on prevailing social norms. Their behaviors and values are thus more likely to be defined, socially and legally, as deviant and in need of legal proscription. In addition, the harm that results from drug use has more obvious adverse consequences for the public when users are poor and have weak attachments to mainstream values. Problems of the poor such as lack of housing or employment options are exacerbated by drug use and may increase their need for services funded by taxpayers. Poor users face more pressure to steal or deal drugs to support a habit than do middle-class users with other sources of income.

Responses to drugs also reflect the larger political environment. Under presidents elected as "law and order" candidates promising to get tough on crime, drug use has been defined as a criminal behavior, and the goal of policy has been total elimination of all illicit drugs. During these administrations, vigorous law enforcement efforts have been coupled with efforts to control the supply of imported drugs. In this context, treatment of addicts, required in some cases by the courts, has been seen as a humane response to users unable or unwilling to desist. Policy research in this climate tends to focus on the effectiveness of law enforcement activities and on rehabilitation of users.

On the other hand, during eras in which the general domestic policy climate has stressed the alleviation of underlying causes of social distress, drug use has been defined as a social and medical problem, and the goal of policy has been to reduce harm based on the dangers of specific drugs. Treatment of addicts has been seen as one component in a public health model of primary, secondary, and tertiary prevention that seeks voluntary control of drug use through persuasion and therapy. In this climate, policy research questions focus on types of harms caused by drug use and on developing a range of prevention and treatment alternatives to reduce these harms.

Thus, influenced by patterns of use and the political context, diverse interest groups and experts have advanced specific policies that encompass a range of drug policy options. In considering these options, certain basic questions for policy research have emerged again and again:

- What drugs are being used, how often, and by whom?
- What are the causes of drug abuse, and what harms are associated with various drugs and drug use patterns?
- What strategies including law enforcement, treatment, and prevention are effective in controlling drugs?

The selection of research topics, the allocation of federal research funds, and the impact of findings have all been influenced by the range of options considered politically viable—a judgment formed by the patterns of use and general political environment. At times, research findings have been ignored in a political arena in which alternatives were posed as moral choices between good and evil—an almost inevitable discussion when influential elements of the public defend extremely severe criminal penalties for drug use. At other times, as the following review indicates, research findings have been at the center of the debate.

APPROACHES TO DRUG POLICY

Philosophically, the government's approaches to drug policy can be ranked along a continuum from more restrictive to less restrictive, using a model proposed by a study for the Institute of Medicine. At one extreme, libertarian policies, which emphasize individual rights and minimal governmental intervention in the lives of citizens, range from free drug markets (laissez-faire policies) to taxation and government regulation of distribution. At the other extreme, criminal policies, which emphasize the responsibility of government to control deviant behavior, range from incapacitation (incarceration) of users or dealers to deterrence through law enforcement and rehabilitation of offenders. In the middle, medical policies emphasize the treatment and stabilization of users to avert severe social and health consequences. Throughout this century, policies have leaned heavily toward the restrictive end of the continuum, despite the centrality of libertarian values in American society.

Another way to classify approaches to drug policy is in terms of the objectives. Strategies to reduce supply attempt to reduce drug use by making drugs more expensive and/or more difficult to obtain. Supply-reduction programs include efforts to disrupt the flow of drugs into the country through shipment seizures, crop eradication, and pressure on foreign governments to control production. Domestically, street crackdowns on dealers through asset forfeiture and undercover buys are tactics used to reduce the retail availability of drugs. On the other hand, demand-reduction strategies attempt to persuade users not to use drugs or to decrease their drug use. Demand-reduction programs educate individuals to the harm of drug use, teach drug resistance skills, increase incentives for avoiding drugs, and offer treatment for users and addicts. Obviously, supply-reduction strategies can affect demand and vice versa.

Two other drug policies—user accountability and zero tolerance— share the demand-reduction objective of reducing individual propensity to use drugs, but do so through coercion rather than persuasion. User accountability programs focus on arresting drug buyers and imposing criminal penalties for drug possession. Zero tolerance programs are designed to impose penalties for use, sale, or possession of any illicit drug, regardless of drug or amount.

HISTORY OF DRUG POLICY

The history presented in the paragraphs following of drug policy during the past several decades has been divided into stages to highlight shifts in drug use and public opinion and the relationship of these factors to each period's dominant drug policy approach and political context. This temporal sequence of events suggests that, for most of these years, policy was *reacting* to changing drug use patterns rather than *causing* significant changes in drug use. Within each stage, I note the role of research, events, and key individuals and organizations in shaping the course of policy.

1967 to 1973: Marijuana, the Campus Revolution, and the Growth of Tolerance

At the start of the 1960s, public agreement on drugs was firm. All illicit drugs from marijuana to heroin were viewed as dangerous narcotics. The users, primarily African-American jazz musicians and Mexican-American migrant laborers, were feared as dangerous addicts who engaged in crime and violence. Marijuana possession for personal use was a felony offense in every state, punishable by long periods of incarceration.

The first winds of change came from the college campus. Experiments with LSD led by Professor Timothy Leary at Harvard and psychedelic drug use by avant-garde writers and artists attracted students of the early 1960s to an intellectual subculture that featured mind-expanding drugs. The intellectual status of drugs then took on political overtones as campus activists adopted marijuana as a symbol of their support for civil rights and their protest against the Vietnam War. For students, marijuana use became a statement against the hypocrisy, racism, and materialism of their parents and the signature of the values of a generation.

Despite their general distaste for marijuana users and their values, a horrified population of older adults reacted in dismay as young college students were sentenced to long prison terms for possession of small quantities of marijuana. The resulting political furor led to a major revision of federal and state narcotics legislation. The Comprehensive Drug Abuse Prevention and Control Act of 1970 abandoned mandatory minimum sentences and reduced first-offense simple possession of drugs to a misdemeanor. Following the Federal Uniform Controlled Substances Act of 1970, 26 states and three territories adopted uniform guidelines making simple possession a misdemeanor. By 1973 every state in the Union had modified its marijuana laws, some more than once.

The 1970 Comprehensive Drug Abuse Prevention and Control Act had other far-reaching effects. It established the system of classifying drugs into five "schedules" based on their abuse potential, known harmfulness, and medical value. Marijuana, heroin, and LSD were all listed as schedule 1 drugs—those with high potential for addiction and no known medical value. Cocaine was listed as a schedule 2 drug, along with other prescription drugs such as morphine—drugs with the potential for severe addiction but acceptable for some medical applications. Drugs in schedules 3, 4, and 5 included medications believed to carry lower risks of abuse. Because most subsequent drug laws and policies were linked to these schedules, policy differentiation with respect to drugs was and continues to be severely constrained by the implicit directive to treat heroin and marijuana use as comparable problems. This has proved problematic because, although public opinion toward marijuana has varied over time, intolerance of heroin has been a constant.

The 1970 act also created the National Commission on Marijuana and Drug Abuse, charged with assessing patterns of marijuana use, evaluating the impact on public health and safety, and examining a range of legal policy options. The commission published two reports that ushered in the era of drug policy research: *Marihuana: Signal of Misunderstanding* (1971) and *Drug Abuse in America: Problem in Perspective* (1972). To assess patterns of marijuana use, the commission funded the first national survey of drug use to answer the question, "What drugs are being used, how often, and by whom?" The survey found that by 1971 an estimated 24 million Americans, most between the ages of 16 and 24 years old, had used marijuana at least once. It confirmed that drug use was entering the mainstream, reporting that users were as likely to be white as black, as likely to have middle incomes as low incomes, and were overwhelmingly under the age of 30.

Evidence on the harm of marijuana was collected from exhaustive testimony. A thorough review of the potential social, political, and economic consequences of three policies—continued total prohibition of marijuana, prohibition of marijuana sales but not possession, and legalized distribution of marijuana through tightly regulated channels—resulted in official endorsement of partial prohibition. The National Commission on Marijuana recommended that marijuana be subject to partial prohibition in which sales, but not possession, would be subject to criminal penalties. This apparent stamp of approval by a panel of respected public officials, combined with the amassed research evidence in the report, endorsed the legitimacy of opposition to restrictive drug policies and framed the political debate on drug policies for the decade.

Strong resistance to the commission's findings came from the Nixon administration. Elected as a "law and order" candidate, President Richard Nixon had launched an all-out assault on heroin early in his term. He received strong support from many voters, particularly those too old to be part of the new generation of drug users and who remained convinced that all drugs from marijuana to heroin posed a serious moral and legal threat to the public.

The Nixon administration policies had two primary goals: cutting off the supply of drugs and treating heroin addicts to reduce crime. Making drugs more expensive and difficult to obtain by cutting the supply was expected to discourage users, at least casual users, and make it less likely that new users would be recruited.

Control of drug imports focused on exerting pressure on the major foreign producers of the U.S. drug supply, primarily Turkey and Mexico. International investigations were launched to disrupt distribution networks. Domestic efforts to cut off the drug supply involved aggressive law enforcement, such as the infamous "no-knock" searches, which permitted law enforcement officials to enter private property without a warrant if they had reason to believe drugs were on the premises. Early results of the drug control efforts were encouraging. Success in cutting off the supply of heroin from Turkey and the heroin distribution network through France (the "French Connection") received widespread acclaim. Unfortunately, subsequent years illustrated how innovative international drug suppliers can be in developing alternative market routes for their drugs.

Treatment for addicts was defended as a strategy for controlling income-generating crimes among heroin users unable to resist their irresponsible cravings for the drug. Recognizing that addicts, the heavy users, would continue using drugs and would commit crimes to finance their considerable expenditures for heroin on the illegal market, the Nixon administration supported legal maintenance of heroin addicts on methadone. This form of addict treatment was highly controversial because it involved using one psychoactive drug (methadone, which was thought to be nonaddictive at the time) to control the craving for another drug (heroin).

Commitment to these objectives was evidenced by the doubling of the federal antidrug budget between 1970 and 1971, and again between 1971 and 1972. The federal antidrug bureaucracy was expanded during these years with the creation of the Drug Enforcement Agency (DEA) as the lead agency in supply reduction, and the National Institute on Drug Abuse as the lead agency in demand reduction. Single state agencies were established to guide federal monies into state and local antidrug programs. Dr. Jerome Jaffe was appointed head of the Special Action Office for Drug Abuse Prevention to coordinate drug activities, making him the first in a series of White House advisers with varying titles, authority, and influence charged with coordinating federal drug control policies. The government issued an official national drug control policy, the "Federal Strategy for Drug Abuse and Drug Traffick Prevention."

Despite the media prominence given to the international supply control efforts and the "war on drugs" rhetoric of this period, budget allocations favored demand reduction. Between 1970 and 1975, two-thirds of the federal drug budget went to prevention, education, and treatment. The result was a flowering of strategies directed at the goal of reducing the number of users and consumption per user through social influence and therapy. Public appreciation of addiction as a medical problem increased, with heavy users increasingly viewed as suffering from a physical affliction, not moral depravity.

Despite expanded demand-reduction spending, the Nixon administration remained adamant that all drug use be defined as a crime, and opposed efforts to decriminalize marijuana. The focus on the enemy abroad as the source of drugs and the heroin addicts and dealers as the primary threat to law and order domestically reduced the political problem of class differences in drug use. It allowed the administration to fight a vigorous war on drugs overseas, on the borders, and against drug kingpins. At the same time, domestic drug policy exercised medical and criminal control over primarily lower-class addicts while using less coercive education and prevention efforts to control middle-class marijuana use.

1974 to 1979: Decriminalization of Marijuana and Expanding Drug Use

The drug policy statements of Gerald Ford's administration were clearly less restrictive in orientation. The goals of drug policy set forth in the white paper issued by the Domestic Council Drug Abuse Task Force in 1975 were drug containment and harm reduction. Specific objectives were to minimize the number of users and the amount of drugs consumed and to reduce problems of addiction and drug-related consequences. Furthermore, containment efforts were to be directed at those drugs that were most harmful, acknowledging the need to differentiate among drugs based on their destructiveness. The task force based the selection of these goals on its review of the restrictive policies of earlier years, which led to the conclusion that government could not achieve total drug elimination. However, little change in actual policy response to drugs occurred as other issues took priority.

President Jimmy Carter's administration departed even further from the prohibitionist stance on marijuana, espousing decriminalization and initiating a review of therapeutic uses of marijuana and heroin to determine whether their classification as having no medical value was appropriate. The less-restrictive policy stance echoed and often cited the research findings and expert opinion contained in the 1973 report of the National Commission on Marijuana. An even more important influence on this policy may have been the continued growth of drug use among young middle-class users, which was documented in a series of national surveys launched in 1975 by the newly established National Institute on Drug Abuse. Marijuana use continued to climb. In 1976, 25 percent of young adults (18 to 25 years old) and 12 percent of youth (12 to 17 years old) had used marijuana in the past month; by 1979, only three years later, these percentages had increased to 35 percent and nearly 17 percent, respectively. Cocaine use took off. In three years the percentage of young adults who had ever used cocaine had more than doubled, from 13 percent to 27.5 percent. Heroin use remained relatively rare and was confined to small population groups.

For marijuana, tolerance increased, fear declined, and legal penalties were reduced. A 1977 public opinion poll showed that 28 percent of the public favored legalization of marijuana, up from 12 percent in 1969. Eleven states passed laws that removed the penalty of incarceration from marijuana possession offenses, and several adopted the use of citations instead of arrests for possession offenses. Nationally, marijuana prevalence was highest and growing least rapidly in states that had reduced fines for possession, and was lowest but growing most rapidly in states that retained larger fines. Moreover, increases in self-reported marijuana use preceded, but did not follow, reductions in the severity of sanctions. By 1978, one-third of the population of the country resided in states in which simple possession of marijuana carried no criminal sanctions.

The move to less-restrictive marijuana laws reflected the unwillingness of legislators to penalize the sons and daughters of middle-class voters, despite widespread disapproval of drug use. One case study of legislation reducing the penalty for marijuana possession in Utah, a state in which Mormon opposition to substance use is formidable, quoted the head of the Utah Bar Association's Committee on Dangerous Drugs and Narcotics as saying, "We would run the risk of classifying vast numbers of our children as felons, with the extremely serious consequences that brand carries."

Federal expenditures increased only modestly during these years and, despite increasing tolerance for marijuana use, the proportion of funds allocated to treatment and prevention actually decreased, from 70 percent in 1970–71 to about 55 percent in 1977–78. This decrease was due primarily to expenditures on international efforts to control the supply of marijuana and heroin, coupled with a more "hands-off" policy domestically. In California, for example, drug offenders constituted 13.8 percent of new prison admissions in 1977, but only 8.5 percent in 1981, as enforcement eased.

In 1974–75, the National Institute on Drug Abuse (NIDA) initiated three major drug monitoring systems to answer the question, "Who is using which drugs?" These included the National Household Survey on Drug Abuse, the Monitoring the Future survey of high school seniors, and the Drug Abuse Warning Network (DAWN), the latter of which reports on drug-related emergency room visits and medical examiner reports of drug-related deaths. Overall, such epidemiological research, together with basic biomedical and neurobehavioral research, received about 70 percent of the NIDA's extramural research grant funds between 1974 and 1979, compared to just over 20 percent for treatment research. Research on the causes of drug abuse, the social consequences of drug use, and strategies for preventing drug abuse received only a small portion of funds.

Despite growing drug use, support for marijuana decriminalization, and increasing tolerance for drugs, the trend toward reducing criminal sanctions for marijuana ground to a halt. Appeals by the National Organization for the Reform of Marijuana Laws to have marijuana removed from the list of schedule 1 drugs failed in the courts. A program of spraying Mexican marijuana crops with paraquat created a public outcry and generated a feud between the administration and pro-legalization advocates. The senior White House drug adviser, Dr. Peter Bourne, who had previously announced that cocaine was a relatively benign drug, left office under fire for illegally prescribing a widely abused sedative. His departure deprived proponents of decriminalization of a strong advocate within the federal bureaucracy and left the Carter administration defending accusations that it was soft on drugs.

At the same time, new political opposition was forming, led by parents of the growing number of young marijuana users. Grass-roots parent organizations began aggressively campaigning against liberalizing marijuana laws, and received federal support from the National Institute on Drug Abuse. Their influence was impressive, and they received a far better reception in state legislatures and Congress than research findings pointing to limited harm in moderate marijuana use. This may have been due to the fact that the research on marijuana focused on the biological effects of the drug, whereas parents' concerns focused largely on the social correlates of marijuana use, including disinterest in school, long hair, rock music, and other behaviors that they saw as threatening to jeopardize the futures of their children. Because the research agenda did not match politically relevant concerns, its impact was diminished.

1980 to 1984: Declining Drug Use and Declining Tolerance

A number of factors combined to create a decline in drug use and in society's tolerance of drugs in the early 1980s. As the early cohort of campus drug users matured, took on jobs, and established families, many discontinued marijuana use. Younger potential users became more aware, through the examples of the 1970s, that excessive drug use might harm their long-term prospects. The vocal and organized opposition of parents and schools caused older adults to suspect assertions that moderate drug use was harmless.

Between 1979 and 1985, marijuana use fell from 35.4 percent to 21.8 percent among young adults and from 16.7 percent to 12 percent among youth, according to the National Household Survey on Drug Abuse. Upward trends in cocaine use leveled off. The percentage of high school seniors who believed smoking marijuana was risky rose from about 50 percent in 1980 to about 70 percent in 1985. Unlike earlier periods in which changes in behavior preceded changes in the law and drug policies, these early 1980s' changes occurred during, and perhaps in response to, a renewal of aggressive law enforcement to control drugs.

The Reagan administration took office in 1981 on a platform of getting tough on crime, and immediately began a decade-long war on drugs based on law enforcement. The 1981 budget of $1.5 billion for drug control grew to $4.2 billion by the end of Reagan's term, and to $10.8 billion in 1991. In 1981, law enforcement, treatment, and prevention received approximately equal allocation, but this was quickly revised. Funding for prevention and treatment was cut by 40 percent in the first year, and over the decade, law enforcement funding accounted for 90 percent of the increases in the growing federal drug budget. For example, funding for interdiction increased from $263 million in 1981 to $605 million in 1986, when it reached a record 38 percent of the federal drug budget.

The war on drugs and the fight against crime became increasingly viewed as synonymous. Drug policy research focused on the question of the relationship between drugs and crime, on the deterrent effects of enforcement strategies, and on the economic benefits of incarcerating (incapacitating) drug offenders. The 1984 Crime Control Act expanded the criminal and civil asset forfeiture laws used to penalize drug traffickers, amended the Bail Reform Act to target pretrial detention of drug defendants, established mandatory sentencing guidelines, and increased federal criminal penalties for drug offenses. A 1980 Defense Department directive, superseding a 1972 directive, reflected the shift away from tolerance and treatment toward the current military policy of zero tolerance for drugs.

During the early 1980s, the government expanded forces for fighting the war against drugs. The Defense Department and the Federal Bureau of Investigation (FBI) were given broadened authority and responsibilities for drug enforcement. Task forces were created to fight organized crime, coordinate interdiction efforts, and improve communication among local, state, regional, and federal law enforcement agencies. A National Drug Enforcement Policy Board was created. Little attention was given to a 1982 report by the prestigious National Research Council of the National Academy of Sciences, *An Analysis of Marijuana Policy*, which recommended that states should regulate marijuana individually, and reported that the evidence reviewed indicated minimal harm from moderate use and a low risk of uncontrolled use if marijuana were legalized.

Federally supported drug research reflected the government's new priorities. NIDA extramural research funding experienced a one-year drop between 1981 and 1982 of 29 percent, before beginning a rise that continued into the 1990s. Although the percentage of funds allocated to prevention research began to rise, the proportion allocated to biomedical and epidemiological studies between 1981 and 1984 increased to 77 percent, from just over 70 percent during the Carter administration. At the same time, federal leadership in drug prevention and treatment services declined as block grants transferred responsibility to the states for distributing funds for alcohol, drug, and mental health services.

1985 to 1992: The Crack Epidemic and the Escalation of the War on Drugs

Crack first appeared on the streets of New York City in 1984. Cheap, highly addictive, and personally destructive, crack spread rapidly among current cocaine users and successfully recruited new users from low-income and minority groups who could not previously afford cocaine. At the same time, the decline in drug use among the general population continued. Between 1985 and 1990, rates of marijuana use dropped in half, from 12 percent to 5.3 percent for youth and from 21.8 percent to 12.7 percent for young adults. Cocaine use rates fell from 7.6 percent to 2.2 percent for young adults.

The result, according to prominent drug historian David Musto, was the emergence of a two-tiered drug culture, divided between a shrinking number of middle-class users and a growing number of lower-income users. Although legitimate questions were raised about the extent to which the survey decline resulted from a growing unwillingness to report use in the face of increased public intolerance for drug use, the weight of evidence indicated a real shift in the characteristics of users. Statistical breakdowns by education and job status showed much greater declines in cocaine use among well-educated Americans and those with jobs than among high school dropouts and the unemployed.

The shift to crack greatly increased the severity of cocaine-related problems. Violence associated with crack distribution and gang warfare erupted. The popularity of crack among women resulted in increased involvement in prostitution to support use, child neglect by addicted mothers, and the birth of crack-exposed infants. Cocaine-related emergency room episodes soared, particularly those in which dependency was given as the reason for needing care.

The devastation being caused by crack received extensive coverage in the media, bringing the problem to the attention of all Americans. Drugs began to move up in the popular poll rankings of national problems. The death of basketball star Len Bias from cocaine overdose in summer 1986 shocked the nation. Statistics provided by the National Institute on Drug Abuse in summer 1985 showed a jump in cocaine-related emergency room episodes and deaths. In fall 1986, the White House responded with a televised message to the American people by President Ronald Reagan and his wife, Nancy, urging collective support for an all-out effort to eliminate drugs from American society. The "Just Say No" campaign was initiated, and zero tolerance became the official drug policy.

New legislation received bipartisan support in Congress. The Anti-Drug Abuse Act of 1986 provided mandatory prison sentences for large-scale marijuana distribution, added synthetic "designer" drugs to the list of schedule 1 substances, created new penalties for money laundering, greatly expanded international drug control efforts, and created a block grant program for distributing drug law enforcement funds to the states. The act also created the Office of Substance Abuse Prevention within the National Institute on Drug Abuse, to increase the funding and visibility of federal prevention activities.

A second Anti-Drug Abuse Act passed in 1988 further expanded federal antidrug efforts. It established the Office of National Drug Control Policy (ONDCP) to be headed by an official with cabinet-level rank, the "drug czar," whose job would be to coordinate national efforts to control the supply of and demand for drugs. The office was required to publish a national drug strategy annually, advise the National Security Council, recommend changes required to implement the strategy, and consult with state and local governments. The act also increased the penalties for drug trafficking, created new federal drug offenses, and expanded the mandate of the Office of Substance Abuse Prevention to education and early intervention.

The annual drug control strategies issued by the ONDCP were weighted in the direction of law enforcement, as were the accompanying federal budgets. Between 1986 and 1990, budget allocations remained at approximately 70 percent for law enforcement and 30 percent for treatment and prevention. The Justice Department's Office of Justice Programs expanded its role in drug control research and services, with drug research funding in 1990 at over 900 percent above the level of drug research funding in 1985, after adjusting for inflation. Programs to demonstrate and evaluate innovative law enforcement programs were supported, as was research on the effects of drug control strategies and the links between drugs and crime. The Bureau of Justice Assistance administered large state block grants for drug initiatives. The National Institute of Justice developed the Drug Use Forecasting System (DUF) to monitor drug use among the criminal population through a program of drug testing in major cities.

Despite the increase in law enforcement focus, NIDA continued to be the dominant federal source of drug research funding. In constant 1982 dollars, the NIDA extramural research grant program increased by over 400 percent between 1985 and 1990. Research on the etiology and prevention of drug abuse rose substantially and accounted for 40 percent of the grant allocations across this period. Increasingly, this research examined the economic and social factors that increased the risk of drug abuse, and focused on interventions at the personal, family, and community levels to reduce the risk of drug use. The proportion of NIDA grant funds for epidemiological, biological, and neurobehavioral studies fell below 50 percent of its extramural research budget for this period. These allocations reflected increased concern with effective intervention efforts as part of the zero tolerance policy focus.

Drug enforcement, coupled with the general emphasis on getting tough on crime, flooded the jails, courts, and prisons with offenders. This placed unsustainable strain on justice systems and increased costs astronomically. Between 1980 and 1990, the number of Americans on probation grew by 126 percent, the number in prison by 134 percent, and the number in jail by 150 percent. By the end of 1990, well over 4 million Americans were under the supervision of the justice system. Between 1988 and 1990 alone, the demand for prison capacity grew to over 1,000 beds a week, outstripping supply despite booming prison construction.

The lion's share of growth in the offender population consisted of drug offenders. Drug possession arrests rose by 129 percent between 1980 and 1989, while arrests for drug manufacturing and distribution grew by 300 percent. In state prisons, drug offenders grew from 6 percent of inmates in 1979 to 22 percent in 1991. In federal prisons, the number of drug offenders doubled between 1988 and 1991, and now comprise the majority of offenders in federal facilities. In California, the percentage of new prison admissions due to drug offenses grew from 8.5 percent in 1981 to 35.4 percent in 1988. Moreover, the average time behind bars per offender increased, adding to the burden.

Concern about the justice and fairness of the system grew. Law enforcement fell heavily on poor minorities. The proportion of jailed drug offenders who were African-American increased from 35 percent in 1983 to 48 percent in 1989. An influential study by the Sentencing Commission reported that nationwide one in four African-American men between the ages of 20 and 29 were under the supervision of the criminal justice system in 1989. The proportion was undoubtedly higher in poverty-stricken inner-city neighborhoods, given the demographics of these areas and the enforcement targeting of street markets in which drug transactions are more easily detected. The result was a deterioration in race relations and public fear that entire areas of cities were out of control.

In this climate, a diverse group of respected public officials began advocating legalization, sparked by a speech by Baltimore Mayor Kurt Schmoke to the U.S. Conference of Mayors in 1988. This prompted two days of hearings by the Congressional Select Committee on Narcotics Abuse and Control in 1989. Advocates for a drastic change argued that legalizing drugs would remove the profits accruing to drug dealers, decrease the violent crime associated with drug dealing, decrease the health risks of use by ensuring uncontaminated drugs, decrease the inequities and lasting harm of criminalizing large numbers of minority youth, and decrease the expense of drugs and thus user incentives to commit income-generating crimes. Testimony from researchers advocated policy initiatives to address the economic and social factors that increased the risk of drug abuse. Led by committee chairman Charles Rangel, members of Congress vigorously dissented to legalization, largely on the grounds that the risk of greatly increased numbers of users and addicts would outweigh the benefits.

Use of restrictive drug policies continued to expand. In a speech at Harvard University in 1989, Bush administration "drug czar" William Bennett lashed out at "whole cadres of social scientists, abetted by vhole armies of social workers, who seem to take it as catechism that ɘ problem facing us isn't drugs at all, it's poverty, or racism, or some ɘr equally large and intractable social problem." He reasserted the ssity for strict criminal penalties in order to make decisions to ᾽ sell drugs simply too unattractive. National drug control strat-᾽om 1989 through 1992 were crafted around a central policy ᾽—user accountability—and endorsed a variety of ways to enhance the chance that users would be identified and face serious consequences through the courts, the workplace, or otherwise. The Crime Control Act of 1990 doubled law enforcement grants to states and localities, expanded asset forfeiture of drug trafficker assets, and supported drug-free school zones, rural drug enforcement, and regulation of the substances used to manufacture drugs.

By the late 1980s, the link between drug use and the transmission of AIDS to female cocaine users (and to their unborn babies) as a result of prostitution and to men and women intravenous drug users was becoming clearer. As the proportion of new AIDS cases attributable to drug use began to rise precipitously, public health efforts to educate users not to exchange needles or have unprotected sex became increasingly important drug control strategies. The crisis prompted heated debate on policies such as these, which stopped short of zero tolerance and focused instead on modifying risk. The AIDS crisis also set the stage for increasing efforts to control the negative effects of drug use from a public health perspective. In late 1992 at the end of the Bush administration, the National Institute on Drug Abuse was transferred to the National Institutes of Health. In this reorganization, nonresearch functions were transferred to a newly created agency, the Substance Abuse and Mental Health Services Administration (SAMHSA), including responsibility for administration of the state block grant programs, federal support for demonstrating model prevention and treatment services, and management of the major drug monitoring systems. SAMHSA's programmatic efforts are directed at supporting state and local drug treatment and prevention programs.

1993 to 1994: A Shift in Focus

Although it is too soon to say that a retreat is underway in the "war on drugs," the years 1993–94 have seen indications of a shift in focus. Much less high-profile policy debate has been directed at illegal drug use, and much more attention has been devoted to the related, but not identical, problem of violent crime, particularly among juveniles. Signals of the shift were apparent early in President Bill Clinton's administration. When President Clinton took office in January 1993, he immediately cut the staff of the National Office of Drug Control Policy from 147 to 25. Although the new drug czar, Lee Brown, is a professional law enforcement official, he is best known as a police chief advocating community policing approaches that stress police-citizen cooperation in drug prevention and enforcement. Early in the administration, the Drug Enforcement Administration narrowly survived a proposal to merge it with other justice agencies. The new attorney general, Janet Reno, made review of mandatory drug sentencing guidelines an early priority and has been a strong supporter of programs like drug courts that emphasize combining law enforcement with medical treatment for addicts.

Emphasis in the 1994 Violent Crime Control and Law Enforcement Act was on fighting drugs as part of a general effort to control violent crime. Enacted just prior to the landmark Republican sweep in the fall 1994 elections, the law provided federal support for drug courts that would offer expanded treatment options for drug-involved defendants, community-based prevention programs, and substantial support for local governments to hire additional police officers to combat crime and drugs at the street enforcement level. These provisions of the law are currently under vigorous attack by the new Republican majority in the House of Representatives.

The new Republican agenda appears aimed at decreasing federal support for drug courts, treatment and prevention programs, and local police officers. These would be replaced by increased federal support for prison construction and block grants to states to use for state and locally designed anticrime and antidrug initiatives. A major feature of the Clinton administration's budget for 1996 is a proposal to combine existing categorical programs in the U.S. Public Health Service into a $1.3 billion program of Substance Abuse Performance Partnerships to support state treatment and prevention services. The 1995 National Drug Control Strategy presents an "Action Plan for Enhancing Domestic Drug Program Flexibility and Efficiency at the Community Level." Together these proposals seem likely to result in transferring much more control over antidrug programs to states and localities, with unknown effects on the balance between demand reduction and supply reduction strategies.

ROLE OF RESEARCH

A major contribution of research to the drug debates has come from the NIDA drug monitoring programs designed to answer the repeated question, "What drugs are being used, how often, and by whom?" As noted earlier, the National Household Survey on Drug Abuse has produced estimates of the prevalence of past and present use among surveyed household members ages 12 and older since the mid-1970s. In addition, the previously mentioned series of surveys of high school students, called Monitoring the Future, has measured drug use, beliefs, and attitudes of youth, while the Drug Abuse Warning Network (DAWN) has counted drug-related emergency room episodes and deaths from participating jurisdictions. In the late 1980s, the National Institute of Justice instituted the Drug Use Forecasting System (DUF) to study drug use among criminals, using urinalysis tests of quarterly samples of arrestees.

These monitoring systems have been attacked for their shortcomings. Only recently has the National Household Survey on Drug Abuse begun to include portions of several relatively large high-risk populations such as students in dormitories, the homeless, or residents of military bases. The Monitoring the Future surveys do not include school dropouts. Neither survey measures drug abuse (as opposed to drug use) very well, and both are subject to the possibility of untruthful denial of drug use. Until recently, DAWN did not include a nationally representative sample and relies, for the emergency room data, on the accuracy of notations of drug involvement found in medical records. The DUF reflects only recent drug use in selected cities among nonrandom samples of arrestees. Nonetheless, despite their limitations, the impact of these monitoring systems has been significant in lending some empirical evidence to what at times has been almost hysterical debate on the nature and pervasiveness of the drug threat.

Federally supported research on causes and harmful consequences of drug use has included a large number of biological and neurobehavioral studies. Such research has exerted maximum impact when respected panels have conducted exhaustive reviews and incorporated the findings into reports with recommendations. The earlier-cited 1971 and 1972 reports of the National Commission on Marijuana and Drug Abuse were perhaps most influential in this regard; least influential was perhaps the earlier-mentioned 1982 report of the National Research Council of the National Academy of Sciences. The impact of the research and these reports was greatly influenced by the extent to which the research addressed current concerns in the contemporary political climate. More recently, studies of the role of social and economic factors in determining risk of drug abuse and negative effects have been triggered by the apparent link of drug abuse to health problems, such as AIDS and crack-exposed infants, crime, child abuse, and other kinds of social distress. This research is now leading the development of programs and antidrug strategies, although funding allocations still favor international and domestic control of the drug supply. The growing focus on questions about drugs' harmful consequences has also led to a call for reevaluation or expansion of basic drug monitoring systems. This is because, as currently constructed, these systems provide more sensitive measures of the prevalence of drug use than do the social, economic, and health problems resulting from drug use.

The impact of drug policy research assessing the effectiveness of strategies (including law enforcement, treatment, and prevention) in controlling drugs has been mixed. Many evaluations of specific programs have not involved robust experimental designs or representative samples. The range of outcomes considered has been less than comprehensive, costs of programs are often not reported, and unintended consequences not addressed. Nonetheless, reviews of multiple evaluations have generated some guidelines based on the preponderance of evidence showing the types of programs that are most effective. Important lessons have been learned, sometimes from combining the findings of multiple studies. For example, data now exist to support the conclusion that interdiction and crop eradication do not reduce the availability of drugs substantially for long time periods and thus do not have the anticipated effect on drug access. The imposition of random drug testing in the military did change the perceived risks of use and lowered drug use in the armed forces. Drug prevention programs that feature community involvement, family focus, comprehensive services, and positive alternative activities are more effective than single-focus prevention programs.

Unfortunately, this type of research has lacked a framework for cross-program comparisons that could be used for national policy formulation. Evaluations of specific programs frequently do not collect the kind of information that could be used to assess the benefits of supply-reduction versus demand-reduction programs, or the trade-offs between targeted and general prevention programs. One promising development has been the increasing attention given by policy journals in the last two years to a cost/benefit framework for this type of analysis. These articles illustrate the difficulties in specifying the intended and unintended consequences of antidrug programs, their direct and indirect costs, and the range of benefits they might offer. Even when these factors cannot be quantified, however, the specification of the likely range of benefits, consequences, and costs promises to elevate the debate over policy choices to a more informed level.

1995: PROSPECTS FOR THE FUTURE

At this writing, there is considerable dissatisfaction with the "war on drugs," even among those who do not favor drug legalization. Drug interdiction, crop eradication, and pressures to control supply have not appeared to affect drug availability reported by respondents to surveys or estimates by the Drug Enforcement Agency based on street purchases. Indeed, some analysts have concluded that these efforts have stimulated domestic production of drugs, the development of more potent substances (to gain more bang for the buck), and the shift from bulky marijuana to more transportable drugs.

Efforts to reduce demand through intensive domestic law enforcement have been criticized as diverting criminal justice resources from controlling more violent offenders. The war on drugs has been blamed by some for creating a whole class of minority youth labeled by the system as criminals (thereby reducing their already poor employment prospects), and for contributing to the growth of violent drug distribution networks and youth gangs. Criminal penalties and tactics such as asset forfeiture have been criticized for being too severe for the offense or inequitable in their impact. Moreover, the costs of the war on drugs, which are projected in the 1996 proposed budget at $14.6 billion, are being questioned in view of the federal deficit and budget constraints.

At the same time, patterns of drug use are once again shifting. There are indications that the crack epidemic has peaked. Ethnographers report a decline in crack use among teenagers and young adults. Cocaine-related emergency room admissions have leveled off, as has the percentage of arrestees testing positive for cocaine. Unfortunately, there are preliminary signs of two trends reminiscent of earlier years. First, a growing number of young people are using marijuana and hallucinogens; second, there is preliminary evidence that heroin use is on the rise among users of other drugs. National survey data show small but significant increases among young adults in the use of marijuana and LSD. The percentage of juvenile arrestees testing positive for marijuana in Washington, D.C., increased from under 10 percent in late 1991 to 43 percent in mid-1993. Heroin prices have been declining and purity increasing for at least two years, and recent DAWN statistics reflect an increase in heroin-related health problems.

The growing pressure to devote attention to violence, not drugs, as the dominant feature of the crime problem, and the budgetary strain of aggressive domestic drug enforcement, are likely to produce renewed efforts to focus on medical solutions and highly targeted drug programs that identify specific harms and risk groups for federal intervention. This trend may be accelerated if we see a rise in the use of marijuana among the middle class and an increase of heroin use among heavy users. Should this occur, the past decade's research on risk factors, treatment, and prevention may play an increasing role in debates over appropriate drug policy.

The assistance of Rose Marie Yu in locating, reviewing, and organizing background information for this chapter is deeply appreciated.

SUGGESTED READING

Bayer, Ronald. 1991. "Introduction: The Great Drug Policy Debate: What Means This Thing Called Decriminalization?" *Milbank Quarterly* 69(3):341–63.

Bertrand, Marie Andree. 1990. "Beyond Antiprohibitionism." *Journal of Drug Issues* 20(4):533–42.

Burke, Anna Celeste. 1992. "Between Entitlement and Control: Dimensions of U.S. Drug Policy." *Social Service Review* 6 (4, December):571–81.

Courtwright, David T. 1991. "Drug Legalization, the Drug War, and Drug Treatment in Historical Perspective." *Journal of Policy History* 3(4):393–414.

Kleiman, Mark. 1992. *Against Excess: Drug Policy for Results.* New York: Basic Books.

Kornblum, William. 1991. "Drug Legalization and the Minority Poor." *Milbank Quarterly* 69(3):415–35.

Mauer, Marc. 1990. "Young Black Men and the Criminal Justice System: A Growing National Problem." Washington, D.C.: The Sentencing Project.

Moore, Mark H. 1991. "Drugs, the Criminal Law, and the Administration of Justice." *Milbank Quarterly* 69(4):529–57.

———. 1990. "Supply Reduction and Drug Law Enforcement." In *Drugs and Crime,* edited by Micheal Tonry and James Q. Wilson. Chicago: University of Chicago Press.

Nadelman, Ethan A. 1989. "Drug Prohibition in the United States: Costs, Consequences, and Alternatives." *Science* 245(4921):939–47.

National Commission on Marihuana and Drug Abuse. 1973. *Drug Abuse in America: Problem in Perspective.* Washington, D.C.: U.S. Government Printing Office.

———. 1972. *Marihuana: A Signal of Misunderstanding.* Washington, D.C.: U.S. Government Printing Office.

National Research Council Committee on Substance Abuse and Habitual Behaviors. 1982. *An Analysis of Marijuana Policy.* Washington, D.C.: Author.

Office of National Drug Control Policy. 1992. *National Drug Control Strategy: A Nation Responds to Drug Use.* Washington, D.C.: The White House.

Reuter, Peter. 1992. "Hawks Ascendant: The Punitive Trend of American Drug Policy." *Daedalus* 121(3):15–52.

Rydell, C.P., and S.S. Everingham. 1994. *Controlling Cocaine: Supply versus Demand Programs.* RAND Report. Santa Monica, Calif.: RAND.

Sharp, Elaine B. 1992. "Agenda-Setting and Policy Results: Lessons from Three Drug Policy Episodes." *Policy Studies Journal* 20(4):538–51.

Sollars, David L. 1992. "Assumptions and Consequences of the War on Drugs: An Economic Analysis." *Policy Studies Review* 11(1):26–39.

Strategy Council on Drug Abuse. 1973. *Federal Strategy for Drug Abuse and Drug Traffic Prevention.* Washington, D.C.: U.S. Government Printing Office.

Substance Abuse and Mental Health Services Administration. 1991. *National Household Survey on Drug Abuse.* Washington, D.C.: U.S. Department of Health and Human Services.

van Mastrigt, Hans. 1990. "The Abolition of Drug Policy: Towards Strategic Alternatives." *Journal of Drug Issues* 20(4):647–57.

Warner, Kenneth E. 1991. "Legalizing Drugs: Lessons from (and about) Economics." *Milbank Quarterly* 69(4):641–61.

The White House, February 1995. *National Drug Control Strategy.* Washington, D.C.: U.S. Government Printing Office.

Chapter Nine

RACIAL DISCRIMINATION
AND SEGREGATION

George Galster

Trends in public policy efforts aimed at reducing racial discrimination and segregation are like a roller coaster that reverses direction and loops back on itself. Three decades ago we saw an unprecedented rise in public attention, policy resources, and judicial and legislative support devoted to the issue. But it was the Civil Rights movement and urban riots, not policy researchers, that raised discrimination and segregation in education, employment, housing, and mortgage finance to the highest levels of concern.

During the 1970s it appeared that this peak of activity could not be sustained, as public, legislative, and judicial support for reforms flagged. Although most policy researchers explicated and quantified the problems of race and the city, the more influential works tended to downplay the role of race and emphasize the role of class in explaining urban inequalities. Such works implicitly confirmed the growing skepticism about the desirability and efficacy of race-based policies. The roller coaster headed downward.

By the 1980s the issues had been turned on their head, with ideological assumptions carrying more weight in policymaking circles than empirical evidence. Declaring that the war on illegal racial discrimination had been won, federal policymakers (and an increasingly conservative Supreme Court) made "race neutrality" the guiding principle. They turned their attack on the supposedly "racist" character of the policy solutions promulgated only a decade earlier: school busing and affirmative action.[1] By 1988 the roller coaster had returned near to where it had begun two decades earlier.

During the last few years a minor counter-reaction to race-neutral policies has occurred, with renewed legislative and regulatory initiatives against discrimination. These have been sparked by an unprecedented body of policy research that has helped reshape how policymakers and the public perceive racial discrimination and segregation and appropriate policy responses to these problems. This impetus has been severely limited, however, by resolute public and congressional opposition to affirmative action programs, on the grounds that they are unfair.

THE 1960s: SLOWING THE MOMENTUM OF RACISM

By the early 1960s the nascent Civil Rights movement had achieved a few victories in gaining equal access to schools, employment, housing, and mortgage finance. In each of these dimensions, however, the victories paled in comparison to the magnitude of the battles still needed to achieve equality.

In education, the landmark 1954 Supreme Court case *Brown v. Topeka Board of Education* had overturned the "separate but equal" doctrine. This doctrine had guided public education for over half a century, and was founded on the principle that racial equality under the law was upheld so long as schools attended exclusively by minorities had the same resources as those attended exclusively by whites. The Supreme Court countered with the principle that separate was *inherently* unequal, citing the case study evidence presented by Kenneth Clark on the psychological damage to black children imposed by segregation. As indicated earlier in this volume, this was one of the rare cases in which research clearly shaped civil rights policy during the two decades following World War II. However, despite the breadth and import of the *Brown* decision, over the next decade relatively little progress in school desegregation was made. By 1964, 99 percent of black children still attended segregated schools.

Progress in relieving segregation and discrimination in employment was also spotty. The military had been officially desegregated after a 1948 executive order, but change on other occupational fronts was less obvious. The trade unions continued to discriminate (that is, treat unequally on the basis of race those who are otherwise equal); in 1964 only 1.3 percent of all apprentices were black. The white-collar world continued to suggest a double entendre: these jobs were for whites wearing white collars. For instance, the first black reporter for a major television broadcast network was not hired until 1962. Average earnings of blacks were slightly more than half those of whites, on average, and their unemployment rates were twice as high.

Housing segregation (that is, the residential separation of different racial groups) continued at the high levels already reached by 1940. In the early 1960s, sociologists developed a mathematical index that could quantify the amount of separation between racial groups in cities and could be used to make comparisons across cities over time. Given the underdeveloped state of computer technology, these calculations were made for only the largest cities. They revealed that the 12 major southern metropolitan areas scored 87 on the segregation scale (100 denotes maximum segregation) in 1940 and 89 in 1960; the 18 major nonsouthern metropolitan areas scored 87 in 1940 and 82 in 1960.

These figures are not surprising, given the prevailing attitudes of the real estate industry and federal policymakers. Real estate agent associations considered it a breach of professional ethics to introduce "inferior and incompatible elements" into white-occupied neighborhoods, because doing so reputedly would lower property values. This same rationale was used by the Federal Housing Administration, which from 1935 to 1950 had made segregation a requirement before suburban housing developers could receive low-interest, government-insured mortgage loans for their new subdivisions. Government policies related to public housing projects that began to be built in larger numbers after World War II further reinforced patterns of discrimination and segregation in housing. One of the few bright lights for housing was the Supreme Court's 1948 *Shelley v. Kraemer* decision, which overturned covenants attached to property deeds that restricted the groups to which any buyers could subsequently sell.

Media Attention and Civil Rights Legislation

Although problems related to race were not geographically confined, prior to the early 1960s the Civil Rights movement focused on attacking the legacy of discriminatory racial laws in the South, which were especially virulent in rural areas. These barriers offended the ethical principles of many Americans. The highly publicized brutality of some responses to nonviolent civil rights activities—beatings and water-hosings of marchers, assassinations of leaders, even dynamiting of churches—fueled public distaste for institutionalized intolerance. Arguably, the visual media played the pivotal role in shaping Americans' vision of "the race problem." By the time of the civil rights march on Washington, D.C., in 1963, which was highlighted by Martin Luther King's "I Have a Dream" speech at the Lincoln Memorial, political pressure for national civil rights legislation had grown irresistible.

Path-breaking laws followed. Falling under the Civil Rights Act of 1964, Title II prohibited racial segregation of any public facilities, services, or accommodations. Title IV authorized the U.S. attorney general to intervene through the courts to achieve school desegregation. Title VII prohibited discrimination in employment on the basis of race, color, religion, national origin, or sex. The Voting Rights Act of 1965 guaranteed the freedom to exercise the right to vote without discrimination, intimidation, or undue registration requirements.

Important as these legislative initiatives were, they were formulated on the basis of a superficial analysis of "the race problem in America" that viewed the issue as primarily a southern and rural problem. Demography was inexorably setting the stage for transforming this perception of the issue from a southern-rural one to a northern-urban one. Although several popular and scholarly analyses of segregated, black-occupied, northern urban neighborhoods had appeared by the mid-1960s (*The Autobiography of Malcolm X*; and Kenneth Clark's *Dark Ghetto* and Karl and Alma Taeuber's *Negroes in Cities*, respectively), public and political perceptions of the issues were more strongly influenced by the media coverage of southern civil rights leaders and activists.

Demography, Civil Disorders, and Visibility of the Ghetto Problem

The migration of blacks from the rural South to northern cities had been occurring throughout the century. The highly segregated urban ghetto, walled in by a host of blatantly racist and officially sanctioned policies, had become a standard ecological feature of the northern city by 1940. But in the three decades following 1940, an unprecedented 1.5 million blacks per decade moved from the South to the North, creating dramatic changes in the racial complexion of cities. In 1960, over one-fourth of the populations of Philadelphia, Cleveland, Detroit, Baltimore, St. Louis, Washington, D.C., New Orleans, and Newark were black. In all cases except New Orleans and Newark, this represented at least a doubling of the proportion of black population since 1940.

Demographic changes alone may not have produced a shift in public perceptions of the issue had it not been for the civil disturbances of the mid- and late 1960s. Beginning with the Watts section of Los Angeles in 1965, continuing through Cleveland and Chicago in 1966, and escalating to 60 cities in 1967 (most notably Detroit, Newark, and Milwaukee), the black community lashed out violently at what it perceived as decades of not-so-benign neglect of the northern ghetto.

Kerner Commission, Coleman Report, and Educational Role of Policy Research

In response to these urban civil disturbances, President Lyndon Johnson appointed a national commission headed by Illinois Governor Otto Kerner and consisting of social scientists, public figures, and elected officials. The 1968 report of the Kerner Commission represents the most comprehensive, influential, and in many respects, still relevant example of policy research in the field of urban racial issues conducted in the last 40 years. The fundamental changes in perspective provided by the report were two-fold: (1) the existence of de facto segregation was just as significant as de jure segregation; and (2) racial oppression assumes distinct and self-reinforcing forms in the context of urban ghettos that are segregated from the larger society. The report argued that to deal with the conditions spawning civil unrest, policies must focus not only on race but also on space. That is, policy should aim both at desegregating ghettos and redeveloping them as viable social and economic areas.

Unlike earlier work, this policy research clearly molded and informed civic debate and legislative and judicial initiatives. It not only responded persuasively to a highly visible social problem but couched its recommendations in easily understood terms that resonated with the optimism and urban focus of the contemporaneous War on Poverty. In retrospect, it is clear that few of the Kerner Commission's specific recommendations were converted into policy. Yet, the 2 million copies of the report that were distributed had an undeniable educational effect on policymakers and the general public, and shaped the scholarly agenda for years to come. In subtle but crucial ways, the change in conception of the problems spawned by the report still influences the civil rights policy debate today.

Another famous example of policy research appeared during this period, although its effect on public enlightenment was quite different. The U.S. Office of Education published *Equality of Educational Opportunity* in 1966, commonly named after its principal author, James Coleman. In the most comprehensive survey of public educational facilities ever undertaken, the Coleman report attempted to quantify 67 separate measures of school quality and to test for interracial differences. Much to the surprise of many, the report found that black and white schools differed on a multitude of measures but, with the exception of science laboratories, textbooks, and specialized clubs, black schools were not dramatically inferior.

The report provoked a firestorm of criticism. It was argued that the educational environment was experienced by the student holistically and that minimal individual deficiencies cumulated to produce significant inferiority overall. It was furthermore pointed out that important aspects of school quality such as socioeconomic status of parents were omitted and other aspects were too subtle to quantify. In addition, it was alleged that the schools responding to the survey represented an unrepresentative sample.

Whatever the methodological weaknesses of the Coleman report, it did force a reconsideration of what "equal educational quality" meant and how much progress had been made since *Brown v. Topeka Board of Education* in reaching that goal. If racially separate schools were not so unequal in measurable characteristics as was commonly believed, then how *were* they unequal and how did these inequalities relate to the cognitive development of students? By raising such questions, the Coleman report shaped an agenda that guided a succeeding generation of educational researchers.

Optimism at Close of Decade

As the 1960s drew to a close, numerous events suggested that the nation was responding seriously to the urban racial crisis. A month after the release of the Kerner Commission report (and four days after the assassination of Martin Luther King), the Civil Rights Act of 1968 was passed. Its most important section, Title VIII, prohibited discrimination based on race, color, religion, national origin, or sex in the rental, sale, advertising, or financing of housing. The presidential campaign of 1968 saw little difference among the candidates in their commitment to economically redevelop the ghetto, except in the particulars. Robert Kennedy, for example, proposed tax subsidies to businesses locating plants in the ghetto, while Richard Nixon backed a scheme for helping black entrepreneurs start new businesses. In the 1969 case *Gautreaux v. Chicago Housing Authority and U.S. Department of Housing and Urban Development*, the federal court found discrimination in public housing tenant allocation procedures and ordered remedies that involved counseling and housing subsidies designed to help black public housing tenants move into suburban dwellings.

Thus, by the end of the decade, there was just cause for optimism. A cogent, well-supported diagnosis of the urban racial problem seemed to be guiding public policy. De jure segregation of schools and race-based differential treatment in most forms of social intercourse finally were rendered illegal by federal statute. New judicial and legislative remedies were beginning to emerge.

THE 1970s: ADVANCES, DISAPPOINTMENTS, AND REACTIONS

By some measures, the decade of the 1970s witnessed continued, if uneven, progress toward eliminating discrimination and segregation in education, employment, housing, and mortgage lending. By other measures, progress was disappointing. Quantitative policy research tended merely to document trends and reconfirm conventional wisdom. The influential policy research was more conceptual and explicitly ideological in approach, and set the stage for a radical reformulation of the race issue during the next decade.

Documenting Racial Trends in Education, Employment, Housing, and Lending

Perhaps the most remarkable changes during the 1970s were observed in education. Desegregation efforts begun with the 1964 Civil Rights Act culminated with the 1971 Supreme Court decision in *Swann v. Charlotte-Mecklenburg Board of Education*, which expressly required the use of busing as a remedy for illegal segregation. As a result of these efforts, the percentage of black children attending desegregated schools increased from 1 percent in 1964 to 44 percent in 1972. Dramatic declines in black-white student segregation indices occurred between 1967 and 1978 in 15 of the 20 largest cities across the nation. For example, Milwaukee's segregation score fell from 86 to 39, Indianapolis's from 78 to 46, Dallas's from 94 to 64, Memphis's from 95 to 60, and Jacksonville's from 92 to 40.

But such rapid change was not to continue. Public opposition to mandatory busing for desegregation escalated, reaching a fever-pitch in places like Boston. Many white parents responded by removing their children from center-city public school systems, either by moving residence to another district or by enrolling them in private schools. As a result, white enrollment in center-city public school districts fell precipitously. From 1967 to 1986, Detroit, Milwaukee, San Diego, Houston, and Dallas lost at least a third of their white students. One option proposed for dealing with such "white flight" was to combine central-city with suburban districts in a common busing effort. This option was dealt a crushing blow by the Supreme

Court in the 1974 *Milliken v. Bradley* case. The Court overturned a lower court ruling that the desegregation of the Detroit public schools would be impossible unless suburban districts were also required to participate; such could not be required, the Court argued, unless it were proven that the suburban districts had also intentionally discriminated. Policy research continued to focus on quantifying the benefits of desegregated education, seemingly oblivious to the fact that resegregation was on the horizon and that desegregation's main policy tool was increasingly being attacked.

In the area of employment, the record of the 1970s similarly represents a mixed bag. By 1973, black poverty rates had fallen to historic lows after continuous declines since the mid-1960s. Affirmative action plans had been widely implemented, and a series of discriminatory labor practices had been litigated and struck down. The fragility of these gains became apparent, however, as the inflation and stagnant growth of the mid- and late 1970s eroded most of the interracial economic indicators to the point where they stood at the beginning of the decade. This erosion reinforced a growing public impression that a robust economy rather than civil rights initiatives was more important for narrowing racial inequalities. President Nixon's attempts to promote "black capitalism" were half-hearted, at best, and the subsequent Ford and Carter administrations developed no strategies for ghetto economic development.

Advances in computer technology allowed researchers the opportunity to employ new statistical tests for wage discrimination. Researchers collected data from workers of different races about their wages, education, gender, occupation, and employment history. Through a statistical method called multiple regression analysis, these data could be analyzed to discern how much of the interracial wage differentials were due to differences in nonracial characteristics (such as education) compared to racial characteristics. Although estimates varied widely depending on samples and methodological idiosyncrasies, this work documented significant interracial wage disparities that could not be attributed to differences in worker productivity.

Racial dimensions of the housing market showed some modest improvements. More and more blacks moved from central cities to suburbs, and the percentage of exclusively white-occupied communities dropped. Segregation scores in 12 major southern metropolitan areas fell from 75 in 1970 to 68 in 1980; the corresponding figures for 18 major nonsouthern metropolitan areas were 85 and 80. These changes were considered glacial by most analysts, and disappointed those who expected a much stronger impact from the fair housing legislation of 1968.

Several important strands of policy research provided explanations for the persistence of segregation. Anthony Downs's *Opening Up the Suburbs* (1973) cited the zoning policies of suburban jurisdictions that worked to exclude lower-income (hence, disproportionately minority) households, and argued for an array of affirmative marketing strategies. In 1971, Thomas Schelling developed his famous model of racial "tipping" of neighborhoods, which demonstrated theoretically how neighborhoods occupied by whites who did not mind having some minority neighbors would, nonetheless, change into all minority-occupied neighborhoods once the fraction of minority residents passed a certain threshold. Subsequent empirical studies of blacks' and whites' preferences for neighborhood racial composition conducted by Reynolds Farley and his associates supported the tipping hypothesis, although examinations of case studies of racial transition were unable to identify a single, universal tipping point.

Finally, the U.S. Department of Housing and Urban Development (HUD) sponsored an investigation of discrimination in 40 metropolitan areas in 1977 (Wienk et al. 1979). It employed teams of black and white "testers," representing the most unusual and important methodological advance in civil rights research during the post–World War II era. In testing, two investigators of different races were trained to pose as bona fide homeseekers, although their sole purpose was to gather information about how they were individually treated. Both were carefully matched by age and gender, and provided essentially similar information to housing agents about their income, family composition, and housing needs. The only feature that housing agents should have perceived as different was the race of the testers. One teammate approached the agent to inquire about vacancies and the other teammate followed after a short period. The testers' separate experiences in dealing with a particular landlord or real estate agent were compared to ascertain whether discrimination had occurred. The HUD study found that discrimination occurred roughly one out of every four times a black dealt with an agent, but typically was too subtle to be detected by the black tester without comparison to the white teammate's treatment.

The area experiencing the most new legislative initiatives during the 1970s revolved around mortgage lending discrimination. The Equal Credit Opportunity Act of 1974 prohibited discrimination in credit transactions based on race, color, national origin, sex, marital status, age, or source of income. The Home Mortgage Disclosure Act of 1975 required large commercial banks, savings and loans, and credit unions to report their mortgage loan volumes for individual census tracts in metropolitan areas. This permitted community groups and researchers to investigate whether certain areas were being unfairly denied credit or "redlined." The Community Reinvestment Act (CRA) of 1977 stipulated that lenders were obligated to "meet the credit needs of all segments of their communities," and mandated that federal financial regulatory agencies rate lenders on their CRA performance; those with poor ratings could be challenged when they sought approval for various business ventures from the regulators. As in the 1960s, this flurry of federal legislation was minimally stimulated and informed by policy research. Instead, it represented a response to the fierce political pressures brought by various community organizers and neighborhood groups.

Policy Research and Transformation from Race to Class

The most powerful impact of policy research during the 1970s was not in documenting trends, expanding understanding of phenomena, or evaluating particular programs. Rather, it was in gradually building a foundation for an altered public perception of the urban race question. In brief, this transformation involved switching the focus from race to "class." The momentum in this transformation was begun by Edward Banfield's *Unheavenly City* (1970). He argued that most urban blacks were "lower class," by which he meant that they were unable to imagine, plan for, and sacrifice for the future. From this perspective, rioting, crime, dropping out of school, and procreating out of wedlock were symptoms of this deeply seated, indelible psychological defect, rather than transitory adaptations to foreclosed opportunities. This theme reverberated even more strongly in William Julius Wilson's *The Declining Significance of Race* (1976). Wilson argued that civil rights laws and affirmative action plans were remarkably successful in opening up employment, education, and housing opportunities for middle-class blacks. The result was their outmigration from the ghettos, leaving behind the ever more desperate lower classes, who were now bereft of the social and economic resources formerly provided by their middle-class brethren. For these people, Wilson argued, it was the limited resources associated with their low socioeconomic status, not their race, that was most influential in shaping their opportunities.

The seeds planted by these analyses blossomed fully under President Ronald Reagan, who took office in 1981. Nevertheless, many of the same principles had already sprouted in the conventional wisdom by the end of the Jimmy Carter administration. Indeed, *Urban America in the Eighties* (1980), written by Carter's Commission for a National Agenda in the Eighties, did not even use the terms *race, discrimination, segregation,* or *ghettos* in its table of contents. Instead, it focused on the emerging urban *"underclass"* and recommended providing training and helping them to move to regions with better job opportunities. Discussion of antidiscrimination, desegregation, or community development policy was eschewed.

1981 TO 1987: THE "POST–CIVIL RIGHTS SOCIETY"

By the close of the 1970s the optimism and hubris that had characterized civil rights policy development only a decade earlier had all but vanished. Economic malaise, soaring inflation and interest rates, rising poverty, welfare dependency, and unemployment (especially among minorities) dominated the nation's attention. White flight from integrated schools and stubborn residential discrimination and segregation levels led many who were sympathetic to the cause of civil rights to question the efficacy of race-based policies. Public opinion polls showed an increasing acceptance of principles of racial equality but growing resistance to putting these principles into policy. For instance, over 80 percent of whites (and two-thirds of blacks) had become opposed to mandatory busing for desegregation.

Capitalizing on Pessimism to Recast the Issue

Perhaps most important, the newly fashionable term *"underclass"* became ubiquitous in public, political, and scholarly circles, generally conveying a lurid stereotype not only of the poor but of the black poor in particular. Simultaneously, enough minorities had moved into previously all-white schools, occupations, and neighborhoods (and had been elected mayors in major central cities) to foment a popular impression that we had, indeed, achieved an equal-opportunity society. Any minorities who did not "make it," therefore, did not deserve to because of some personal flaw such as *"underclass"* behavior.

The conservative forces in power skillfully capitalized on this mixture of public pessimism and skepticism about policy and on selective examples of minority success. By portraying the ghetto problem as one of individual failure that was impervious to public intervention, the Reagan administration erased the moral and pragmatic rationale for ghetto policy initiatives. Even more radically, by arguing that discrimination was a thing of the past, Reaganites justified the notion that to maintain (as opposed to create) an equal-opportunity society, the government needed to be "race neutral" in all its policies. Thus, affirmative action and desegregation policies of the previous era were redefined as "racist" and "discriminatory" and were systematically dismantled. President Reagan's appointments to the Supreme Court shared this vision and were influential in circumscribing the power of antidiscrimination laws and overturning a variety of race-conscious remedies.

As noted earlier, much of the intellectual foundation for the Reagan civil rights program was laid during the 1970s, but was given substantial reinforcement by such authors as George Gilder and Charles Murray, writing in the early 1980s. Their work was discussed fully in the context of poverty in chapter 3. Suffice it to note here that these authors' influence can be attributed to the fact that their conclusions resonated with the prevailing ideology in power, not because they were based on careful scholarship or rigorous statistical investigations. On the contrary, subsequent policy research has convincingly rebutted most of these writers' central assertions, as noted in chapter 3. This is a key illustration of how research can be used as a political weapon, even when it has little credibility by conventional standards of social science.

A final ingredient was added to the recipe for the "post civil rights" era: the rise of the so-called black conservatives. In previous decades the leadership of the Civil Rights movement had a unified intellectual foundation based on the principles of nondiscrimination, integration, and government activism. In the 1980s these principles were severely shaken by the conservative writings of several black policy researchers, most notably John Calmore, Thomas Sowell, Walter Williams, and Robert Woodson. They argued that, beyond enforcing civil rights laws, the federal government should scale back a vast range of its programs and regulations, from minimum wage laws to welfare to public housing, because they were having unintended adverse impacts on the minority community. Integration as an end in itself was denigrated; instead, self-help programs in the context of reinvigorated (but segregated) institutions within the minority community were advocated.

Retrenchment on Multiple Fronts

The combined effects of these emergent forces were apparent in education, employment, and housing. In education, resegregation proceeded unabated: by 1985 one-third of black children attended schools that had 90 percent or more black enrollment. By the end of the decade, enrollment in the country's 47 largest central-city districts consisted of 25 percent white, 42 percent black, 27 percent Hispanic, and 7 percent other minority students. By the 1980s the earlier system of separate (and unequal) schools within a district was thoroughly supplanted by separate (and unequal) school districts—central-city (predominantly minority) and suburban/private (predominantly white) districts. At the end of the decade the interdistrict segregation scores for white and black students were 72 in Philadelphia, 77 in Chicago, 79 in Cleveland, 81 in Newark, 90 in Detroit, and 91 in Gary, Indiana. Segregation scores for white and Hispanic students in the areas where most Hispanic students resided were 53 in Dallas, 54 in New York, 55 in Los Angeles, 59 in San Antonio, and 69 in Chicago. These districts were not only separate but also unequal: central-city districts had much higher concentrations of students from low-income backgrounds, yet spent substantially less per pupil due to their more limited fiscal capacity.

The situation was not quite so bleak in the area of employment. Policy research showed that the interracial wage differentials between those of equal age, gender, education, and occupation virtually disappeared, although the racial gap in nonemployment for males rose. Additional policy research showed that affirmative action plans in the 1970s did have a significant impact in opening up occupations and promotion options previously foreclosed to minorities. Ironically, the Supreme Court chose this area of relative success to focus its decisions. In *Bakke v. Regents of the University of California* (1984), the Court drastically limited the scope of affirmative action and ruled that rigid racial quotas were not permissible. In eight cases, culminating in *Patterson v. McLean Credit Union* (1989), the Court made it more difficult for plaintiffs to win employment discrimination suits and limited the damages they could be awarded. In *Wards Cove Packing Co. v. Atonio* (1989), the Court reversed a 1971 ruling that prohibited employers from discriminating racially by utilizing job requirements that were unrelated to the successful performance of the task. Henceforth, aggrieved parties would be required to demonstrate how each individual hiring practice both had an adverse racial impact and was unrelated to job performance.

On the housing front, the assault on prior policy initiatives was spearheaded by the Department of Justice. Especially noteworthy were department suits against two apartment complexes, one in New York and one in Chicago, that employed racial quotas as a means to achieve stable racial integration. Although it can be argued that such quotas

are unwise because they serve primarily to restrict housing opportunities available to minorities, the denigration of the value of integration
and a strict adherence to race-neutrality principles seemed equally
important motivations for the department.

Yet Another Reformulation of the Race Issue

At the close of the 1980s, once again William Julius Wilson's research
heralded an emerging conception of the race question. His 1987 book,
The Truly Disadvantaged, provided a cogent, if often speculative,
analysis of the growing "underclass" in the ghettos. The fundamental
force currently shaping the ghetto was posited as deindustrialization:
the loss of manufacturing jobs in or near the ghettos that provided the
main avenue for those of modest skill to achieve middle-class status.
As the ranks of the ghetto unemployed swelled, alternative forms
of income (welfare, illegal activities) and dealing with frustration
(substance abuse, violence) became more attractive. As the pool of
"marriageable" males evaporated, women were encouraged to bear
children out of wedlock. Ironically, argued Wilson, the very successes
of the earlier civil rights initiatives in opening housing and employment opportunities for minorities deprived the ghetto of the role
models, networks, and resources provided by their middle-class
neighbors. As social, economic, and physical isolation intensified, a
tangle of pathologies erupted in the ghetto, rendering its residents
"truly disadvantaged."

Wilson did not blame ghetto residents for their own problems, as
did much of the "underclass" literature of the time. It was not merely
"bad values" but the social structure that kept many urban blacks
impoverished. However, his emphasis on the pivotal force of deindustrialization ultimately proved resonant with the prevailing spirit of
race neutrality. That is, Wilson argued that further efforts at antidiscrimination and affirmative action policies would prove ineffective in
aiding the truly disadvantaged in the ghetto.

1988 TO 1994: REDISCOVERY OF RACE

Despite the prevailing conventional wisdom of race neutrality, during
the 1980s a significant body of new conceptual and empirical research
was accumulating. Much of this was incorporated in the National
Research Council's *A Common Destiny: Blacks and American Society*

(1989), called "the most definitive report card on race in 20 years." Unlike in the 1960s, when policy researchers were rather passive respondents to legislation spawned by popular movements, during the late 1980s policy researchers were instrumental in igniting long-dormant public interest and in shaping politicians' perceptions of the race issue. The result was a flurry of new programmatic initiatives in all aspects of the urban racial issue: education, employment, housing, and lending.

Education

In education, Gary Orfield was the central figure disseminating the facts of resegregation between school districts, and the consequent concentration of minorities in big-city districts that had weaker in-structional resources and higher concentrations of needy students. Jonathan Kozol's *Savage Inequalities* (1992) illustrated the abysmal level of resources available to some center-city school districts. Though less statistically rigorous than the Coleman report of 25 years earlier, *Savage Inequality's* vignettes better captured the cross-group differences in educational quality and shifted public opinion through its dramatic portrayals. The focus of legal suits began moving toward multiple-district remedies and statewide school funding allocation schemes that would better equalize fiscal resources across districts.

Employment

Employment discrimination was restored to public attention by two well-publicized Urban Institute studies that employed paired testers who posed as job seekers. Hispanic-Anglo tests conducted in San Diego and Chicago in 1989 found that Hispanic male testers were offered 36 percent fewer entry-level jobs than their equally well-qual-ified Anglo teammates; the comparable figure for black-white tests conducted in Chicago and Washington, D.C., in 1990 was 23 percent (Fix and Struyk 1994). New surveys of employers confirmed a hard-ening of their racial stereotypes, especially as they related to young black males. Partially in response to this evidence and in reaction to the previously mentioned Supreme Court rulings, Congress passed the Civil Rights Act of 1991, which restored many of the standards of proof of employment discrimination that only three years before had been stripped by the Court.

Policy researchers also provided important new evidence on the role of residential segregation in perpetuating interracial economic disparities. "Spatial mismatch," a concept originally introduced by John Kain in 1968, argued that minorities confined in central-city ghettos had less access to burgeoning job opportunities in the distant suburbs, and this was reflected in their lower rates of employment (Kain 1992). Keith Ihlanfeldt's sophisticated statistical studies of this phenomenon in the 1980s indicated that spatial mismatch was an important economic barrier (1994). James Rosenbaum (1995) and his associates studied the experiences of black welfare mothers and their families who moved to the Chicago suburbs pursuant to the 1969 *Gautreaux* decision, and found persuasive evidence of their increased educational, social, and economic opportunities. Such evidence prompted Congress in 1992 to authorize the Moving to Opportunity Program, a demonstration to replicate the *Gautreaux*-type desegregation plan in five additional metropolitan areas.

The most comprehensive attack on the race-neutral view of interracial economic differentials was provided by Douglas Massey and his colleagues. Massey and Denton's *American Apartheid* (1993) tested the theses advanced in Wilson's *The Truly Disadvantaged* and found several wanting. Massey and Denton found that data did not reveal a major outmigration of minority middle-class households from the ghetto as a result of civil rights laws, and that deindustrialization only concentrated poverty spatially where there was a high degree of racial residential segregation.

Housing

Legislative enhancements flowing from policy research also occurred in the area of housing. In 1988 the Fair Housing Amendments Act was passed, primarily on the strength of policy research involving paired testing that showed continued high levels of discrimination. The act expanded protection to include family status and disability, accelerated the complaint adjudication process by instituting a HUD-sponsored system of administrative law judges, empowered the Department of Justice to initiate investigations of systemic patterns and practices of discrimination, and increased penalties for violators. The Fair Housing Initiatives Program was instituted by HUD in 1987 to fund private, nonprofit fair housing groups to conduct testing and litigate suspicious findings; funding for the program has subsequently been increased. The need for these initiatives was rendered indisputable by the HUD-sponsored paired testing study conducted in 1989 by The Urban Institute in 25 metropolitan areas (Turner, Struyk, and Yinger 1991). That study found that both blacks and Hispanics in both rental and sales markets faced some degree of discrimination in half of their contacts with landlords and real estate agents. Blacks (and Hispanics) in the sales market had, on average, 21 percent (22 percent) fewer homes recommended or shown to them than their otherwise identical white teammates. In the rental market, the comparable figure was 25 percent (11 percent) fewer apartments.

Mortgage Lending

Both journalistic articles and policy research reawakened interest in mortgage lending discrimination in 1988. These studies examined Home Mortgage Disclosure Act data from lenders and found that the numbers of applications from and mortgage loans to predominantly minority-occupied neighborhoods were significantly less than those from and to comparable, predominantly white-occupied neighborhoods. Mainly because of these provocative findings, the Financial Institutions Recovery, Reform, and Enforcement Act of 1989 (or the savings and loan bailout bill) included strengthened Home Mortgage Disclosure Act reporting requirements that, for the first time, publicly detailed the disposition of individual loan applications; the race, gender, and income of the applicant; and the location of the property. Analyses of the first set of such data in 1991 revealed that minority applicants were rejected at roughly twice the rate of white applicants of the same gender and income.

Skeptics in the federal financial institution regulatory community, which is charged with examining lenders to ensure civil rights compliance, argued that these findings were not conclusive proof of discrimination because the data did not control for other differences among applicants, such as employment history and credit worthiness. A crucial piece of policy research conducted by the Federal Reserve Bank of Boston answered these skeptics (Munnell et al. 1992). The bank's analysis of applications from over 300 Boston lenders statistically controlled for all relevant differences among applicants, and concluded that blacks and Hispanics were 60 percent more likely to be rejected than comparable white applicants. The proof was bolstered by the Justice Department's findings of discrimination by major mortgage lenders in five major suits filed during the 1990s. Currently, the regulators are attempting to better detect and deter what has been revealed to them as a major failure to meet their mandate.

Paired testing, a methodology that was first developed in the housing field and later extended to employment, was also applied to the field of mortgage lending during the late 1980s. Pilot studies revealed cases in which prospective minority borrowers were misinformed and discouraged from filling out applications by loan officers. At this writing, paired testing investigations of lenders in several metropolitan areas are being conducted by fair-housing organizations under the sponsorship of HUD.

Holistic Views of Urban Racial Issues

Beyond studies that focused on particular dimensions of the race question, the late 1980s and early 1990s also witnessed a growing understanding and statistical quantification of the complex, mutually reinforcing elements of the ghetto, best embodied in *The Metropolis in Black and White: Place, Power, and Polarization* (Galster and Hill 1992). The book's thesis is as follows: segregated schools provide minority students inferior opportunities for intellectual achievement and the attainment of credentials. These constrained opportunities increase the probability that minorities will be the least likely to be hired and, even if hired, will be segregated into less-rewarding occupations. School segregation also contributes to housing segregation because the existence of predominantly minority student bodies often repels white parents who might otherwise move into the community.

Employment discrimination contributes to minorities' inferior rates of employment and wage levels. Discrimination in housing and lending is a prime contributor to residential segregation. This segregation limits minorities' access to high-quality, desegregated educational opportunities. It also limits their information about and access to suburban jobs that hold the promise of stability, on-the-job training, decent pay, and advancement potential.

Thus, by limiting physical access to work, the means by which people become productive workers, and the occupations that help them attain economic success, discrimination and segregation in schools, employment, and housing systematically create and perpetuate a host of socioeconomic inequalities among racial and ethnic groups. These disparities manifest themselves in many ways, but perhaps most dramatically in higher rates of poverty, unemployment, school and labor force dropouts, welfare dependency, crime, and substance abuse for minority individuals.

These economic and social inequalities reinforce the stereotypes held by some whites. They legitimize whites' prejudices about the "undesirable characteristics" supposedly possessed by all members of a minority group. Such reinforced prejudices make it more likely, in turn, that white households will want to perpetuate all dimensions of segregation, and will be motivated to continue discriminatory acts.

This conceptualization of the issue holds daunting implications for policymakers: the ghetto must be attacked on a variety of fronts simultaneously. Piecemeal efforts will not sufficiently unravel the nexus of relationships to significantly address the problems. The need for an all-out attack on the ghetto has been often articulated by the secretary of HUD, Henry Cisneros. His philosophy is to fight self-destructive behaviors and racism, deconcentrate racial and economic ghettos, and "build community" from presumably diverse communities sharing common civic values.

CONCLUSION AND PROSPECTS

During the 1950s and 1960s there was an increasingly common public view of the race issue: severe inequality and segregation were the result of individual and institutional acts of discrimination directed against people of color. These acts were documented more potently by the media than by researchers. Buttressed by a prevailing ideology of legislative and judicial activism, this diagnosis led in the 1960s to a plethora of civil rights legislation and court-imposed remedies, all of which were quite uninformed by systematic policy research or analysis regarding the dynamics of the emerging urban racial ghetto. The civil disturbances of 1965 to 1968 brought these urban issues to the forefront. Although the Kerner Commission provided an insightful diagnosis and changed public understanding of the issues, insufficient political will could be mustered to undertake the significant desegregation and community development policies that it advocated.

By the 1970s it had become clear that civil rights laws and court-ordered remedies were creating enough tangible social changes—some desirable and some not—to generate a shift in public perceptions. Equality of treatment under the law seemed to be widely supported, but seeking remedies for past discrimination through affirmative action and school busing generated resentment and counterproductive reactions among many whites. Quantitative policy research during this period did little to inform or alter this changing perception of the desirability and effectiveness of governmental intervention in this area. On the contrary, the most influential works were more theoretical and speculative in nature, and reframed the debate over urban racial issues into one of class rather than race.

The conservative ascendancy of the early 1980s drew strength from three elements: inadequately designed prototype policies of the 1960s, growing public dissatisfaction with governmental intervention in the area of civil rights, and emerging policy research that downplayed the significance of race. The resulting transformation of the issue into "race-neutral" terms led, in turn, to a dismantling of the policies and legal interpretations initiated years earlier.

Policy research contributed greatly to yet another reformulation of the race issue in the late 1980s. Policy research has shown the essential vacuousness of the race-neutral approach by clearly documenting that racial discrimination still occurs frequently in many contexts; that segregation in schools, occupations, and neighborhoods persists (although in different forms than before); and that urban racial phenomena are interwoven in a complex web of mutually supportive interrelationships. These understandings appeared to be motivating the deliberations of both the Departments of Justice and HUD during the early 1990s.

At this writing the first signs of yet another trajectory of the roller coaster are emerging. In his July 1995 speech, President Clinton promised a dismantling of affirmative action programs that gave preference to the unqualified, involved reverse discrimination, and continued indefinitely. A court in Hartford, Connecticut, has ruled that vast discrepancies in educational quality between city and suburban school districts do not violate state constitutional protections and are not the purview of legal remedy because school segregation can be explained by residential segregation, not de jure school board policies. Funding for the second year of the Moving to Opportunity Program, a multicity demonstration allowing public housing residents to move into nonpoverty areas, was canceled due to racist backlash in suburban Baltimore. Proposals to weaken Community Reinvestment Act requirements for many lenders and to eliminate funding of the Fair Housing Initiatives Program are before Congress. None of these initiatives have been driven by policy research; rather they have been motivated by critical perceptions of affirmative action as the sine qua non of civil rights policy and by a growing ideology that promotes a reduced federal role in a panoply of issue areas. Time will tell how the ideological and political constraints prevailing in 1995 will shape, and be shaped by, the next round of policy research, but the current direction toward scaling back anti-discrimination, desegregation, and affirmative action policies is clear.

Note

1. *School busing* refers to efforts to desegregate schools by busing children from their homes to schools outside their own neighborhoods. *Affirmative action* refers to initiatives to increase employment and education opportunities for minorities and women.

SUGGESTED READING

Darden, Joe, Harriet Duleep, and George Galster. 1992. "Civil Rights in Metropolitan America." *Journal of Urban Affairs* 14(3/4):469–96.

Farley, Reynolds, and Walter Allen. 1987. *The Color Line and the Quality of Life in America.* New York: Alfred A. Knopf.

Farley, Reynolds, and William Frey. 1994. "Changes in the Segregation of Whites from Blacks during the 1980s." *American Sociological Review* 59(February):23–45.

Fix, Michael, and Raymond Struyk, eds. 1994. *Clear and Convincing Evidence: Testing for Discrimination in America.* Washington, D.C.: Urban Institute Press.

Galster, George. 1992. "Research on Discrimination in Housing and Mortgage Markets: Assessment and Future Directions." *Housing Policy Debate* 3(2):639–84.

Galster, George, and Edward Hill, eds. 1992. *The Metropolis in Black and White: Place, Power, and Polarization.* New Brunswick, N.J.: Rutgers University, Center for Urban Policy Research.

Holzer, Harry. 1994. "Black Employment Problems: New Evidence, Old Questions." *Journal of Policy Analysis and Management* 13(4):699–722.

Ihlanfeldt, Keith, and David Sjoquist. 1990. "Job Accessibility and Racial Differences in Youth Employment Rates." *American Economic Review* 80(1):267–76.

Jargowsky, Paul. 1994. "Ghetto Poverty among Blacks in the 1980s." *Journal of Policy Analysis and Management* 13(2):288–310.

Jaynes, Gerald, and Robin Williams, eds. 1989. *A Common Destiny: Blacks and American Society.* Washington, D.C.: National Academy Press.

Lemann, Nicholas. 1991. *The Promised Land: The Great Black Migration and How it Changed America.* New York: Alfred A. Knopf.

Massey, Douglas, and Nancy Denton. 1993. *American Apartheid: Segregation and the Making of the Underclass.* Cambridge, Mass.: Harvard University Press.

North Carolina Law Review Association. 1993. "Symposium: The Urban Crisis—The Kerner Commission Report Revised." *North Carolina Law Review* 71(5):1283–1786.

Orfield, Gary, and Carol Ashkinaze. 1991. *The Closing Door: Conservative Policy and Black Opportunity.* Chicago: University of Chicago Press.

202   *Reality and Research*

202   *Reality and Research*

Rosenbaum, James. 1995. "Changing the Geography of Opportunity by Expanding Residential Choice: Lessons from the Gautreaux Program." *Housing Policy Debate* 6(1):231–70.

Schuman, Howard, Charlotte Steeh, and Lawrence Bobo. 1985. *Racial Attitudes in America*. Cambridge, Mass.: Harvard University.

Wilson, William. 1987. *The Truly Disadvantaged*. Chicago: University of Chicago Press.

Yu, Corinne, and William Taylor, eds. 1995. *New Challenges: The Civil Rights Record of the Clinton Administration Mid-Term*. Washington, D.C.: Citizens' Commission on Civil Rights.

Other References

Banfield, Edward C. 1970. *The Unheavenly City: The Nature and Future of Our Urban Crisis*. Boston: Little, Brown.

Clark, Kenneth. 1965. *Dark Ghetto*. New York: Harper and Row.

Downs, Anthony. 1973. *Opening Up the Suburbs: An Urban Strategy for America*. New Haven, Conn.: Yale University Press.

Haley, Alex, and Malcolm X. 1976. *The Autobiography of Malcolm X*. Amereon Ltd.

Ihlanfeldt, Keith. 1994. "The Spatial Mismatch Between Jobs and Residential Locations Within Urban Areas." *Cityscape: Journal of Policy Development and Research*. Washington, D.C.: Office of Policy Development and Research, U.S. Department of Housing and Urban Development.

Jaynes, Gerald Davis, and Robin M. Williams, Jr., eds. 1989. *A Common Destiny: Blacks and American Society*. Washington University: National Academy Press.

Kain, John. 1968. "Housing Segregation, Negro Unemployment, and Metropolitan Decentralization." *The Quarterly Journal of Economics* 82:175–97.

Kozol, Jonathan. 1992. *Savage Inequalities: Children in America's Schools*. New York: Crown.

Munnell, Alicia, Lynne Browne, James McEneaney, and Geoff Tootell. 1992. "Mortage Lending in Boston: Interpreting the HMDA Data," Working Paper. Boston: Federal Reserve Bank of Boston.

Taeuber, Alma and Karl. 1965. *Negroes in Cities: Residential Segregation and Neighborhood Change*. Chicago: Aldine.

Turner, Margery, Raymond Struyk, and John Yinger. 1991. *The Housing Discrimination Study* (multiple volumes). Washington, D.C.: The Urban Institute/U.S. Department of Housing and Urban Development.

Schelling, Thomas. 1971. "Dynamic Models of Segregation." *Journal of Mathematical Sociology* 1: 143–86.

U.S. Office of Education. 1966. *Equality of Educational Opportunity: Summary*. Washington, D.C.: U.S. Government Printing Office.

U.S. President's Commission for a National Agenda for the Eighties. 1980. *Urban America in the Eighties: Perspectives and Prospects—A Report of the Panel on Policies and Prospects for the Metropolitan and Nonmetropolitan America.* Washington, D.C.: U.S. Government Printing Office.

Wienk, Ronald, Clifford Reid, John Simonson, and Fred Eggers. 1979. *Measuring Racial Discrimination in American Housing Markets.* Washington, D.C.: U.S. Department of Housing and Urban Development/Policy Development and Research.

Wilson, William Julius. 1978. *The Declining Significance of Race: Blacks and Changing American Institutions.* Chicago: The University of Chicago Press.

Chapter Ten

INTERGOVERNMENTAL FINANCIAL RELATIONS

George E. Peterson

Most domestic policy in the United States, even if formulated in Washington, must be implemented by state and local governments. A new policy agenda therefore must include a strategy as to how the federal government and state and local sector will work together. In recent years, the most problematic element of this strategy design has been the intergovernmental financing plan.

In principle, it might seem that the logical sequence in which to attack domestic policy issues would be first to identify what effective governmental policy would be, examine the costs of implementing the policy, then analyze the capacity to pay of the different governmental partners and allocate costs accordingly. If necessary, the policy approach could be revised to bring it within overall budget constraints. In reality, financing questions have never been so straightforward. Taxpayers' willingness to pay for government programs always has intruded at the earliest stages of policy discussion, and no level of government has had the fiscal detachment to view costs paid by it as equivalent to costs paid by other levels of government.

Over the last 25 years, the financing side steadily has become more important to public policy debate. The most heated controversies have dealt with tax rates, tax structure, and the type of aid programs that the federal government should be providing to state and local governments. As we approach the 21st century the budget debate is focusing almost exclusively on federal deficit reduction. Other aspects of policy design are being relegated to a distinctly second tier of importance.

In this chapter, we look at financing strategy as a policy choice. We use national urban policy to illustrate how the balance between financing and programmatic content has shifted over time. A quarter century ago, the financing issues surrounding cities seemed conceptually simple, even if filled with political difficulty. By the late 1960s cities had become the locus of society's most severe social and environmental problems and the home of those most urgently in need of public help. At the same time, older cities in particular had begun to decline as manufacturing and economic centers. Their tax bases were eroding relative to the rest of the nation. In short, a mismatch had emerged between where the nation's problems were located and where the ability to pay for solutions lay—a mismatch that Walter W. Heller, chairman of the Council of Economic Advisors during the Kennedy and Johnson administrations, summed up with the aphorism "prosperity gives the national government the affluence and local governments the effluents."

To most observers at the time, this situation seemed to argue for shifting part of the urban financing burden to the country at large. Policy advocates might differ on how this should be done, or on the appropriate mix that should be struck between program-specific targeting of intergovernmental aid and a laissez-faire grant policy that trusted local or state governments to make their own decisions about how to spend federal dollars. But the principle that federal, state, and local budgets should be combined to attack urban problems went fundamentally unchallenged in policy circles.

Over time this consensus vanished. Angry citizens focused more and more on the tax burdens they were being asked to assume. The tax revolt started with local governments, then spread to the state and federal level. Constitutional tax limitations and organized demands for tax cuts restricted the public sector's ability to raise funds, and placed voters in more direct control of tax and spending decisions. A distrustful citizenry (and later, under Ronald Reagan, a distrustful presidency) used aggressive controls on government's revenue-raising capacity as a way to limit the scope of government, both at the federal and state-local levels. Concentration on tax cuts and deficit reduction has continued to erode the possibility of policy innovations that cost money. The cost of government has become the primary political concern.

The primacy of the cost and financing side of the budget has left its mark on policy research, as well. Because of the importance voters give to pocketbook issues, public finance analysis has been conducted closer to the reality of politics than analysis in many functional policy areas. However, the users of studies have changed over the last quarter century. Initially, public finance studies were offered as technical support for Washington-inspired policy reforms, and aimed largely at an audience of professional policy designers. But the tax revolt popularized public finance. As frustrated citizens grappled to find ways to control public spending, a new body of public finance theory—"public choice" theory—evolved to assist (and reflect) this movement. Suddenly public finance became the stuff of newspaper editorial pages and referenda campaigns. Many well-known analysts shortened the distance between research and policy by taking their conclusions directly to the public, rather than waiting for their results to filter into public discourse via the professional literature.

THE WAR ON POVERTY AND THE GREAT SOCIETY

For the first six decades of this century, city finances rested largely undisturbed. A municipal officer who dozed off in 1900 and reawakened in 1960 might not have recognized the physical structure of the city but would have found few surprises in the city budget. The local property tax still was the principal source of city revenue. Traditional local functions such as police protection, firefighting, public schooling, and local road maintenance still accounted for the great majority of city government expenditures. Direct aid from the federal government was inconsequential. There was little controversy over what city government should be doing or how it should pay for its spending.

The first challenge to business as usual came from the War on Poverty and the associated response to the "urban crisis" of the 1960s. Poverty, racial discrimination, economic decline and attempts at revitalization, welfare dependency—all the critical issues confronted by the War on Poverty and the Great Society—seemed to assume their most acute form in cities, especially big cities. The War on Poverty became, in effect, an urban program, but one that challenged the traditional presumption that local authorities bore the responsibility for dealing with local problems.

To those in Washington, city governments seemed to lack both the resources and, often, the policy skills to cope with the newly perceived problems. As a consequence, federal officials felt obliged to design a strategy of external intervention. This required finding a way to deliver federal dollars, as well as federal programs incorporating federal policy solutions, to the local level.

Designing Urban Aid

In retrospect, it is remarkable how little policy debate took place over how federal aid to cities should be structured. A desire for comprehensive reform may have inspired the War on Poverty, but the war was fought as hundreds of individual battles and minor skirmishes over programmatic specifics. Each new problem area, as it was identified, tended to give rise to its own narrowly targeted intergovernmental program. Central-city redevelopment was financed by one set of intergovernmental programs (urban renewal and Model Cities), housing construction and community development by another set, and myriads of smaller initiatives such as community legal services or regional planning by still other sets of programs.

From a fiscal perspective, the principal instrument for implementing intergovernmental policy was the categorical grant-in-aid. Categorical grants deliver federal money to states or localities in return for implementing specific federal programs. At least in the beginning, virtually all categorical grants were designed as matching grants. To obtain federal dollars, city governments had to spend some of their own locally raised resources on the federal program. The more of its own money a local authority was willing to spend, the more federal aid it qualified for.

The *system* of categorical grants that evolved from this approach targeted hundreds of different federal grant programs on hundreds of separately identified local problems. This result was not really intended by any of the program authors. Rather, it was the cumulative product of finding the quickest, seemingly most direct means of financing separate federal initiatives.

Impact of the Poverty War on City Finances

Intended or not, the War on Poverty and Great Society transformed urban public finance in the following ways.

First, city government spending, especially in big cities, accelerated at a record rate. Between 1962 and 1972, big cities' spending per capita almost *tripled*, keeping pace with the revenue growth of America's premier growth company of the era, IBM. In cities that were losing population, generally the cities with the highest concentrations of social problems, the number of city employees per 1,000 residents climbed from 25.4 in 1964 to 35.8 in 1973.

Second, federal aid fueled the greatest part of this growth. Cities suddenly became dependent on external aid for large portions of their budgets. Federal aid to state and local governments surged by 14.7 percent per year between 1965 and 1970, then grew still faster to a rate of more than 22 percent growth per year between 1970 and 1973. In cities such as Baltimore, Boston, Buffalo, Detroit, Newark, New York, and Philadelphia, external aid accounted for well over half of all the expansion of government spending that occurred, while another part was financed by cities' growing indebtedness.

Third, direct grants from Washington to cities displaced the more traditional federal path of aid to states, whereby states assisted cities to the extent they (states) deemed appropriate. This trend toward direct federal assistance to cities reflected a deep skepticism on the part of those commanding the War on Poverty about states' willingness to face up to the problems of the poor, of racial minorities, or of large urban centers. The new federal aid programs often deliberately bypassed the states. Federal money was sent directly to the local level or even to community organizations, carrying federally defined programmatic objectives.

Last, the breadth of city government responsibilities vastly expanded. Most of the newly assumed functions were in the area of social welfare. In New York City, between 1961 and 1969, the share of primarily redistributive functions in the city budget (public assistance, social services, health, and housing) rose from 25.8 percent to 35.8 percent—by historical standards representing a massive change in budget allocation. The share of developmental functions in New York City's budget (infrastructure and transportation) fell by half over the same period. The relative change in government spending was even larger in some other cities. Often the new responsibilities were accepted by local public officials without much enthusiasm. Some of the new federal aid went to community organizations that were not accountable, or perhaps even hostile, to city hall. Part of it was used to coax local governments into delivering social programs that lacked broad voter support. Even at a later date, when federal funding for social programs was being cut, surveys found that local government officials were essentially indifferent to, or even favored, federal spending reductions in such parts of city budgets as community legal services, regional cooperation, low-income public housing construction, and temporary youth unemployment programs. These were viewed by local governments as federal programs that federal agencies should operate and pay for directly if they wanted to pursue them.

THE DEBATE OVER CATEGORICAL GRANTS

The experience gained with categorical grants under the War on Poverty and Great Society programs shaped a generation's view of intergovernmental finance. At the time categorical grants were adopted, however, little systematic thought was given to the shape of the grant structure. The only analysts who seemed to notice the evolving character of grant design were political scientists, who for the most part viewed it as a demonstration of the federal system's capacity to adjust to the realities of twentieth century interdependence. In a famous article, Martin Grodzins likened the reality of modern federalism to a marble cake, in which the responsibilities of different levels of government were tied together in overlapping swirls, rather than rigidly separated as the traditional textbooks would have it. The basically favorable attitude that political scientists had toward the new arrangements was conveyed by the labels chosen to describe them. The binding together of different levels of government through categorical program grants was dubbed "Cooperative Federalism," and Washington's extension of federal funds to local community groups was labeled "Creative Federalism," presumably because it reached directly to the people without the regimenting intermediation of government.

What appeared to political theorists as "cooperative" and "creative," however, increasingly appeared to those tracking implementation in the field as intergovernmental paralysis. A series of studies followed the grants designed in Washington through to local impact. The authors of the best known work of this genre, Jeffrey Pressman and Aaron Wildavsky, aptly summarized their conclusions in the title (abbreviated here) *Implementation: How Great Expectations in Washington Are Dashed in Oakland; or, Why It's Amazing that Federal Programs Work at All.* . . . Martha Derthick demonstrated that it was not distance alone that hobbled implementation. When Lyndon Johnson announced a grant program to build model new communities on surplus federally owned land in cities, he decided to start with a demonstration project just a few miles from the White House. Derthick's title, *New Towns In-Town: Why a Federal Program Failed*, also reflects her conclusions.

Studies of federal program implementation such as these contributed significantly to the next generation's redesign of intergovernmental financial aid, because they demonstrated it was not feasible to construct detailed grant programs in Washington and expect that they would be implemented in the field as planned (or perhaps at all).

Categorical grants to local governments also posed federal management problems. Between 1962 and 1967, the number of federal formula or project grants to state and local governments skyrocketed from 160 to 379. The challenge of administering this number of grant programs was overwhelming. Recipients were supposed to comply with all of the (sometimes conflicting) regulations. Federal managers were supposed to monitor compliance, a task made immensely more difficult now that monies were being paid directly to thousands of local governmental units and countless additional community organizations, rather than to 50 states. No one at the federal or local level could maintain a coherent overview of the totality of federal aid and the incentives it created. There was even less chance that local officials, constrained by detailed grant regulations, could construct a genuinely *local* strategy of response to the priority concerns that lay behind federal program design.

Matching Grants and the Federal Budget

The matching grant strategy, which seemed so appealing as a way to augment federal resources with local funding, proved to be a fiscal loose cannon for the federal budget. Federal officials discovered that they could not control, or even predict accurately, how much local officials would choose to spend on matching-grant programs. Federal budget spending was being driven by thousands of local spending choices, each of which, once made, gave rise to a federal matching obligation. Rather quickly, federal officials moved to "cap" most of the matching grant programs. That is, the federal government promised to match local spending only up to a certain level. This approach had the advantage of limiting Washington's budget exposure, but reduced the attractiveness of local spending, which could no longer be used in unlimited amounts to leverage federal dollars. Local governments began to cut back on their spending for federal priorities. In response, Washington began to rewrite grant legislation to *require* that local governments spend minimum amounts on programs as a condition of receiving *any* program aid, or sometimes as a condition of receiving other types of federal assistance. What had begun as a federal incentive strategy, attractive to localities because it offered new budgetary resources, ended as a series of federal spending mandates. By the beginning of the 1970s, the administration of categorical grants had become a morass of federal directiveness.

THE REVENUE SHARING ERA

A growing appreciation of the fragmentation brought on by the categorical grants system stirred several observers to reconsider how the federal government should relate fiscally to lower levels of government, especially the cities. The intellectual work of this re-examination began under Lyndon Johnson, but it did not bear political fruit until Richard Nixon came to office in 1969.

The Fiscal Basis of Urban Problems

The rethinking began by attempting to construct a more general analysis of cities' problems. The recurring problems of cities (especially larger cities) were seen to stem from an imbalance between their spending responsibilities and their revenue sources. Cities were saddled with the most difficult, nearly intractable problems of the time: concentrations of poverty, welfare dependency, racial strife, and deteriorating public education. Spending on these problems should have been rising rapidly, reflective of their importance to the nation. Yet cities were tied to inelastic tax bases that prevented their revenues from rising even at the rate of national income. Thus, the gap between expenditure needs and revenue sources continually widened, causing the problems to become greater and leading the cities periodically into financial crises. Simultaneously, the federal government's tax structure generated ever larger revenue collections and threatened to place a fiscal drag on the economy through escalating budget surpluses. Budget surpluses at the federal level, it was thought, would become especially pressing once the peace dividend from ending the Viet Nam War was realized. In the words of Patrick Moynihan, who had been director of the MIT-Harvard Joint Center for Urban Studies, then became Special Assistant for Urban Affairs to President Nixon (and is now the senior U.S. senator from New York): "The basic equation, as it were, of American political economy is that for each 1 percent increase in the Gross National Product (GNP) the income of the federal government increases 1.5 percent while the normal income of city governments rises .5 to .75 at most."

This diagnosis of the underlying urban problem swiftly gained widespread bipartisan political and intellectual consensus. The same argument is found, in essentially the same words, in Walter Heller's writings, in the Brookings Institution's annual federal budget analyses, in political science essays of the time, and in the publications of the Advisory Commission on Intergovernmental Relations. The resulting policy prescription was no less widely shared. Fiscal imbalance could be cured only by a fundamental change in the assignment of national revenues. Cities needed to have automatic access to nationally collected revenues that would grow with inflation and the economy.

When the idea of revenue sharing, as it came to be known, was first proposed, it was taken for granted that the state and local sector, and especially cities, should claim a continually increasing share of national income. Early revenue-sharing proposals emphasized the desirability of giving state and local governments a fixed percentage of the federal government's highly elastic tax collections. This proposal became known as the Heller-Pechman plan, so styled because Walter Heller, chairman of the Council of Economic Advisors, and Joseph Pechman, director of economic studies at the Brookings Institution and chairman of a task force to study federal-state-local fiscal relations for Lyndon Johnson, urged similar revenue sharing plans as early as 1964. In the Heller-Pechman proposal, state and local spending was explicitly singled out as warranting priority over the two alternative uses for increased yields from the federal tax structure. These alternatives were to return money to the private sector by cutting federal tax rates or to increase direct federal spending. The magnitude of new revenue sought for state and local governments was substantial. In endorsing the revenue-sharing plan, Patrick Moynihan argued that the share of federal funding in state and local budgets should roughly double from the 17 percent share it represented in 1967 to more than one-third.

The revenue-sharing debate tacitly accepted the prevailing ideology of the time: that the public sector share of national spending should rise as incomes grew. The proposal to shift some of the public revenue and spending growth from the federal level of government to states and localities was seen as imaginative and innovative. However, the more sweeping alternative—to cut tax rates so as to keep incomes earned in private hands—was scarcely considered in policy circles. It was included as a logical possibility in the Heller-Pechman writings, but was judged to be unreasonable on its face because there remained so many unmet public needs in the cities and elsewhere. Policy debate turned quickly to the question of which *level* of government should deploy the additional resources.

Administratively, revenue sharing had the advantage of extricating the federal government from detailed programmatic involvement in local spending of the kind the implementation studies had criticized. Recommendations for "general" revenue sharing were usually accompanied by proposals to simplify the rest of the grant system by eliminating some of the smaller categorical grants and consolidating them into broader program areas, called block grants.

Results of the Revenue-Sharing Experiment

To a surprising degree, the revenue-sharing agenda was implemented as designed by the Heller-Pechman plan. "General Revenue Sharing" was introduced and passed as one of Nixon's first policy initiatives.

True, by the time it was enacted, it had lost some of its urban focus. Revenue sharing was extended to state governments as well as cities, and was budgeted for specific amounts rather than a percentage of federal revenue collections. Still, revenue sharing brought a significant increase in flexible funds for local governments. It was reinforced by some block grant consolidation, most notably in the Community Development Block Grant of 1974.

Although revenue sharing was a short-term political success, the underlying argument as to why revenue sharing was critical to cities' fiscal health and the country's social policy eventually collapsed on all fronts. This happened for several reasons.

First, state and local revenues ceased to be inelastic in the 1970s. With the explosion of the real estate market in that decade, the property tax suddenly became a tremendously elastic revenue source. For many years the property tax base grew faster than any other tax base in use in the United States, including that for the income tax or for general and specialized sales taxes. When property assessments were adjusted regularly to reflect market values (as happened in the most efficient property tax systems), property tax collections soared, as they did in California. Progressive state income taxes likewise became immense revenue generators in the high-inflation environment of the 1970s. It is true that tax base growth in a few big cities continued to lag, but this was the result of the cities' economic decline, not tax-base inelasticity. The fundamental premise that the urban tax base inevitably lagged national economic growth ceased to be true in the 1970s, just at the time national domestic policy embraced this notion.

Second, though city revenues grew at unprecedented rates from both local resources and revenue sharing, this growth turned out not to provide a cure for city financial crises. In fact, the 1970s brought the first true collapse of big-city finances since the Depression. New York City fell into a deep financial emergency in 1975 and had to be bailed out by extraordinary state intervention. Cleveland defaulted on a bond issue in 1977, the first big city to do so since the Depression. Instead of providing local governments with a financial cushion that protected them against crisis, the steady growth in external revenues seemed to dissolve local will to balance the city budget. Expenditures climbed even faster than revenues. In many big cities, the feeling solidified that external funders always would come to the rescue. This conviction led many economically declining cities to surrender control of city spending.

Third, city governments disappointed some urban advocates by their reluctance to use unrestricted federal monies to launch profound policy reforms of their own design. Cities always regarded revenue sharing as possibly temporary, and so used the federal transfers to purchase capital equipment, award wage increases, or otherwise pay for traditional types of spending. There were few local attempts to take on a new mission in tackling urban problems.

Finally and most fundamentally, the view that governments' historically assigned tax bases were immutable and that tax rates, at most, were subject to adjustment at the margin, proved utterly false. The Heller-Pechman-Moynihan view of fiscal reality was that each level of government had its legislatively or constitutionally assigned tax sources. Tax rates were also essentially fixed, since legislatures modified them only at a glacial pace. In this world, the tax "system" automatically generated revenues, much like a machine left on automatic pilot.

As elastic tax structures rolled out increasing tax collections during the 1970s, however, the nation's revenue system suddenly ceased to be a "given," and became the object of taxpayer revolt. As will be discussed below, tax limitation initiatives swept across the nation, slashing property tax rates and setting severe limits on future taxes and government spending.

Federal aid to cities peaked in 1978. That year the Carter administration released its national urban policy, calling for much greater federal support for large and old cities. To many contemporaries, it seemed that the cities and their problems were finally receiving political priority commensurate with the attention that policy analysts had been giving them for a decade and a half.

In the fall of 1978, however, Proposition 13—which greatly limited state and local governments' ability to freely implement new or raise existing taxes—passed in California. Traditional urban policy and intergovernmental finance strategies collapsed overnight. Federal assistance for cities reversed course as rapidly as it had risen. Virtually none of the Carter urban policy measures ever saw the light of day. Indeed, six months after the urban policy statement had been issued it already read like a document from another epoch, filled with expectations about federal funding and the redistributive role of federal programs that belonged to an earlier age of intergovernmental politics.

Reflections on the Revenue-Sharing Era

The tax revolt that began in 1978 ended the prevailing paradigm underlying urban policy and much of the rest of domestic policy of the era: namely, that the tax system could be counted on to generate revenue growth "automatically," and that policy experts and national leaders were free to decide on their own how to allocate these national revenues to tackle the domestic issues of greatest urgency. The tax revolt was in some ways a populist rebellion. It was a message sent by the taxpaying majority, indicating that it wanted less redistributional spending by government and, in fact, less government spending of all kinds.

As it turned out, policy analysts had underestimated almost all the elements of "choice" in state and local budgets. If a city government's spending needs and local tax receipts were in fact externally determined, an injection of federal revenue-sharing funds *would*, as hypothesized, improve the city's budget balance. However, both elements in this equation proved to be subject to choice. Cities had a large reservoir of program "needs." As their revenue picture improved, they began to fund new programs that met some previously unmet needs. Federal grants also turned out to substitute partially for local revenue collections. One use to which localities put federal general revenue sharing was to cut local taxes. As a result, the transfer of federal revenues to the local level did not substantially improve local fiscal conditions.

Role of Policy Analysis

Mainstream public finance research of the period failed to anticipate the debate that was about to erupt over public sector revenue levels and tax structure. The largest portion of research funding was tied up in formal monitoring studies of federal grant programs. Networks of local analysts painstakingly monitored the spending uses to which federal grant monies were put at the local level. The Brookings Institution alone launched multi-year, multi-site monitoring studies of General Revenue Sharing, the Community Development Block Grant, and the Comprehensive Employment and Training Act. These projects documented local spending patterns for the historical record. They helped resolve some arguments as to how local authorities respond to federal grant signals. Occasionally, local monitoring results influenced changes in federal grant formulas. For example, the targeting of the Community Development Block Grant (CDBG) was altered, in part because monitoring studies showed that the share of CDBG funds received by distressed cities was not as large as many believed it should be.

On broader questions of grant reform, however, monitoring studies encountered a basic paradox. The philosophical premise of General

Revenue Sharing was that local governments should be free to decide how to spend their transfers. The same argument, with some limitations, applied to CDBG and other block grants. Under these conditions, monitoring studies could document local spending choices and call attention to unexpected spending outcomes. But since there were few federal rules about how the money should be spent, and few specified program objectives beyond augmenting the revenues of fiscally straitened jurisdictions, there were correspondingly few policy questions to be answered by detailed monitoring of how funds were spent. Policy research became focused on increasingly narrow questions at a time when the basic landscape of public finance was about to be transformed. In this case, policy research failed to lead to a reconceptualization of the problem at hand, or even to recognize that such a reconceptualization was occurring elsewhere.

PUBLIC CHOICE THEORY AND THE TAX REVOLT

The tax revolt was a distinctively American phenomenon. It relied on instruments such as citizen initiative and public referendum that are virtually unique to the United States. The provisions for direct voter expression were installed, especially in western states, as protections against the remoteness of government and the perceived tendency of public officials, once in power, to cozy up to big business interests.

Generations had passed since initiatives and referenda actually had been used as policy tools on critical issues. When the first attempts were launched to revive referendum politics (in California—a state that is often the first to experiment with political and social reforms), mainstream policymakers patronizingly dismissed the tax limitation movement. After all, the chief architect of Proposition 13, Howard Jarvis, had led a checkered career that invited parody. He had founded his own transitory Conservative Party in California; he had raised money for Republican presidential candidate Barry Goldwater in 1964 until postal inspectors intervened on the grounds that all of the money raised was being used to pay salaries to Jarvis and his associates; and, by the 1970s, he had launched four other petition drives for tax limitations that had failed to get on the California ballot.

Circumstances in California in 1978 were different, however. The "inelastic" state and local tax system seemed to have burst out of control with the real estate boom. In Los Angeles, the heart of the tax revolt, 500,000 homes were reassessed in 1978 for property tax purposes as part of the region's triennial reassessment cycle. The assessments on these homes, based on market value, increased by an *average* of 125 percent. The state government revenue system in that year alone generated $5 billion more than projected, leading to a state budget surplus of similar magnitude. Governor Jerry Brown's plans for using the excess revenue to fund a $300 million housing program, alternative energy development, and even a state-operated space satellite suddenly seemed like parodies of government as usual. Jarvis and his supporters gathered 1.25 million signatures to place Proposition 13 on the California ballot. The initiative was approved by voters by an overwhelming margin of 65 percent to 35 percent. It rolled back property taxes to 1 percent of market value; limited year-to-year increases in property assessments to 2 percent per year as long as homeowners occupied the same homes; stipulated that any future increase in state taxes must receive approval by a two-thirds vote of the state legislature; and allowed cities, counties, and local special districts to introduce new taxes, or raise rates on existing taxes, only if they could secure two-thirds voter approval at a local referendum.

Within 18 months, similarly inspired constitutional or legal tax and spending limits were ratified by voters in Tennessee, Texas, Michigan, Massachusetts, Arizona, Hawaii, New Jersey, and large numbers of local jurisdictions. All in all, 11 different statewide tax or spending limitations were ratified in 1978, affecting either state government or all local governments in a state. Another 13 limitations were approved in 1979 and 7 in 1980, before the movement suddenly evaporated, replaced by tax-cutting pressure at the federal level. Many of the initiatives went beyond Proposition 13 to limit *all* sources of state or local revenues or to limit aggregate government spending. States and localities not subjected to formal tax limitations scrambled to "voluntarily" curb spending.

Intellectual Foundations of the Tax Revolt

Although the tax revolt had its populist roots, it also drew heavily on conservative political theory and conservative theorists' critique of traditional public finance. Several strands of conservative writing were woven together. One strand emphasized the tendency of government bureaucracies to aggrandize themselves by constantly expanding government activities and attempting to insulate the bureaucracy from public accountability. The best-known (and most insightful) volume in this vein was William Niskanen's *Bureaucracy and Representative Government* (1971). A second strand of writings built on James

Buchanan's public choice theory. It argued that most public sector activities should be viewed in the context of a collective market. Taxpayer-voters exchanged their taxes for services that they wanted the public sector to provide. Under constitutional systems that allowed direct referendum voting, taxpayer-citizens could express their demand for public services directly. The more indirectly voter preferences were represented, the more likely these preferences were to be distorted by intervening government institutions that inserted their own "demand" for spending. This line of argument, represented by *The Calculus of Consent: Logical Foundations of Constitutional Democracy*, by Buchanan and Tullock (1962), and *The Theory of Public Choice*, edited by Buchanan and Tollison (1972), emphasized the critical importance of the "constitutional rules" by which government decisions were made, and the fact that in a democracy the rules could be modified by citizens to establish the kind of relationship between taxpayer and public service provider that voters wanted. Finally, a more traditional fiscal conservatism that favored less government spending and lower tax rates was incorporated in the new coalition.

There were ironies in the way this coalition waged its tax limitation campaigns. Simple majority voting, exercised at state referendum, was used to seize fiscal power. But Proposition 13 and several of the other state initiatives then changed the basic rules so that a future generation that might want to spend more through the public sector would have to muster super-majority votes (two-thirds or three-fourths) to raise taxes. By the standard norms of public choice theory, this imposition of super-majority requirements would result in too little public spending, frustrating the majority of taxpayer-voter preferences as surely as the previous system had resulted in excessive spending. However, the super-majority voting requirements did serve to hold down taxes.

One of the most remarkable aspects of the public policy analysis supporting the tax revolt was its willingness to go outside the normal channels of dissemination. Previously, public finance studies, like those in other domestic policy areas, influenced public policy through two routes. They either became part of the professional literature and influenced the analytical perspective on policy issues, or they were prepared specifically at the request of federal government commissions, federal agency policymakers, or Congress. In the latter role, expert analysts in academia or policy research organizations communicated directly with experts in government.

But in this case, public choice theorists entered actively into the populist campaign supporting tax limitations. When Ronald Reagan was governor of California, he had appointed a task force on tax reduction that recommended Proposition 1, a measure placed on the state ballot (and ultimately defeated) that would have permanently limited state spending. Among the members of this task force were William Niskanen, then a professor of public policy at the University of California at Berkeley, W. Craig Stubblebine, a student of James Buchanan and a professor at Claremont College, and Milton Friedman, the country's most renowned conservative economist. All these figures later played prominent roles in the campaign for Proposition 13. When Niskanen moved to Michigan as chief economist of Ford Motor Company, he became a key figure in Michigan's successful tax limitation referendum, the Headlee Amendment.

The tax limitation message was spread through political journals and other publications that reached general policymakers more quickly than standard economic journals. The conservative journal *The National Review* became a principal vehicle of dissemination. New journals were formed specifically as instruments of dissemination of the new public policy analysis.

The Legacy of the Tax Limitation Movement

By 1981 the tax limitation movement had virtually disappeared from the state and local scene. Tax-cutting enthusiasm had not died, however, but merely changed address. Ronald Reagan carried California's message to the nation as a whole, and focused taxpayer resentment on the federal tax system.

The tax limitation movement also left a lasting legacy of government by public opinion poll. The change in the state and local tax structure that was produced by the tax revolt could be interpreted as a direct response to voter preferences. With one year's exception, between 1972 and 1978 the annual public opinion polling conducted by the Advisory Commission on Intergovernmental Relations (ACIR) and Opinion Research Corporation had identified the property tax as "the worst tax . . . that is, the least fair." Most of the tax limitation initiatives singled out the property tax for tax cutting. By May 1979, after approval of Proposition 13, the federal income tax surged to the top of public resentment and stayed there through 1981, when the federal government responded by slashing its own tax rates.

For local officials, the taxpayer revolt was a frightening experience. Local authorities began to take informal polls on tax and spending issues before acting, in an effort to anticipate taxpayer-voter demands. Governments became terrorized at the prospect of going to the electorate with tax or spending proposals that might be rejected. In about half the states, for example, general municipal bond issues used to finance infrastructure investment had to be approved by local voters. After Proposition 13, the volume of bond proposals submitted to the public for voter approval plummeted, and remained at unprecedentedly low levels throughout much of the 1980s. The fear of bond referenda played a large role in the decline of infrastructure investment, as the traditional financing sources for state and local capital investment dried up, and local governments allowed their capital stock to deteriorate rather than risk taxpayer anger at the ballot box.

THE REAGAN YEARS AND FEDERAL FISCAL RETRENCHMENT

Ronald Reagan came to office against the backdrop of this tax revolt. He had two domestic priorities: to cut domestic spending and to restore to the states the responsibilities and authority that he believed the federal government had usurped. These two goals were, in principle, compatible with each other. States were "closer to the people" than the federal government. As long as the people wanted less government spending, decentralization of fiscal choices to the state level should help curtail domestic spending. In practice, however, conflicts sometimes arose between the goals of expenditure reduction and federalism reform. When they did, the Reagan administration usually gave priority to cutting back federal spending. Congress and the states rejected Reagan's more sweeping proposals for achieving both goals at once, such as the New Federalism proposals to turn over a large part of domestic program responsibility to the states while drastically reducing federal aid. Nonetheless, by the time Reagan left office he had made considerable progress in restructuring intergovernmental relations and cutting back federal support for local programs.

The depth of the transformation in state-local relations that the Reagan administration proposed is best illustrated by a single comparison. In 1980 federal aid constituted almost 25 percent of state and local expenditures. If all the administration's New Federalism proposals had been adopted, by 1991—a scant decade later—the federal aid share in state and local budgets would have been reduced to 3 to 4 percent, the same level that existed prior to the Depression.

Although changes of this magnitude never were achieved, the initial Reagan budgets did saddle intergovernmental grants with the largest part of the domestic spending reductions. In constant dollars, grants to governments fell by 36.3 percent between 1978 and 1983. Such grants declined 32.8 percent as a share of the total federal budget and 29.7 percent as a share of the federal domestic budget. One hundred and ten project grants—or more than one-third of the total—were eliminated altogether. Direct grants from the federal government to local governments (and especially big cities) were hardest hit.

The 1990s

By 1993 when Bill Clinton came to office, the United States appeared to have completed a full cycle of experimentation with different ways the federal government, states, and localities could collaborate to pay for domestic programs. The Reagan Revolution had not succeeded in turning back the clock to before the New Deal, but it had restored much of the intergovernmental financing philosophy that had existed prior to the War on Poverty initiatives.

Bill Clinton became president in a political system that is more comfortable with an explicit sorting out of roles for the different levels of government, rather than indiscriminate ad hoc cooperation. In this new world, the direct partnership between Washington and cities has virtually disappeared. This development essentially ratifies in budget allocations the Reagan conception of American federalism in which the states, not Washington, have the primary responsibility for inter-acting with the cities, while the states also can decide how much importance to assign to the issues of poverty and urban problems.

Cities have gone back to a more traditional conception of the services local government should provide. The expansion of city social functions triggered by the federal aid programs of the 1960s and 1970s has left a permanent legacy of broadened responsibilities. However, the most ambitious service expansion efforts have been abandoned or curtailed. Cities in the 1990s no longer build significant amounts of public housing or use city payrolls for anti-cyclical employment pol-icy. They have cut back substantially on city-funded public hospitals. At the same time, there has been a strong resurgence in city spending on such traditional functions as infrastructure investment and main-tenance, and police protection. Federal aid once again is a minor presence in city budgets.

Until the 1994 election, many observers would have predicted that the Reagan legacy had worked itself out, and that we were in for a relatively stable period in intergovernmental financial arrangements. They would have been wrong. Taxpayer resentment at current federal tax rates, combined with a new determination not only to reduce but to eliminate the federal deficit, has led to another paradigm shift. This time it has affected federal grants for what were individual entitlement programs.

Entitlement programs are so named because individuals meeting the eligibility criteria are automatically entitled to receive payments. Among the programs affecting lower income households, welfare (Aid to Families with Dependent Children), Medicaid, food stamps, school lunch assistance, and many other programs were operated as entitlements. Many of the programs also were operated in partnership with the states, co-financed by federal grants that passed through the states and the states' own funds. State cooperation was sought in implementation and financing but not in program design, which remained a federal responsibility.

The Reagan reforms never tackled the federal entitlements budget or the state grants that helped finance it. Every year since 1978, including the Reagan and Bush years, there has been a steady increase in the share of federal grants to states and localities used for payments to individuals, as entitlements have squeezed out other federal program initiatives. Between 1978 and 1994, individual entitlements rose from 31.8 percent of the federal grants budget to 63.3 percent. Grants for payments to individuals have grown rapidly enough to overwhelm expenditure restraint on other intergovernmental programs. From 1955 to 1978, programmatic grants grew much faster than individual entitlement grants (for much of this period, grants to cities and other local entities grew fastest of all). But since 1978, entitlement grants for individuals have dominated the intergovernmental grants picture.

As this book goes to press, the 104th Congress is rapidly putting together legislation that takes a dramatically different approach. Included in the proposed changes is replacement of the AFDC and Medicaid entitlements with capped block grants that would give states more responsibility for managing these programs but at the same time drastically reduce the funds that would have been available to the states for these programs under current law.

Block granting, even at its most extreme points in the past, never sought to change more than a sixth of the federal grants-in-aid budget. The block granting initiatives of the 104th Congress would shift the structure of two-thirds or more of the federal grants budget not already block-granted. *Business Week* has called the proposed legislation "the most radical transfer of power since the New Deal." Never before has there been a restructuring of the intergovernmental budget on this scale. And never before has the United States, or any other country, devolved income transfer or health care entitlement programs to the state or local level. Movement has always been in the opposite direction, toward more national responsibility.

The intent of the changes is to curb federal financial obligations and at the same time give states new opportunities to find creative solutions to society's problems. It will be years before the full impacts of this shift will become clear. Fiscally, a major question is whether the conversion to block grants and elimination of open-ended federal entitlements will permanently slow the growth of Medicaid, AFDC, and other income support programs in the federal budget, as has happened in the past when categorical programs were block granted, and whether the eliminations of federal cost sharing will lead states to reduce "welfare" expenditures as much as possible.

Behaviorally, two contrary predictions of state responses to block granting have been offered. Advocates of policy devolution have argued that 50 state experiments will be unleashed, and that states will quickly sort out both distinctive policy designs for anti-poverty programs and different levels of funding. In this case, state variation should increase. Some critics of block granting, in contrast, have argued that block granting will set off a "race to the bottom." The fear of becoming welfare magnets and attracting households in search of higher transfer payments, it is asserted, will prevent states from paying even the benefit levels they think appropriate. Instead, each state will be forced by competition to be as mean-spirited as its cheapest competitor. This analysis predicts *less* variation in the level of welfare financing, and a sharp reduction in average levels of support once governors and state legislatures are freed from federal constraints on program design. (Just *how* free states will be to design their own programs in the short run remains to be resolved. Some versions of current legislation call for maintenance-of-effort requirements that would limit states' ability to make immediate cuts.)

CONCLUSION: POLICY FORMULATION AND POLICY ANALYSIS

Chapter 1 of this book raises questions about the interconnection among domestic policy formulation, professional policy analysis, and ideologically oriented politics. The review of 30 years of public finance policy in this chapter suggests some answers to these questions.

Policy analysis in public finance has been mostly backward-looking and narrow in its focus. Much of the formal work has been descriptive—that is, concerned with how the intergovernmental system has reacted to external events, such as federal aid cutbacks or taxpayer-inspired limitations on tax rates. These studies have deepened our understanding of how the intergovernmental finance system as a whole operates, and why it is overly simplistic to think that a policy change introduced at one level of government will directly change policy without triggering offsetting reactions at other levels of government. Formal policy analysis has played a role in policy formulation, but mostly at the edges. Research findings have led to changes in federal grant allocation formulas and in grant eligibility criteria, as well as to much better understanding of the realities of city finances.

New program directions, fundamental policy reforms, or what might be called paradigm shifts have not come from such policy analysis. At least in the public finance field, however, such shifts often *have* come from people who are (at least during part of their professional lives) policy analysts. The most influential writers have been those who, having achieved professional credibility through close analyses, set out to communicate to a broader audience, using other tools. These writings (or oral advocacy) have been leavened with more political awareness, but also with basic public finance theory. The analytical ideas behind revenue sharing or the tax revolt can best be described as informed points of view on public finance that were supported primarily by background theory and a political orientation. Detailed data analysis helps apply these points of view to particular issues, but only clutters the general argument for a new paradigm.

The recent history of public finance debate suggests that the most effective way to bridge the gap between analysis and policy is not so much by changing the character of "policy analysis" by making it more political or less empirical and analytical. Rather, the policy analysts who have most profoundly affected policy have done so by complementing their technical studies with writings that seek a broader grounding in politics and other forms of civic interaction. A parallel exercise probably is appropriate for all policy research. It would not only help clarify the policy implications of policy research, but oblige policy researchers to ask themselves whether they are addressing questions that have significance for policy application.

Note

1. A marble cake is made by alternating separate vanilla and chocolate batters in the pan and then swirling them together with a knife.

SUGGESTED READING

Brecher, Charles, and Raymond D. Horton with Robert A. Cropf and Dean Michael Mead. 1993. *Power Failure: New York City Politics and Policy Since 1960*. New York: Oxford University Press.

Ladd, Helen F., and John Yinger. 1991. *Ailing Cities: Fiscal Health and the Design of Urban Policy*. Second edition. Baltimore, Md.: Johns Hopkins University Press.

Nathan, Richard P., Fred C. Doolittle and Associates. 1987. *Reagan and the States*. Princeton, N.J.: Princeton University Press.

Peterson, George E., ed. 1994. *Big City Politics and Fiscal Constraints*. Washington, D.C.: Urban Institute Press.

Peterson, George E., and Carol Lewis, eds. 1987. *Reagan and the Cities*. Washington, D.C.: Urban Institute Press.

Chapter Eleven

SUMMARY AND CONCLUSIONS

George Galster

As stated in chapter 1, this book's purpose has been to present a comprehensive overview of how we as a nation have endeavored over the last 35 years to make our metropolitan areas more livable places and to explore what these attempts tell us about the interactions between policy research and the policymaking process. The conceptual framework I introduced hypothesized that the role of policy research can be elucidated by positing mutual interactions among research, policymakers' conception of the problem, and past public policies; all interactions are constrained by dominant ideology. Some recapitulations and conclusions are now in order.

THREE DECADES OF AMERICAN URBAN POLICY AND SOCIAL RESEARCH

Economic Development

Two ideological underpinnings have been the foundation upon which all urban economic development policies have been built: faith in decentralization of political authority and faith in the outcomes generated by private investment, according to Christopher Walker and Patrick Boxall, in chapter 2. The Urban Renewal Program represented the first post–World War II policy manifestation; it granted funds to locally controlled redevelopment authorities to acquire land, demolish property, relocate businesses and residents, and promote new commercial and housing developments in their place. Though modestly effective in certain locations where combined with coherent renewal strategies, the program generated considerable local opposition and drew fire from numerous policy studies, eventually winding down after two decades of operation.

The Model Cities Program, enacted during the Johnson administration's War on Poverty, attempted to coordinate both physical revitalization in the style of the Urban Renewal Program and social service enhancements and coordination. The companion Economic Development Administration targeted business investment in central cities through direct capital subsidies. Together they reflected, in the opinion of Walker and Boxall, the confident assumption of the era that social science could devise effective solutions to complex urban problems. The manifest failure of these programs shattered this belief. Although this failure undoubtedly stemmed from the sheer complexity of the problems involved compared with our inadequate understanding of them, it was abetted by the fragmented nature of urban governance and service delivery systems and the general underfunding of the programs.

By the early 1970s there was a growing consensus that previous economic development efforts had been piecemeal and ad hoc and, therefore, ineffective as well as needlessly complex administratively. In response, the Nixon administration embarked on a program of "New Federalism" that consolidated the welter of development programs into block grants and devolved decision-making authority. Suggesting some residual confidence in the ability of the federal government to affect local economic development, President Nixon also created a council of executive branch department heads (now known as the Domestic Policy Council) to formulate urban strategies. Policies stemming from the former policy thrust evinced modest successes. The Community Development Block Grant (CDBG) Program, initiated in 1974, built local capacity to deliver housing and community redevelopment programs, although it was never funded sufficiently and the funds typically were too geographically dispersed to arrest decline in many decaying inner-city neighborhoods. The Urban Development Action Grant (UDAG) initiative of the Carter administration represented a further evolution that emphasized formal cooperation between public and private investors and produced several notable examples of downtown commercial real estate redevelopment.

The latter thrust met a dead end, inasmuch as by 1980 there was widespread belief that the federal government could not plan and execute effective solutions for local economic development problems. On the contrary, the Reagan administration's view was that spatially targeted programs generated no net increase in wealth and thus should be abandoned. Reagan's policies emphasized the removal of regulatory barriers and general reduction of taxes, as epitomized by his "enterprise zone" proposal. Although never adopted as national policy, most states enacted variants of the enterprize zone idea. These zones, and the downtown office booms spawned by favorable tax policies during the 1980s, however, could not noticeably dent the rising unemployment problems associated with the spatial and skill mismatches afflicting inner-city labor markets.

Spatially targeted development efforts have seen a renaissance with the advent of the Clinton administration. Empowerment Zones were awarded to 6 central cities in 1994, based on their preparatory comprehensive plans. These $100 million grants provide for tax incentives, wage subsidies, and service delivery coordination in a specified high-poverty area. Community Development Banks and enhanced lending standards for the 1977 Community Development Act represent additional new initiatives aimed to expand urban economic development.

Walker and Boxall posit that research has had less influence upon the formulation of these economic development initiatives than in any other urban policy area. Here policy has been driven primarily by politically expedient definitions of problems uninformed by rigorous social science. Perhaps, Walker and Boxall suggest, this is due to the underdeveloped state of economic development policy evaluation research and the lack of a consensual model of what key factors influence business location and general economic growth.

Poverty

My scan of the landscape of federal antipoverty policy in chapter 3 reveals a jagged terrain of varied positions about the importance, definition, and causes of poverty. Poverty was "rediscovered" in the early 1960s as a pressing national dilemma as social research and theoretical debates over the cultural versus structural causes of poverty infused policy discussions. The hubris of the era was reflected in the Johnson administration's War on Poverty; perhaps an even more potent (if less visible) attack on poverty consisted of the expansion of coverage and outlays for cash and in-kind transfers, such as Social Security, Medicare, Aid to Families with Dependent Children (AFDC), Medicaid, and Food Stamps. These efforts were encouraged by the growing conceptual dominance of thinkers who espoused the structuralist view that poverty was a result of macroeconomic conditions in conjunction with human capital deficiencies that were correctable through education and training programs.

By the mid-1970s it was clear that second thoughts about activist federal antipoverty policy abounded. Despite an unusual research consensus that a negative income tax system providing guaranteed minimum cash incomes to all would be the fairest and most efficient means of attacking poverty, growing public ambivalence over the "de-servedness" of the poor deterred its implementation.

These second thoughts were transferred into a widespread antipathy toward federal antipoverty efforts during the 1980s. Supported by a welter of theoretical and modest empirical treatises, conservative politicians shifted the dominant conception of the problem to one of government policy that caused poverty through its encouragement of dependency. Numerous analyses of this period focused attention on a core of reputedly multiproblem, welfare-dependent, mainly minority poor residing in central cities: the "underclass." Despite several accompanying analyses suggesting that the ultimate source of the "underclass" was structural, the net effect was to reinforce the growing perception that the poor were different from mainstream America, suffered from personal and/or cultural defects that kept them poor, and deserved minimal public largess.

I thus conclude that the effect of research here on antipoverty policy was mainly to shape the conception of the problem: first in one way in the early 1960s and then in another way two decades later. But in both cases the influence was visible only because it was reinforced by a dominant political ideology emanating from the White House. In other venues poverty research's influence has been constrained by the deep-seated American ambivalence toward the poor.

Family Support and Social Welfare

Understanding the way in which the nation has chosen to address the thorny policy of Aid to Families with Dependent Children is the key to analyzing the broader issue of welfare reform and family policy over the last three decades, argues Pamela Holcomb in chapter 4. Narrowly focused efforts to reform AFDC have garnered support because critiques of the program have remained remarkably consistent; however, more comprehensive strategies have always failed to be adopted. Initial attempts to provide comprehensive social welfare coverage in the early 1960s were spearheaded by social workers who stressed a services-and-counseling-dominated approach aimed at rehabilitating women on AFDC. This approach quickly inspired disenchantment as AFDC caseloads continued to rise, so in 1967 programs were instituted to train single mothers for gainful employment. These thrusts were informed primarily by personal vignettes, not by sophisticated social research.

Spawned by impressive theoretical research and bipartisan support, numerous proposals for replacing AFDC with a comprehensive entitlement of a guaranteed annual income for all Americans appeared in the late 1960s and early 1970s, culminating in President Nixon's proposed Family Assistance Plan. These social welfare proposals and those forwarded later by the Carter administration were never enacted. Holcomb argues that part of the reason can be traced to the ambiguity and scholarly controversy surrounding the results from the unprecedented income maintenance experiments conducted by social scientists in the 1970s and 1980s with the intent of obtaining precise answers to theoretical questions surrounding guaranteed incomes and negative income tax strategies.

By the 1980s, discussion of social welfare and family support policy had abandoned the notion of income guarantees and had returned to an enhanced employment and training strategy coupled with required work by single mothers. The 1988 Family Support Act required states to expand programs designed to move AFDC recipients off welfare, and a spate of new experiments for doing so emerged. Researchers evaluated these state programs and—because they presented their results in a timely and nontechnical fashion—were crucial in convincing Congress of the value of a mixture of employment, training, education, and supportive services. Holcomb also stresses, however, that the impact of research was enhanced because it supported the preexisting political rhetoric of the time.

Recent Clinton administration proposals for welfare reform have relied heavily on research findings, primarily because key poverty investigators have been appointed to powerful policymaking positions in Washington, D.C. Nevertheless, the tenuousness of the putative research consensus was made manifest by the Republican congressional ascendancy of 1994; ideology, not social scientific evidence, has guided the Republican leadership's formulation of social welfare policy at this writing.

Housing

As with the reluctance to broadly reform AFDC, one component of national housing policy has remained constant over many decades: an unswerving fealty to the goal of increasing home ownership. Indeed, a host of significant direct and indirect subsidies has been provided in pursuit of this goal despite, according to Jennifer Daniell and myself in chapter 5, remarkably little social scientific evidence to undergird its social value. By contrast, in other dimensions the perception of the "housing problem" and appropriate policy responses has been quite variant and malleable by research.

Post–World War II perceptions of general housing shortages spawned massive construction programs of both private, nonsubsidized dwellings and public, subsidized dwellings. By the 1960s the residual housing problem was seen as concentrated in central city ghettos, partly as a consequence of ill-conceived concentrations of public housing there, as diagnosed by several important scholarly studies. A switch to subsidies for private developers of low-cost housing ensued.

Research continued to play an important role in shifting the focus of subsidized housing policy away from supply-side and toward demand-side solutions. Particularly influential were analyses of the elasticity of housing supply and demand functions and the Experimental Housing Allowance Program. Other research documenting changing trends in housing conditions also was influential, however, in shaping perceptions of which housing problems were the most severe. Such research was instrumental, for example, in refocusing attention on the emerging problem of housing affordability in the 1970s and homelessness in the 1980s. But, as we point out, equally high-quality research on the inefficiencies and inequities associated with sprawling suburban development and the filtering process have had no noticeable impact on the headlong rush toward the "American Dream" of a single-family, detached home on a large lot.

Transportation and Land Use

In the view of William A. Hyman and G. Thomas Kingsley, authors of chapter 6, there typically has been a disjuncture between transportation and land-use policies, and both sets of policies have tended to be passive reactors to the broader forces shaping metropolitan decentralization trends. Transportation and land-use policy research has rarely had a decisive impact, either in evaluating particular policies or in framing the conception of the problem.

The construction of the Interstate Highway system was motivated by a highway engineering focus serving the interests of national defense; small wonder, then, that its enormous impacts on central cities was neither anticipated nor assessed. It took citizen outrage in the 1960s over the environmental consequences of unbridled highway construction to force federal legislation requiring more metropolitan-wide, "coordinated, comprehensive, and continuous" planning. These "3C" processes had little impact because, in the authors' opinion, no consensus ever emerged that higher-density land-use patterns were a desired goal of transportation and land-use planning. They also note, however, that the cause of comprehensive planning was not aided by the dominant transportation research studies of the period, which focused on rush-hour congestion as the main problem to be tackled, and portrayed land use as an independent variable in the process.

The oil embargo of 1973 served as another external force that drastically altered the conception of the main problem, this time to one of energy conservation. Even in this era, land-use patterns were not often seen as central to the discussion, perhaps owing to the fact that scholarly debate indicated a lack of consensus over the existence of significant social costs of sprawl. Continuing worries during the 1970s and 1980s over transportation congestion produced volumes of research about how highways should be priced with tolls that would achieve optimal usage levels. This research, too, was ignored, as overriding equity concerns over ability to pay such tolls dominated concerns over economic efficiency of usage.

More recently, a major concern about budget constraints has produced both a policy emphasis on how better to manage and maintain transport infrastructure and a growing awareness that land use and transportation must be viewed as interrelated in the policymaking process. This perspective was codified in the Intermodal Surface Transportation Efficiency Act of 1991, which granted unprecedented flexibility to use highway funds for mass transit, imposed planning procedures requiring metropolitan planning organizations and states to consider transportation impacts on land use and pollution, and mandated the use of management systems for improving planning and capital budgeting. Implementation of this act, argue Hyman and Kingsley, provides a venue for an increased impact of holistic, social science research. Nevertheless, the continuing lack of a consistent, consensual theoretical foundation regarding the causal links between transportation and land use may well prove to be a significant limitation on the impact of such research, as it has in the past.

Education

Paul T. Hill's presentation in chapter 7 demonstrates how urban educational policy has been driven more by lawsuits, local politics, and fragmented control attempting to undertake crisis management than by rational problem-solving. As a consequence, the impact of research has been limited, seldom in ways that scholars anticipated, and often not for the better.

For example, research in the 1950s and 1960s documented educational inequalities associated with racial segregation in schools and, more recently, in curriculum tracking schemes. Unfortunately in the latter case, notes Hill, the results were sometimes carried to the extreme of justifying the abolition of all tracking and advanced courses. In the area of school finance, research on interdistrict inequalities spawned many lawsuits and statewide equalization legislation. Yet, major inequalities in outcome associated with intradistrict inequalities in amount and direction of spending have generally been overlooked by researchers. Researchers have carefully circumscribed a limited agenda and role for standardized tests, yet "simple" measures have nevertheless proved irresistible as drivers of educational policy; the notion of "measurement leads to improvement" continues to hold sway, despite attacks by researchers.

Perhaps no more profound impact of federal educational policy can be found than that created by the Elementary and Secondary Education Act (ESEA) of 1965. Although not fully grounded in the educational research of the era, the act was crucially guided by the concept of "compensatory education" current at the time. Research associated with the ESEA produced little directly to change policy, but led indirectly to tightened regulations in the early 1970s in the hope of generating measurable results. Fragmentation of school programs and management resulting from the ESEA has not yet been overcome because, according to Hill, research on such adverse effects fits no one's advocacy agenda. Researchers have tried to counter the negative impacts of regulation and fragmentation with their work on school effectiveness, resulting in proposals ranging from charter schools to educational vouchers. Again, however, such efforts to create more autonomous and entrepreneurial schools have run afoul of the current of test-based accountability that standardizes curriculum and instruction. Hill concludes that if research can explain how undesirable outcomes occur and how they are embodied in the structures and incentives of urban public education, policymakers are far more likely to understand and use points of leverage for progressive change.

Drug Abuse

As detailed by Adele Harrell in chapter 8, antidrug policy has evinced wide swings in approach, from a focus on punishment, incapacitation, and deterrence of users and sellers of all types of illegal drugs to treatment and prevention coupled with differentiation among types of controlled substances. These swings have been associated with changing definitions of the drug abuse problem that, in turn, were strongly related to the class dimension of drug use. When drug use was more popular among nonpoor groups, a more tolerant approach that emphasized individual rights was adopted; in other eras, a crackdown was justified out of concern for "public safety."

Policy research has tended to respond to the overall political-perceptual climate surrounding the drug issue. When public safety was the dominant issue, research was funded that focused on the effectiveness of law enforcement agencies; when rights were held paramount and drug use was perceived as a result of some deeper social distress, research focused on the effectiveness of public health efforts toward therapy and persuasion aimed at treatment and prevention.

As an illustration, Harrell cites the increasing tolerance of marijuana from the late 1960s to the late 1970s as it became the "drug of choice" for a wide spectrum of Americans. Efforts to decriminalize marijuana ground to a halt as the political backlash against increasing permissiveness mounted. What seemed crucial in this backlash was the public's perception of the social correlates of marijuana use, against which the research evidence about its minimal biological effects could not hold sway. As the 1980s proceeded, both the use and tolerance of all sorts of drugs declined. Federal antidrug policy dollars were shifted from treatment and prevention programs into enforcement programs. The fight against drugs became synonymous with the fight against crime and moral decay in general.

The advent of the crack epidemic in 1985 led to the formation of a two-tier drug culture based on class and race, with crack being concentrated among poorer, minority users. Increasing media attention on the unsavory social and criminal effects of crack catalyzed public opinion that culminated in drug control acts in 1986 and 1988. These acts emphasized "zero tolerance" and provided increased federal funding for prisons to house the skyrocketing number of drug felons. Research in this period focused on causality and prevention of drug abuse, as well as innovative control strategies.

By the early 1990s, policymakers' attention turned to violent crime; the primary evils of drug use were seen in this light. The 1994 Violent Crime Control and Law Enforcement Act supported drug courts that offered expanded treatment options for offenders. Although at this writing Congress has threatened to revoke this act, Harrell speculates that intensified concerns over violence may yield a renewed focus on medical solutions and targeted drug programs as a strategy to reduce drug usage and, thereby, the incidence of violence-producing drug trafficking.

Against this historical perspective, Harrell sees research as primarily performing three roles, only the first of which suggests substantial efficacy. First, research documented trends in drug-use patterns and thus helped to shape the perception of the problem. Second, it uncovered the consequences and, to a lesser extent, the causes of drug use, but here the impact was limited by the contemporaneous ideological climate. Third, research investigated the effectiveness of alternative strategies for drug control, but produced only piecemeal implications because it lacked a framework for cross-program comparisons that could be used for national policy formulation.

Racial Discrimination and Segregation

An unprecedented panoply of critical legislative initiatives and court decisions effectively addressed the institutionalized, legalized discrimination and segregation that characterized the United States in the early 1960s, especially in the South. In chapter 9, however, I contend that these initiatives were far more influenced by media coverage of grass-roots civil rights campaigns than by social scientific research.

The focus of racial issues shifted to the North concomitant with continued mass migrations of blacks from the rural South; this shift in focus was punctuated by the central city civil disturbances of the late 1960s. The most influential piece of research in response to these disturbances, the 1968 Kerner Commission report, proved ineffective in generating a coordinated, large-scale policy reaction, but did succeed in recasting the conception of the race problem as one of de facto segregation most virulently manifested in the self-reinforcing social form known as the urban ghetto.

During the 1970s, research continued to document trends in and new measurements for discrimination, segregation, and interracial disparities, and there was some continued momentum for new civil rights legislation. However, the more powerful intellectual forces of the era were provided by ideologically driven treatises that served to reconceptualize the race issue into one of class. This recasting complemented the emerging conservative doctrine of the 1980s that America had reached a "post–civil rights society." New scholarly and popular studies of the "underclass" further served to reinforce the notion that racial minorities who did not succeed failed purely due to their own personal inadequacies and moral failures. Indeed, the final hurdle to achieving a truly color-blind society, conservatives argued, was ill-conceived, race-conscious federal policies that promoted desegregation and affirmative action.

I argue, however, that social research demonstrated its capacity to alter public and policymakers' opinion during the late 1980s and early 1990s, despite an unfavorable ideological climate. Powerful, easily understood evidence derived primarily from paired testing studies demonstrated that discrimination continued at high levels in education, employment, housing, and lending. These studies resulted in significant increases in civil rights enforcement efforts promulgated by several federal agencies.

Intergovernmental Financial Relations

During the mid-1960s there was a consensus that the federal government should shoulder the main burden of financing urban policy, inasmuch as cities faced disproportionate shares of the nation's social problems yet had limited revenue-raising capabilities. As explained by George Peterson in chapter 10, federal aid that initially took the form of categorical grants eventually was shifted into revenue sharing and block grants. Such federal aid proved increasingly crucial for cities in the late 1970s, as tax revolts restricted their ability to raise revenues. Yet, over time the consensus about the federal responsibility for financing a wide range of urban policies conducted by lower levels of government has dissolved. This dissolution emerged during the Reagan administration, when federal tax cuts and budget deficit limitations ushered in the era of fiscal restraint. Recent legislative initiatives sponsored by the Republican congressional majorities represent unprecedented changes in intergovernmental fiscal relationships that will further erode federal responsibilities for urban policy. Support to state and local governments would be slashed as part of a broader strategy to shrink the size of the federal government. At least two-thirds of federal grant expenditures not already block-granted would become so, including Aid to Families with Dependent Children and Medicaid. Never before has such a massive devolution of transfer programs to the state and local levels been proposed, raising the specter of whether these governments will be driven by a concern for competitiveness to cut back their own support for these programs.

Policy research contributed only marginally to the aforementioned changes, in Peterson's analysis. During the period of categorical grants, research on the implementation weaknesses of the program did help shape the succeeding generation of consolidated block grants, according to Peterson. But the research myopia of the 1970s made no contribution to the emerging populist redefinition of the problem, and arguably took a reactive stance to the "tax revolt." Although the conservative fiscal initiatives of the 1980s and 1990s nominally were built upon the intellectual foundation laid by public choice theorists, it was researcher/advocates who led the charge.

In sum, in Peterson's view, no fundamental paradigm shifts or significant policy reforms have come from policy research on intergovernmental financial relationships. By contrast, more power has been exerted by analysts in the role of advocates who could command significant media attention and whose views were sympathetic with the prevailing political winds.

RESEARCH AND REALITY

Influence of Policy Research

In chapter 1, I postulated that the role of policy research in the last three and one-half decades of American urban policymaking could productively be understood as a mutually causal set of linkages among policy research, the conception of the particular urban problem in question, and past and present programmatic attempts to respond to that problem. Here I recapitulate the support for this view that has emerged in the foregoing chapters.

I believe that policy research has, indeed, had an independent influence on the policymaking process. But such influence has neither been frequent, equally spread across all policy areas, nor typically dramatic or obvious. This book's recounting of urban policymaking since 1960 suggests that the influence of policy research has been both direct and indirect, but that such influence has only been significant when: (1) policymakers are interested in the answers, are uncertain about them, and open to new definitions of problems; and (2) research results are conveyed in a nontechnical and persuasive fashion with little scientific dissent.

Policymakers have used policy research when they have adopted a "problem-solving approach" in response to a situation in which there was widespread agreement about policy goals but uncertainty about the most effective means to attain them. In these circumstances, policy research has had important, direct effects. One illustration was the case of the Experimental Housing Allowance Program, which demonstrated the most effective programmatic rules for delivering demand-side subsidies to alleviate housing problems for the poor. Another example was the evaluations of the multistate experiments with welfare-work-training reforms. Similarly, negative program evaluations of the early categorical grant programs lent impetus to a consolidated block grant strategy for providing federal financial aid to states and localities.

The direct influence of policy research can also be seen by its "political" use as a weapon in support of predetermined positions. For instance, evidence from child developmental psychology was marshaled to show harm from racially segregated schools in the context of desegregation legal suits. The casual empiricist studies of George Gilder, Charles Murray, and others in the 1980s were used effectively by conservatives in justifying their attacks on the social welfare system. A decade later, the results from the Gautreaux experiment in Chicago were central props for advocates of metropolitan-wide deconcentration of the poor in their successful efforts to enact the Moving to Opportunity Program.

The indirect influence of policy research in the past should not be discounted, however. Arguably, the role of policy research as a shaper of the agenda by revealing previously unknown facts and trends has been at least as important as its more direct roles noted here. Michael Harrington's work can fairly be credited with resurrecting poverty as an important issue worthy of national attention. By shifting attention to the "underclass," more recent analyses have reshaped this vision into one that commands a quite different public sentiment: the "undeserving poor" whose problems are the result of their own shortcomings, not failures in educational systems, macroeconomic activity, or civil rights enforcement. Less rhetorically volatile but no less important has been the ongoing stream of statistical studies that documented and forced policymakers to recognize the change in "the housing problem" from one of absolute shortages of decent-quality dwellings to one of lack of affordability of such dwellings. Perhaps the most powerful example of the ability of policy research to alter a perception of the problem is the set of HUD-sponsored paired testing-based discrimination studies conducted by The Urban Institute during the Bush administration, and which led to an enhancement of civil rights enforcement actions, a generally hostile political climate to the contrary notwithstanding (see chapter 9).

These illustrations of direct and indirect influence of policy research are also indicative implicitly of three necessary, but not sufficient, conditions: simplicity, persuasiveness, and consistency of the research thrust. The form of policy research presentation appears to be crucial, because results that are couched in highly technical terms and that rely upon arcane methodologies appear to have attenuated potential impact. The alternative is illustrated by the nontechnical fashion in which influential results from state workfare evaluations were forwarded. Closely related to simplicity is persuasiveness. To be powerful, the findings must be dramatic and produced by a transparently credible methodology; the paired testing findings of racial discrimination in housing and labor markets represent this characteristic. Finally, this book has described numerous examples in which the inconsistency of results produced by a body of policy research destroyed any chance that elements of the work would be efficacious: uncertainty over structural versus cultural causes of poverty; alternative interpretations of statistical results from income maintenance experiments; lack of consensual causal theory connecting land use and transportation; inadequate frameworks for evaluating the effectiveness of alternative drug control and educational strategies; and no persuasive theory of urban economic development and business location. Put differently, policy research that produces a message that is complex or diffuse seems unlikely to be influential.

Finally, as these chapters have noted, policy research has not always yielded positive or intended consequences, even when it has proven influential. Research results have been misinterpreted, misapplied, or generalized inappropriately. For instance, William Julius Wilson's widely publicized work on the "truly disadvantaged," although positing at root a structuralist argument about the causes of the "underclass," unwittingly may have given ammunition to those holding culturalist views about the "undeserving poor" that would justify further federal withdrawal from the area. Similarly, research on the harms of racially discriminatory curriculum tracking programs was misappropriated by some as a rationale for eliminating all tracking and advanced courses.

Influences upon Policy Research

Of course, policy research is not an independent variable but, rather, a product of society's intellectual enterprise. Thus, the momentum of history as embodied in past policy initiatives guides the course of contemporary policy research, both directly and indirectly. Directly, a consistent policy thrust over an extended period will draw the attention of policy researchers, especially if evaluation research funding accompanies this thrust. Many illustrations have been provided here: the 1980s' emphasis on the "war on drugs" spawned much research on effective enforcement; the 1991 Intermodal Surface Transportation Efficiency Act requirement for infrastructure management systems stimulated research on such systems; the Family Support Act of 1988 generated evaluations of state workfare experiments; and numerous housing and community development programs have been scrutinized in HUD-sponsored evaluations, including the Community Development Block Grant Program and the HOME Investment Partnership Program.

The indirect effect of past policies is that they can subtly narrow and enshrine a particular perception of the problem and thus constrain what policymakers see as reasonable new strategies. For example, recent research on more autonomous and entrepreneurial schools has often been thwarted or ignored because it flies in the face of a longer-standing focus on test-based measures of performance and accountability that create biases toward standardization and bureaucratic rigidity.

The current conception of the urban problem at hand also acts as a powerful director for policy research, as this book has manifestly shown. For instance, the perception that housing affordability was the predominant emerging problem led to the commissioning of the Experimental Housing Allowance Program; the view that past social welfare programs were contributing to poverty spawned research on the work incentive and the fertility effects of public assistance; an emphasis on interschool district variations in financial resources led to a research myopia in which equally severe intradistrict inequalities long went uninvestigated; and the notion in the 1970s that drug use was a symptom of a larger social problem yielded research on the effectiveness of public health services for therapy and prevention.

But perhaps the clearest conclusion that can be drawn from this book is the pervasive influence wielded by ideology. Ideology clearly constrains what research accomplishes and whether it has any direct or indirect impact upon policy. Our deep-seated beliefs about individual responsibility, the value of work, and the importance of raising children have led to an ambivalence toward the poor that has been impervious to consensual, research-based proposals like the negative income tax or family allowances. Similarly, nostrums about the evils of "big government" and the advantages of government "close to the people" have recently led to a wholesale discounting of a significant body of research findings in a headlong rush to convert social welfare entitlements into a block grant program for the states. In addition, convincing research on the costs of suburban sprawl has foundered on the shoals of the "American Dream" of single-family detached homeownership on large lots. And moral revulsion over drug use and the implications of a panoply of permissive behaviors have produced a widespread and consistent discounting of scientific evidence on the consequences of marijuana usage.

IMPLICATIONS FOR RESEARCHERS AND FUTURE ROLE OF POLICY RESEARCH

In the course of their chapter discussions, various contributing authors to this volume have suggested several ways for policy researchers to enhance the influence of their work. These may be summarized as follows. First, the research should focus on the questions being asked by policymakers or that they arguably should be asking. Second, researchers should explain explicitly how their work bears on the larger policy context of the day and, by implication, the limits on its applicability. Third, technical results should be made as accessible as possible, but with appropriate caveats to minimize the dangers of misunderstanding or misuse. These recommendations by no means guarantee influence, nor do they guarantee that the results of policy research will not be misunderstood or distorted. But, as Paul Hill noted, because no policymaker wants his or her work to be futile, an opening remains for policy research to be effective if it meets the preceding criteria.

Although this book closes on a note of cautious optimism about the potential role of policy research in shaping the future American city, two emerging trends could well render even this conclusion more circumspect. First is the move led by the current Republican Congress to decentralize policymaking to the state and local levels across a wide range of urban-related topics. If this decentralization were to be accompanied by a corresponding fragmentation of decision making (as has been the case with educational policy), the audience capable of generating decisive policy change on the basis of persuasive research might be badly eroded. In addition, local governments may be less inclined to marshal the resources needed to sponsor large-scale evaluation research directed at their own programs, let alone consistent cross-local evaluations that might provide the basis for identification of "best practices."

Second, the proliferation of ideologically based "think tanks" creates another worry. Often these organizations, much in the style of "creation science," begin with conclusions and conduct investigations aimed only at uncovering evidence in support of their preordained positions. Although such research may be employed to great effect in political combat, the cacophony of research weapons being fired by contrary sides on an issue may serve to obfuscate more than enlighten. As we have often seen in the past, a body of research is least effective when it lacks a consensual view on a topic and thus permits policymakers to fall back on conventional wisdoms and ideological nostrums because, "after all, even the experts don't agree."

If, then, policy research is to avoid becoming an unwitting tool of anti-intellectualism and scientific nihilism, it must constantly renew itself by returning to its roots. It must be a discipline characterized by: free inquiry into all aspects of social problems; a willingness to test conventional conceptions and conclusions; the application of the most appropriate, rigorous, and sophisticated analytical methodologies available; an objective, accessible reporting of the results; and an explicit discussion of the potential uses, misuses, and limitations of the research by those who would shape American urban policy in the 21st century.

SUGGESTED READING

Wilson, William Julius, 1987. *The Truly Disadvantaged: The Inner City, the Underclass, and Public Policy.* Chicago: University of Chicago Press.

ABOUT THE EDITOR

George Galster is a Program Director and Principal Research Associate at the Urban Institute. He has published widely on the topics of racial discrimination, segregation, neighborhood dynamics, urban poverty, and community lending patterns.